John Dickson presents a bigger picture of evangelism than most of us are used to. We should, he insists, recognise worship, love, prayer, and generosity as all part of "gospel" work. Still more refreshing is the heart of the book: a treatment of Jesus and the Kingdom of God — the message of the four Gospels — as the centre of "the gospel." God's good news is about the entire new creation, and ourselves caught up into it; it is not just a mechanism for getting individuals into heaven. Dickson explains the whole picture with so many real-life stories that one cannot fail to be drawn in to the excitement of this many-sided gospel work. Here is a book offering fresh energy for the whole task of the whole people of God.

— N. T. Wright, Bishop of Durham

Whereas so many books on evangelism are filled with techniques and strategies, the first and most heartwarming thing to commend about this book is that it is biblical — excitingly, eye-openingly biblical from start to finish, moving backwards and forwards within the Bible and between the Bible and abundant "case studies" in today's world. The book's second great feature is that it is balanced — showing us in just how many ways the Bible speaks about what we can do to promote the gospel. Everything from being bold to being beautiful is there (yes, even that is biblical), from doing good to doing worship. Here is a book that takes us beyond merely talking about the gospel (though without ever leaving that behind) to really living it, and also makes sure that when we *do* talk about the gospel, we actually have in mind something that the gospel writers and the apostle Paul would recognize.
Biblical, balanced, and — well, brilliant.

— Christopher J. H. Wright, International Director,
Langham Partnership International and Author of
The Mission of God and *The Mission of God's People*

This book has the potential to radically change for good your perspective on evangelism. It is required reading at Parkside.

— Alistair Begg, Senior Minister, Parkside Church,
Cleveland, Ohio

This is as lively and sensible a book on evangelism as I have seen, especially valuable for bringing out the wide range of activities that all need to be carried on in effective Christian witness in contemporary society. It encourages congregations to recognize the varied gifts of their members and to enable each one to be involved in evangelism even though not all of them may be called to be evangelists in the narrower sense of the term.

— I. Howard Marshall, Emeritus Professor of
New Testament, University of Aberdeen

When I was asked to review this new book on evangelism, I didn't know what to expect. But I soon discovered: this is a terrific book! Without compromising or reducing the gospel to pious platitudes, Dickson presents evangelism as the Christ-centered imperative of biblical faith. Theologically rich and practically helpful.

— Timothy George, founding dean of Beeson Divinity School
of Samford University and senior editor of *Christianity Today*

John Dickson's *The Best Kept Secret of Christian Mission* was not only a great stimulus to my own thinking about evangelism but also proved a real help to our congregation at St Ebbe's, Oxford, as we thought through how we could best fulfill our role as Christ's witnesses. It's a wonderful mix of thoughtful reflection on the Bible and down-to-earth practical application.

— Vaughan Roberts, Rector of St Ebbe's Oxford and
President of The Proclamation Trust UK

Even — or perhaps especially — if you do not consider yourself to be a gifted evangelist, John Dickson will encourage you from Scripture with many varied ways to promote the gospel of Jesus Christ.

— Collin Hansen, *Christianity Today* editor-at-large and author of
Young, Restless, Reformed: A Journalist's Journey with the New Calvinists

John Dickson shows that taking seriously the church's message, worship, and ecclesiology, along with the biblical call for Christians to impact the social and cultural world around them, does not negate the mandate and high calling of evangelism. In fact, to be ambassadors for the gospel of the kingdom is at the heart of what it means to be a Christian and to change the world. This is a message that needs to be heard.

— Jim Belcher, author of *Deep Church*

Dickson offers a thoroughly biblical account of evangelism, informed and enlivened by stories from his own experience. For many who are weary of what often goes by the name evangelism, this book will be a most refreshing and inspiring experience.

—Richard Bauckham, Senior Scholar,
Ridley Hall, Cambridge

John Dickson has given us a biblically rich and powerfully written book on evangelism. His views are deeply embedded in Scripture and well-rounded. He does not fall into formulas, but encourages us toward a life-style of living and speaking the gospel in our culture today. I recommend this book to those whose passion for evangelism has flagged as well as for those who are actively sharing Christ with their friends and neighbors.

— Tremper Longman, Robert H. Gundry Professor of
Biblical Studies, Westmont College

For any twenty-first-century Christian who has felt the dread of prosely-tizing people into the faith, read John Dickson's empathetic, confessional treatise on Christian mission. He combines the mind of a scholar with the heart of a pastor to talk to us as fellow Christians about the compelling wonder of Christ for the twenty-first-century world.

— David Livermore, thought leader in cultural intelligence
and global mission, Executive Director of Global
Learning Center, Grand Rapids, Michigan

Some years ago John Dickson ran an excellent evangelism training course in our local church. The course material—now available in this book—is biblical, liberating, and practical. I commend it as a stimulating resource for congregations and church leadership teams.

— Christopher Ash, Director of Cornhill
Training Course, London

A biblical, practical, warm, and encouraging book that does exactly what it sets out to do: equips us as the Christian community to promote the gospel. Should become a standard text on the subject.

— Michael Frost, Director, Centre for Evangelism and Global Mission, Morling College, Sydney

Having read Dr. Dickson's published doctoral thesis, I am delighted that he has now produced this highly readable book for all church members in the biblical art of mission today. The style is down-to-earth and lively. I warmly recommend it.

— Donald Robinson, former Archbishop of Sydney and Vice Principal, Moore Theological College, Sydney

Here is a compelling case for the involvement of all believers in promoting the gospel, not based on hype or overwrought exegesis but on a profound understanding of Scripture and illustrated with contemporary and moving human experience. A must read.

— The Rt. Rev. Robert Forsyth, Bishop of South Sydney, Anglican Church of Australia

I warmly recommend this book. I have learned from reading it, and I have no doubt that others will as well. It challenged me, encouraged me, and often inspired me. And at my age that's quite an achievement! (from the foreword)

— Alister McGrath, President of the Oxford Centre for Christian Apologetics

In *The Best Kept Secret of Christian Mission*, John Dickson winsomely demonstrates how each of us can be part of the greatest story ever: God's mission to our hurting world. He insightfully observes that proclaiming the gospel is not only about witnessing to the reality of God's worth and uniqueness with our lips but with our very lives — through such everyday but life-transforming acts as prayer, faithfulness, compassion, and worship ... I wholeheartedly commend John's book to you and know you will be richer for his insights. (From the foreword)

— Ravi Zacharias, author and speaker

The Best Kept Secret of
Christian Mission

Promoting the Gospel with More Than Our Lips

The Best Kept Secret of
Christian Mission

Promoting the Gospel with More Than Our Lips

JOHN DICKSON

ZONDERVAN®

ZONDERVAN.com/
AUTHORTRACKER
follow your favorite authors

ZONDERVAN

The Best Kept Secret of Christian Mission
Copyright © 2010 by John Dickson

This title is also available as a Zondervan ebook. Visit www.zondervan.com/ebooks.

This title is also available in a Zondervan audio edition. Visit www.zondervan.fm.

Requests for information should be addressed to:

Zondervan, *Grand Rapids, Michigan* 49530

Library of Congress Cataloging-in-Publication Data

Dickson, John.
    The best kept secret of Christian mission : promoting the gospel with more
than our lips / John Dickson.
        p. cm.
    ISBN 978-0-310-32863-6 (hardcover, jacketed)
        1. Missions. I. Title.
BV2061.3.D53 2009
248'.5 — dc22   2009040162

All Scripture quotations, unless otherwise indicated, are taken from the Holy Bible,
Today's New International Version™, TNIV® Copyright © 2001, 2005 by Biblica, Inc.™
Used by permission of Zondervan. All rights reserved worldwide.

Any Internet addresses (websites, blogs, etc.) and telephone numbers printed in this
book are offered as a resource. They are not intended in any way to be or imply an
endorsement by Zondervan, nor does Zondervan vouch for the content of these sites
and numbers for the life of this book.

Cover design: Kirk DouPonce
Interior design: Mark Sheeres

Printed in the United States of America

10 11 12 13 14 15 16 /DCI/ 20 19 18 17 16 15 14 13 12 11 10 9 8 7 6 5 4 3

For Glenda Weldon,
who taught me the gospel
and showed me how to pass it on.

Contents

Foreword by Professor Alister McGrath 13
Foreword by Ravi Zacharias 15
Introduction: Confessions of an Evangelist. 17

1. The One and the Many:
   Why Get Involved in Mission? 25

2. The Many and the One:
   The Challenge of Pluralism 38

3. Following the "Friend of Sinners":
   The Missionary Mind of the Ordinary Christian 46

4. The Hidden Mission:
   Promoting the Gospel with Our Prayers 61

5. Partners for Life:
   Promoting the Gospel with Our Money . , ...76

6. Being the Light of the World:
   Promoting the Gospel through the Works of the Church. . .85

7. Being Beautiful:
   Promoting the Gospel through Christian Behaviour 97

8. What Is the Gospel?
   The Message We Promote 111

9. The Few and the Many:
   Evangelists and the Local Church 141

10.   Heralds Together:
      Promoting the Gospel through Our Public Praise...... 155

11.   The Apt Reply:
      Promoting the Gospel in Daily Conversation 172

12.   A Year in the Life of the Gospel:
      Bringing It All Together 190

Appendix 1: Gospel Bites........................ 203
Appendix 2: A Modern Retelling of the Gospel........... 211
Notes 219
Scripture Index................................ 230
Subject Index 234

Foreword

I READ THIS BOOK WITH ADMIRATION and excitement. Rarely have I seen such a wonderful combination of enthusiasm and expertise, passion and reflection. John Dickson writes winsomely and elegantly, drawing his readers into his vision for the future of evangelism. It is one of the best books I have read on evangelism. A new star has clearly risen in Australia.

Why is it so good? I think it is the way in which Dickson inspires the confidence of his readers, explaining the mistakes he made along the way and how others can learn from them. Many, many readers will identify with his concern about technique-based evangelism courses, which make evangelism into a human skill comparable to car mechanics. Dickson offers his readers something very different—a vision for evangelism, opening up the full riches of the gospel and allowing its many facets to radiate through every believer, not just the gifted evangelist.

It is a tribute to Dickson's experience as an evangelist and skill as a writer that he manages to combine theoretical reflection and practical advice. Where some authors leave their readers wondering how on earth they are going to apply their ideas, Dickson offers wise advice, clearly based on experience, as to how best to do this.

His emphasis on the importance of the local church is theologically astute and immensely practical. Dickson's approach will energise both individuals and churches to promote the gospel, while emphasizing the importance of the church at every level in sustaining the ministry of individual evangelists. His appeal to the worship of the church reminds us that the power of the gospel lies not merely in its words, but in its capacity to transform people's lives.

I warmly recommend this book. I have learned from reading it, and I have no doubt that others will as well. It challenged me, encouraged me and often inspired me. And at my age, that's quite an achievement!

ALISTER MCGRATH
President of the Oxford Centre
for Christian Apologetics, and
Professor of Historical Theology,
Oxford University.
Oxford, March 2006

Foreword

HAVING TRAVELED THE GLOBE for over thirty years proclaiming the gospel of Christ, I have encountered the gamut of curious questioners, struggling believers, skeptical onlookers and strident atheists. Yet when the Scriptures are proclaimed, time and again I have witnessed the awesome power of God's Word melting away one's resistance and convicting another with openness to the gospel message. At the same time, with soberness I have often said that I have little doubt that the single greatest obstacle to the impact of the gospel has not been its inability to provide answers but the failure on our part to live it out.

Thus, when I encounter someone living out the gospel with great passion, serious mindedness and a heart of joy, I am blessed to meet them and want to share them with others. I have known and worked alongside John Dickson for several years, and I am thrilled to introduce one of his many books to a North American audience. John is an historian from whom I've learned much and whose authenticity I greatly admire. A musician, well-respected scholar in the scriptural texts and father, he is a uniquely gifted man in the range of topics he addresses and in the depth of his commitment to Christ and his church.

In *The Best Kept Secret of Christian Mission*, John winsomely demonstrates how each of us can be part of the greatest story ever: God's mission to our hurting world. He insightfully observes that proclaiming the gospel is not only about witnessing to the reality of God's worth and uniqueness with our lips but with our very lives — through such everyday but life-transforming acts as prayer, faithfulness, compassion and worship. He brings such arenas to life with his biblical exposition, transparency and profound understanding of the human heart.

Moreover, John's words are reinforced by a life of ministry and scholarship, engaging people across cross-cultural lines through television, lectures, sermons and music.

I wholeheartedly commend John's book to you and know you will be richer for his insights.

RAVI ZACHARIAS, author and speaker
November, 2009

Introduction

Confessions of an Evangelist

FOR THE FIRST COUPLE OF YEARS of my faith I was a passionate promoter of the Christian message. I was fifteen years old and spoke about Christ to everyone who would listen. Without any background in Christianity I just assumed everyone would want to hear what I had heard. I shared my new beliefs with my mother, my friends, my football team, strangers on the street and even the crowds of other teenagers I met on the holiday camps my mum used to send me on (regularly!).

In those early years as a believer I had no idea Christians could be coy about their faith. No one had told me I was meant to feel awkward about spreading the good news. That was something I learnt only after mixing with Christians for a while. But I learnt it soon enough.

Because of my obvious enthusiasm for sharing the faith with others, my church decided I should be trained in "evangelism". I had never heard of "evangelism"; I just wanted others to discover what I had discovered. I did not know there was a word for it or that courses and books had been written on the subject.

So, off I went to special classes once a week for several months where I was trained in one of the popular evangelism training tools. There I learnt a carefully prepared gospel outline, a set of illustrations to explain the message and a list of Bible verses to back it all up.

At the end of the course I was turned loose on the public of Sydney. I took part in prearranged home visits, systematic door knocking and even "cold turkey" walk-ups at the local shopping centre.

Suddenly, my joy and ability at passing on the faith evaporated. I had previously delighted in sharing Christ with others, but now it seemed a burden: a burden on my emotions as I felt the weight of the moment I had been trained for, on my memory as I tried to recall all of the points of the gospel and, perhaps most of all, on my poor unsuspecting evangelistic "targets". This enthusiastic, natural promoter of Christ had been transformed into a nervous and unnerving "Bible-thumper".

I do not blame the course itself. Many Christians around the world have been helped by this and other programs. I still see a place for evangelistic and apologetic training. But I suspect the way the course was run in my church, combined with my over-eager personality, left me with several unhealthy perspectives on what it means to promote Christ to others. I have since discovered just how common these perspectives are in modern church circles.

The Curse of Self-Consciousness

First, I had become self-conscious about reaching out to others with the news of Christ. When I first became a Christian, promoting Christ was a perfectly natural orientation of my whole faith. It was similar to the way I felt about football (or what Australians and Americans call "soccer"). I loved football. I played it almost every day. I watched every televised English Premier League match. I talked about it and asked friends to come up to the local oval for a kick-around. I never dreamt that football-lovers might be self-conscious about mentioning it or coy about inviting others to play it.

But after attending this evangelism course, that is exactly how I felt about my faith. Suddenly, mentioning God and inviting people to church had become a specialised compartment of the faith. It had its own name — evangelism — its own propositions and jargon, and even its own multiweek courses. Whereas I once talked of God as freely as I talked about my favourite TV show, now I found myself switching into "evangelism mode" — where the heart beats faster, the palms get sweaty and you feel the pressure to steer the conversation in a most unconversational manner. What was once a natural outflow of faith, something requiring little concentration, now felt like a cross between a theological exam, an acting class and a knife-edge rescue operation. It is a bit like the *Australian/American Idol* television competition. One of the most frequent criticisms from the judges, especially in the early stages, is that contestants' performances are self-conscious. "I could see the cogs turning in your mind," say the judges, "as you concentrated on the notes, scrambled for the lyrics and counted out the dance moves, instead of just enjoying the song and engaging the audience." The parallel with evangelism is obvious. Sometimes we concentrate so hard on steering the conversation and remembering the correct content that we forget the joy of the good news and the privilege of sharing it with another human being. At that point we have become overly self-conscious.

Let me reiterate: evangelism courses per se are not the problem. Some Christians undergo such training without ever feeling self-conscious; others feel self-conscious without ever being trained. Nevertheless, I suspect many would agree that this evangelistic self-consciousness is common amongst modern believers (with or without the help of evangelism training courses).

Thankfully my own evangelistic self-consciousness soon passed. After months of trying to "perform" as I had been taught, I decided to relax. I forgot about getting it "right", getting it "in order" and getting my conversation partner "over the line". Instead, I decided to approach my gospel opportunities as if they were friendly conversations about my favourite topic. It was not long before I realised again that this is exactly what sharing the faith is.

Part of my hope in writing this book is that a fresh, biblical look at the topic of evangelistic mission will go some way toward dispelling Christian self-consciousness.

The Gospel "Download"

The second outlook I inherited from my days as a budding evangelist was equally unhelpful. I began to think that if I had an opportunity to say something about Christianity, I ought to say everything about it. I had spent months learning a gospel outline, complete with analogies and Bible verses. I somehow got it into my head that it was my duty to download the whole thing no matter how passing the conversation about Christianity might have been. I don't know how many poor souls had to endure my sermonettes before I realised the glazed look in their eyes was not the look of spiritual wonder!

In reality, most of our opportunities to speak about Christianity will occur in passing, in the to-and-fro of daily conversation. It should not surprise us, then, that the two clearest passages in the Bible calling on all believers to speak up for the Lord urge them simply to "answer" for the faith—to respond to people's comments, questions or criticisms with a gentle and gracious reply (Colossians 4:5–6 and 1 Peter 3:15).

Most Christians are not "evangelists" (in the technical, New Testament sense of the word) and should not be made to feel the pressure to be something they are not. The Scriptures certainly urge us all to be open about our faith whenever opportunity allows, but doing "the work of an evangelist" (2 Timothy 4:5) is something God's Word asks only of some of us.[1]

Of course, if you have a chance to explain the whole message of Christ, please go for it! Evangelists do not have a monopoly here. My point is simply this: far more frequent than the full gospel opportunity will be the passing opportunities to offer brief nuggets about the faith to those around us—a relative at the Christmas lunch, a friend at the café, a parent on the sideline of the sporting field and so on. On occasions like these a gospel "bite" will usually prove more useful to your hearer than a gospel download.

Reducing the Gospel

The third unhelpful perspective I picked up in my early evangelism training concerns the gospel message itself. The particular
course I studied summarised the gospel in the theological con-
cepts of sin and grace. The goal of the presentation I had memo-
rised was to convince my hearers (1) that they were unworthy of
God's acceptance because of their rebellion and (2) that God's
acceptance was offered on the basis of faith alone, not through
good works. The gospel, in other words, was condensed to two
doctrines with little attempt to connect these ideas to the flesh-
and-blood story of Jesus' birth, teaching, miracles, death, resurrection, appearances and return for judgment.

Some gospel preaching today—including some gospel conversations we have with friends—forgets that, at its heart, the gospel
is the news about Jesus as narrated in the Gospels. This is why
the four Gospels are called "Gospels"—because they, more than
any other part of Scripture, tell the gospel. This is why the apostolic preaching in the book of Acts generally narrates the story of
Jesus, including his birth to King David's line, baptism by John,
miracles, arrest and so on (Acts 2:22–39; 4:8–12; 10:34–43;
13:16–41). This is why when Paul explicitly summarises the
content of the gospel in his letters, he does so by outlining the
key events of Jesus' life from birth to exaltation, including of
course his atoning death, burial in a tomb and glorious appearances (Romans 1:2–4; 1 Corinthians 15:1–8; 2 Timothy 2:8).

Of course, sin and grace are central to any true gospel presentation (as they are in the four Gospels themselves), but the
gospel cannot be reduced to these themes any more than it can
be reduced to a simple retelling of Jesus' "biography".

I will say much more about this in the overly long chapter 8,
"What Is the Gospel?" For now, let me just say that the gospel
is not a theological idea or two. It is theology grounded in the
actual events of Jesus' life. The gospel and the Gospels are one.

Let me offer a concise summary of what I mean by the "gospel" throughout this book:

> The gospel is the announcement that God has revealed his kingdom and opened it up to sinners through the birth, teaching, miracles, death and resurrection of the Lord Jesus Christ, who will one day return to overthrow evil and consummate the kingdom for eternity.

Any account of the Christian gospel that does not narrate the basic content of the books we rightly call the Gospels does not deserve to be called a "gospel outline". It might be a true and accurate statement of biblical truths—and, for that reason, valuable and useful for our hearers—but it is not the gospel that Jesus said must be preached to all nations (Mark 13:10).

Underestimating the Mission

There is a fourth unhelpful perspective I developed in those early days. This one was probably the result of my personality as much as any training I received. Somehow I came to assume that the only important means of promoting Christ was talking about him. Reaching out to others became for me an entirely verbal activity.

But perhaps the best kept secret of Christian mission is that the Bible lists a whole range of activities that promote Christ to the world and draw others toward him. These include prayer, godly behaviour, financial assistance, the public praise of God (in church) and, as already mentioned, answering people's questions. All of these are explicitly connected in the Bible with advancing the gospel and winning people to Christ. They are all "mission" activities, and only a couple of them involve the lips at all.

I do not want to diminish the role of speaking. As I have said already, the New Testament urges us to be open about Christ in our regular conversations. To push our faith below the level of daily speech is unnatural and a sure sign of Christian ill health. At the same time, downplaying the range of mission activities listed in the Bible creates its own set of problems. It can make those who do not have a flair for speaking feel inadequate in their contribution to God's work in the world. Perhaps more worryingly – and this was certainly so in my case – it can make those who do have the "gift of the gab" feel they are fulfilling God's plans just by talking. The Lord wants more than our lips in the grand task of taking his mercy to our friends and neighbours. To think otherwise, as I did for years, is to greatly underestimate what God's mission involves.

In light of this, I want to make a distinction throughout this book between the specific activity of *proclaiming the gospel* and the broader category of *promoting the gospel*. The former is properly called "evangelism", a word that derives from the New Testament term *euangelizomai*, which only ever means "announcing (grand) news". The wider category of *promoting the gospel* includes any and every activity that draws others to Christ (including, of course, evangelism). People sometimes use the words "mission", "outreach" or "witness" for this larger work, but I prefer the expression "promoting the gospel" (I'm sure I pinched this from someone else but I can't remember from whom) because it reminds us that at the heart of our mission to the world is the news about Christ, the gospel. In my view, when "mission" becomes disconnected from the gospel, as it sadly does in some church circles, it no longer deserves to be called Christian mission.

The concept of promoting the gospel obviously includes evangelism, but it also tries to give a proper place to things like prayer, godly behaviour and answering for the faith, all of which are explicitly connected in the New Testament with God's plan to save his people. Such activities are not separate from the work of the gospel; they are supportive of it and vital to it. Praying that your friends and neighbours would come to know Christ is no less a promotion of the gospel than speaking to them about Christ. Both activities are evangelistic, even if only one of them is evangelism in the strict sense. This does not mean that those who pray for their friends need not worry about speaking to them any more than it means that those who speak to their friends need not worry about praying for them. My point is that both activities are full contributions to the promotion of Christ in the world.

For years, both as a public evangelist and as a personal encourager, I urged other Christians to evangelise (announce the gospel) as if this were the only significant thing they could do to promote Christ. In a sense, I was projecting my own ministry and personality onto believers in general. I was an evangelist; everyone else should be as well. That was the logic.

The problem is: God's Word does not quite put it that way, and attempts to argue otherwise usually involve stretching biblical passages beyond their plain meaning. I used to do it myself both in sermons and (I am embarrassed to say) in my first book.[2] The motivation was honourable – I wanted more Christians to be more involved in the work of the gospel – but, as with so many other issues, a worthy goal does not give me permission to handle the Scriptures poorly. We are involved in *God's* mission, and so we must allow his Word to shape our part in it. The slogan "Every Christian an evangelist" has a noble purpose, but it is not a biblical way of speaking.

For Christians in general – as opposed to evangelists in particular – telling the gospel to others (evangelism) could be described as the icing on the cake of mission. It is certainly the most conspicuous part, and, once tasted, it will often be the sweetest part too, but for the typical Christian it is not the bulk of the task. It is not where most of our opportunities to promote Christ to others will be found.

A central aim of this book, then, is to show just how all-encompassing is the Bible's call to be involved in God's mission. I hope and pray that what follows will inspire you to see everything you do in life as a tool in God's hands for the benefit of those who don't yet know Christ.

Before we explore the Bible's multifaceted approach to the promotion of the gospel, we should stop to ask the most obvious question: Why get involved in God's mission?

CHAPTER 1

The One and the Many

Why Get Involved in Mission?

He is to be feared above all gods.

Psalm 96:4

A FEW YEARS AGO, I was having coffee with a friend in a café at my local beach. I was explaining to him what our church was doing to promote Christ among the residents of the area. At one point, I noticed a woman a few tables away looking inquisitively at me. I assumed she was a fellow Christian interested in listening into our conversation. I just kept on talking.

A few minutes later, the woman got up from her table, paid her bill, walked straight across to me and, at what seemed like the top of her voice, said: "So, you want to convert the world. How dare you!" And off she stormed. It was at that point I realised she probably wasn't a Christian.

I thought of the perfect comeback – about an hour later! At the time I was dumbfounded. For a moment, I even wondered: "Maybe our mission is presumptuous. Perhaps promoting the news about Christ is the stuff of fanaticism rather than a reasoned, modern faith."

I am sure many of us at times have wondered similar things. The rhetoric of our world, which insists you keep your faith to yourself, is powerful and sometimes leaves us cringing at the thought of getting overly active in God's mission to "convert the world".

So, I want to step back and ask: Why do we reach out to others with the news of Christ? What ultimately is the driving idea behind God's mission to the world?

There are plenty of good, biblical answers to this. You could say we promote Christ because he means so much to us personally, and that's true. You could say we promote Christ because in the Great Commission he commands us to do so (Matthew 28:18–20), and that's true as well. But I want to suggest that a more comprehensive reality drives our desire to make Christ known to the world. Not surprisingly, this driving force of mission also happens to be the fundamental idea of the Scriptures, Old and New Testaments.

The Bible's Most Basic Doctrine

Please pause and reflect about what you would regard as the most basic doctrine of the Bible. Go back through your mental list of theological big ideas and try to arrive at the starting point (this is not a test of true faith, by the way).

There may be different ways of expressing it but I think I would have to answer this question with the simple statement: *there is one God.*

From Genesis to Revelation the Bible makes the resounding, unapologetic declaration that there is just one Creator and Lord of the world. It begins in the Bible's opening line: "In the beginning God created the heavens and the earth" (Genesis 1:1). To ancient readers, this was not simply a sensible way to start a holy book. It was a huge swipe at the entire religious outlook of the time. The opening lines of the Babylonian creation story, *Enuma Elish,* to give just one example from the period, list no fewer than nine separate gods, each with its own part to play in the events leading up to creation. Saying that "*God* created the heavens and the earth" was tantamount to saying that no other deity was involved in the universe.

And that's exactly what the rest of the Bible affirms. The central creed of the Old Testament was the Shema (still recited twice daily by Orthodox Jews). It proclaims an uncompromising monotheism, or belief in one God:

> Hear [Hebrew: *shema*], O Israel: the LORD is our God, the LORD, the One and Only.[3] (Deuteronomy 6:4)

In the New Testament, the apostle Paul reworked the Shema (which he himself would have recited daily since his youth) in light of the lordship of Jesus:

> We know that "An idol is nothing at all in the world" and that "There is no God but one." [the original language here is very close to the *Shema*]. For even if there are so-called gods, whether in heaven or on earth (as indeed there are many "gods" and many "lords"), yet for us there is but one God, the Father, from whom all things came and for whom we live; and there is but one Lord, Jesus Christ, through whom all things came and through whom we live. (1 Corinthians 8:4–6)

Monotheism, crystallised in the universal lordship of Jesus Christ, is the Bible's most basic doctrine.

What has monotheism got to do with mission? How is it that the most basic doctrine in the Bible is also the fundamental idea behind promoting the gospel? The answer may be obvious but let me spell it out. If there is just one God in the universe, everyone everywhere has a duty to worship that Lord.

Psalm 96 and the Universal Duty

This brings us to the main Old Testament text I want to reflect on. Psalm 96 is one of those Bible passages made famous by countless hymns and songs of praise (I hear a tune every time I look at the text). The words are well-known but they must not be taken for granted. The truths contained in this portion of God's Word are crucial for a biblical understanding of why we promote the Lord to the world. For in this psalm we have not only a strident affirmation of the lordship of one God, but also a plea to God's people to publish this reality throughout the world (for the two ideas are related):

> Sing to the LORD a new song;
>> sing to the LORD, all the earth.
> Sing to the LORD, praise his name;
>> proclaim his salvation day after day.
> Declare his glory among the nations,
>> his marvellous deeds among all peoples.
> For great is the LORD and most worthy of praise;
>> he is to be feared above all gods.
> For all the gods of the nations are idols,
>> but the LORD made the heavens. (Psalm 96:1 – 5)

The opening lines of the psalm are directed to the ancient people of God, the Jews, urging them to "sing to the LORD" and "praise his name" within earshot of the pagans or non-Jews around them. In the words of verse 3, they were to "declare his glory *among the nations*, his marvellous deeds *among all peoples*".

This might be hard to imagine at first: how could non-Jews (or Gentiles) overhear Jewish praises of God? The answer is simple: ancient Jerusalem was a bustling international city in the ancient world, and the temple drew not only Jewish visitors but Gentiles as well (see 1 Kings 8:41 – 43). Later, when Jewish synagogues began to spring up all around the Mediterranean (300 BC – AD 100), a psalm like Psalm 96 took on special significance, since now Jews were singing their praises on pagan turf. In Jesus' day, the Jerusalem temple had a large Court of the Gentiles designed specifically for Gentiles to experience the praise of the true God. For ancient Jews this was a kind of evangelism.

It may sound odd to speak of "evangelism" in the Old Testament, but these opening verses of our psalm make clear that

The word translated "proclaim" in verse 2 ("proclaim his salvation day after day") makes the same point. It is the Hebrew term *basar,* meaning "announce grand news". It is the same word that appears in the famous "evangelism" passage of Isaiah 52:7: "How beautiful on the mountains are the feet of those who bring good news" (Hebrew: *basar*). This term always refers to an announcement that is news to the hearers. It is the very term that (via the Greek translation of the Old Testament) gave us the words "gospel" and "evangelism".

this proclamation of salvation and of God's glory is intended for those for whom it is "news", the pagan nations around Israel. Israel's praise of God – in the temple and the synagogue – was meant to be overheard by the pagans around about. This is "evangelism" through our public praise, something I will be discussing at length in chapter 10. If we were in any doubt about all this, verse 7 of the psalm takes up this call to proclaim God's glory to pagans and begins to address the Gentiles directly:

> Ascribe to the Lord, all you families of nations [that's the
>   Gentiles],
>   ascribe to the Lord glory and strength.
> Ascribe to the Lord the glory due his name;
>   bring an offering and come into his courts.
> Worship the Lord in the splendour of his holiness;
>   tremble before him, all the earth. (Psalm 96:7–9)

These verses provide the lyrics of the "new song" Israel was instructed in verse 1 to sing among the nations. The song turns out to be an invitation to the nations to come and worship the God of Israel, to "bring an offering and come into his courts" (verse 8). The same thought appears in Psalms 57, 66, 108 and the lovely Psalm 117:

Praise the LORD, all you nations;
    extol him, all you peoples.
For great is his love toward us,
    and the faithfulness of the LORD endures forever.
Praise the LORD. (Psalm 117)

This is nothing other than the fulfilment of King Solomon's inaugural prayer for the Jerusalem temple. After pleading with the Lord for blessings on Israel, Solomon asks for the same blessings (through the temple) to be poured out on non-Israelites:

> As for the foreigners who do not belong to your people Israel ... when they come and pray toward this temple, then hear from heaven, your dwelling place. Do whatever the foreigners ask of you, so that all the peoples of the earth may know your name and fear you, as do your own people Israel. (1 Kings 8:41–43)

What King Solomon prayed for, Psalm 96 (and others) invites: all people everywhere to come to the place of God's presence (the temple in the old covenant; the Lord Jesus in the new) and "worship" him.

Psalm 96 and the Great Mission Equation

There are so many interesting things we could explore in this important psalm. For instance, it is often said that the Old Testament has no interest in seeing Gentiles join God's people. That idea, say some, developed only in the New Testament. But Psalm 96 (among others) shows that this is not true. Several Old Testament texts, and many Jews of the pre-Christian era, were keen to invite the nations to know and worship the one true Lord. If this were a different sort of book, I would enjoy detailing the way in which large numbers of ancient pagans found themselves drawn to Jewish "worship services" to learn about the true God.[4]

But let me return to the main question of this chapter. *Why* were God's people to declare his praises within earshot of the Gentiles? What is the logic behind the call of Psalm 96 to promote God's glory and salvation to an unbelieving world? Verses 4–5, beginning with the Hebrew conjunction *ki* or "because", provide the all-important answer:

> For [or "because"] great is the LORD and most worthy of
>   praise;
>   he is to be feared above all gods.
> For all the gods of the nations are idols,
>   but the LORD made the heavens. (Psalm 96:4–5)

The splendour and majesty of the Lord must be promoted throughout the nations for the simple reason that there is no other Lord of the nations, no other Creator of the universe. All of the so-called gods are "idols". The Hebrew word for "idols" (*elilim*) basically means "nothingness/worthlessness". The Bible does not so much denigrate pagan gods as insist they are non-existent. Here we arrive at the fundamental equation of mission, the driving force behind all our efforts to bring the news of the one true Lord to our friends and neighbours:

> If there is one Lord to whom all people belong and owe their allegiance, the people of that Lord must promote this reality everywhere.

Monotheism and mission are intimately related. The existence of just one God makes our mission to the many essential.

This is not to say there are not other reasons for promoting the gospel as well. There are. For instance, the fact that our friends and neighbours need salvation from the coming judgment provides a real motivation to promote the news of a Saviour. Indeed, the final paragraphs of Psalm 96 itself remind us of this theme:

> The world is firmly established, it cannot be moved;
>   he will judge the peoples with equity.
> Let the heavens rejoice, let the earth be glad;
>   let the sea resound, and all that is in it.
> Let the fields be jubilant, and everything in them;
>   let all the trees of the forest sing for joy.

> Let all creation rejoice before the LORD, for he comes,
>   he comes to judge the earth.
> He will judge the world in righteousness
>   and the peoples in his faithfulness. (Psalm 96:10 – 13)

People in the West (even Christians) sometimes object profoundly to the idea of God's judgment. Part of the reason for this, I think, is a justified revulsion at the "fire and brimstone" preaching in some quarters of the church. But there is another reason: people just don't like it. Cognitive dissonance theory in psychology tells us that people tend to modify, or create, beliefs to suit their tastes. This is sometimes thrown at religious people in the form: "You just want a big daddy in the sky, so you invent a god to believe in." But the boot is often on the other foot: the inconvenience of the idea of a just God, especially one who might be displeased with the way we live, is a powerful motivation for many to exclude such a god from their thinking. They replace him with a more palatable image – the vague, distant God of peace and equilibrium, the One who always thinks happy thoughts about us. But the God of the Bible does not dispassion-

While Christians often think of the coming judgment as a key motivation for evangelism (as no doubt it is), the Bible does not make the connection between the two as obvious as we might have thought. The one passage that comes closest to connecting God's judgment with a motive or reason for evangelism is Paul's description of his apostolic ministry in 2 Corinthians 5:10 – 11: "For we must all appear before the judgment seat of Christ, that everyone may receive what is due them for the things done while in the body, whether good or bad. Since, then, we know what it is to fear the Lord, we try to persuade people." In context, however, Paul appears to be saying that he evangelises not out of fear *for others* (going to hell), as

ately view the world in all its injustice and godlessness. He is deeply outraged by the evil in the world and is coming to "judge the world in righteousness and the peoples in his faithfulness".

Having said all this, while the coming judgment is part of the *message* proclaimed in Psalm 96 to the nations (as it is in our new covenant gospel), it is not the *reason* for proclaiming the message. The rationale for this worldwide promotion of God's glory and salvation is clearly stated in verse 4: "For great is the LORD and most worthy of praise; he is to be feared above all gods." The fundamental reason for spreading the news of God is that he is the only one worthy of praise, the only God deserving of allegiance among all people. He is the One for the many.

Matthew 28:16–20 and the Mission Equation

Not surprisingly, the logic is exactly the same in the most famous New Testament passage about the gospel mission, the so-called Great Commission. When Jesus sends out his apostles to make

real as that must have been, but out of fear *for himself*. As the apostle to the Gentiles, Paul had received a weighty responsibility from the Lord. He therefore tries to persuade everyone about the gospel, lest he be found to have shirked his divine commission and fall under God's wrath.

Exactly the same idea is found in 1 Corinthians 9:16 ("Woe to me if I do not preach the gospel!"). This is not to say that God's judgment does not provide a strong and healthy motivation for getting involved in promoting the gospel. I am simply observing in passing that this is not a logic clearly spelled out in the Bible itself. The primary rationale for mission is the lordship of God/Christ.

disciples of all nations, the single reason offered for this task is the universal lordship of God or, more accurately, the lordship that God now exercises through his Messiah. Follow the Lord's logic:

> Then the eleven disciples went to Galilee, to the mountain where Jesus had told them to go. When they saw him, they worshiped him; but some doubted. Then Jesus came to them and said, "All authority in heaven and on earth has been given to me. *Therefore* go and make disciples of all nations, baptizing them in the name of the Father and of the Son and of the Holy Spirit, and teaching them to obey everything I have commanded you. And surely I am with you always, to the very end of the age." (Matthew 28:16–20, my emphasis)

There is debate about how much of this Great Commission applies directly to individual Christians today. Are we all to "teach"? Are we all to "baptise"? My own view, for what it's worth, is that while Matthew would have thought the specifics refer directly to the "eleven disciples" and those entrusted with the apostolic mission afterward (teachers, evangelists, etc.), the broad thrust of the Lord's command applies to all who know him. We might not all "go" throughout the nations, "teach" everything Jesus commanded and "baptise", but we do all promote the gospel – through our prayers, good works, public praise, financial support of gospel workers and daily conversations – and so contribute to making disciples of all nations. We all share in the aptly called Great Commission.

My main point, however, is thoroughly uncontroversial. Notice the reason Jesus gives for getting involved in this mission. It is made clear by the all-important "therefore": "All authority in heaven and on earth has been given to me. *Therefore* go and make disciples" (verses 18–19). The reference to "heaven and earth" obviously recalls Genesis 1:1 and refers to every part of creation. The one true God has given universal authority to the one true Lord, and for this reason we are to make disciples throughout the world. At the risk of sounding like a scratched CD, let me repeat the mission equation: if there is one Lord to whom all people belong and owe their allegiance, the people of that Lord must promote this reality everywhere.

We promote God's glory to the ends of the earth not principally because of any human *need* but fundamentally because of God's/Christ's unique worthiness as the Lord of heaven and earth. Promoting the gospel to the world is more than a rescue mission (though it is certainly that as well); it is a reality mission. It is our plea to all to acknowledge that they belong to one Lord.

In passing, I want to quote another passage that underlines the same theme. I will reflect more deeply on 1 Peter 3:15 in chapter 11, where we will explore the importance of giving an answer for the faith in everyday conversation. For now it is worth observing the reason offered by Peter for speaking up for Jesus: "But in your hearts revere Christ as Lord. Always be prepared to give an answer to everyone who asks you to give the reason for the hope that you have." In Greek this is one sentence: "But in your hearts revere Christ as Lord, always being prepared to give an answer . . ." In other words, Peter, who was an original recipient of the Great Commission, not only urges his readers to play a part in that mission but also motivates them with precisely the same rationale: the lordship of Jesus. It is because Jesus is Lord of heaven and earth that the apostles were to go and make disciples of all nations; it is because believers in general likewise revere Christ as Lord that they are now to "give an answer" in their daily lives.

Why promote Christ to your atheist friend with a nice car and the self-confidence to match? Not simply because he would be happier or more fulfilled with Jesus, but because in reality your friend belongs to the one true Lord (revealed in the gospel). Why take the gospel to cynical retirees with a lifetime of worldly experience and a fat nest egg to enjoy? Not simply because they will soon face eternity, but because right now they exist for the pleasure of the one true God. Why reach out to the super-student with the first class honours degree and wardrobe of designer clothes? Not simply because Christianity will make her more moral or productive in life, but because in reality she is the possession of her one and only King. Why send out (and support) missionaries to Mongolia or Burkina Faso? Not only because Asians and Africans need rescuing from God's judgment (as we all do) but because they too are creatures of the one Creator, and he alone deserves their worship.

The people of the world do, of course, have all sorts of needs of their Creator – it would be strange if it were otherwise – but more fundamental than their felt need of God is the reality of their duty toward him, to "ascribe to the LORD the glory due his name" (Psalm 96:8). This, above everything else, necessitates God's mission to the world.

An apparently true story is told of three young men who hopped on a bus in Detroit during the 1930s and tried to start a fight with a man sitting by himself at the back of the vehicle. They insulted him. He didn't respond. They turned up the heat of the insults. He said nothing. Eventually, the bus arrived at the stranger's stop, and he stood up. The lads realised he was much bigger than they had estimated from his seated position. He reached into his pocket, handed over his business card and walked off the bus. The lucky young men gathered around the business card and read the words: JO LOUIS, PROFESSIONAL BOXER. It turns out they had just tried to start a fight with the man who would soon become the world heavy weight boxing champion for more than a decade. How lucky they must have felt that day!

But imagine we were friends of Jo Louis on the bus that day, and these boys carried on in this way. Even if Louis said nothing – he was known for humility – we surely would have. But why? Well, partly I guess out of fear for the three young men. Louis was said to be able to knock out a horse with one blow (though I have no idea how one gains that reputation). But there is a deeper answer. These lads were in the presence of greatness and did not know it. They had to be informed. His sheer greatness demands it. We would surely have chimed in, "Excuse me, may I tell you who this is!"

Our friends and neighbours live and breathe in the presence of the greatest Lord. Yet, they do not know it. We, the people of the Lord, who know his majesty over heaven and earth, must stand up on the bus, so to speak, and, in whatever way is appropriate to our gifts, personality and circumstances, promote his glory.

The next time you're in a café and someone protests, "So, you want to convert the world. How dare you!" don't be dumbfounded as I was; don't begin to question the rationale or beauty of God's mission. Just remind yourself of the mission equation crystallised in the Great Commission and in 1 Peter 3:15 and sung about in the Psalms:

> Declare his glory among the nations,
> > his marvellous deeds among all peoples.
> For great is the LORD and most worthy of praise;
> > he is to be feared above all gods.
> For all the gods of the nations are idols,
> > but the LORD made the heavens. (Psalm 96:3 – 5)

CHAPTER 2

The Many and the One

The Challenge of Pluralism

For all the gods of the nations are idols, but the
LORD made the heavens.

Psalm 96:5

AFTER GIVING A RECENT SERMON on Psalm 96, exploring some
of the themes discussed in the previous chapter, I was approached
by a Christian man who said, "Thanks for that, John. I really
liked it . . ."—from the tone in his voice I could tell what was
coming next—"*but* isn't it possible that the one God worshiped
by us is the same Lord worshiped in different ways by Buddhists,
Hindus and Muslims?" His logic was: if everyone has their own
version of the Lord, we don't really need to promote our version
to them.

In terms of what Psalm 96 teaches, the answer is fairly
straightforward, as I pointed out to the gentleman. The psalmist insists that the "gods" of the nations are mere "idols", noth-
ingness. Moreover, those who worship such things are urged:
"Ascribe to the LORD the glory due his name; bring an offering and come into his courts" (verse 8). The word "LORD" used

here (in capitals in our Bibles) is the Hebrew word *Yahweh*, the personal name of the God of Israel: "God" (*elohim*) and "Lord" (*adonai*) are different words altogether. Those outside of Israel are asked to worship God as Yahweh, that is, as he has revealed himself to Israel. The fact that they are also urged to "come into his courts" (the Jerusalem temple) makes clear that from the psalmist's perspective those without biblical faith are meant to give up their religions and embrace the one God of the Bible. It is difficult to square this teaching with the idea that "the one God worshiped by us is the same Lord worshiped in different ways by Buddhists, Hindus and Muslims".

But my friend's question is not quite so easily answered. He was not asking for more exegetical details about Psalm 96. He was wondering out loud what many today have begun to think: perhaps the religions of the world are different paths up the same mountain. This is the challenge of "pluralism", the popular belief that spiritual truth (unlike most other truths) appears in many forms (hence: "plural"), not just one. If true, pluralism would provide a monumental defeater to the idea of Christian mission as I have expounded it. So, some comments are in order. I have written a book or two on this topic, and so I ask those who have read my previous material to bear with me in the next few pages as I cover some of the same territory.[5]

There are two forms of pluralism, "popular" and "sophisticated". Both challenge the mission equation taught in Psalm 96 and potentially undermine Christians' confidence in the reasonableness of the task of promoting the gospel to the world.

Popular Pluralism

Popular pluralism is the pluralism you meet in the café, the workplace and sometimes even over morning tea after church. It basically states that all religions teach essentially the same thing. Sure, they differ on what name to give God (Yahweh, Allah) or how to approach him in prayer, but basically they agree on the big issues – God's existence, the afterlife, the need for human kindness and so on.

The basic problem with popular pluralism is that in trying to affirm all religions, it pays close attention to none of them. For the most part, the great religious traditions of the world make claims that are entirely at odds with each other. Superficially, they agree – most of them, for instance, say prayers – but at the more basic level they tend to refute each other. Let me list some of the more obvious contradictions:

Hinduism teaches that many gods, or *devas*, exist in the world, each reflecting some aspect of ultimate reality (Brahman) but nonetheless possessing individual existence. Guru Nanak, however, a one-time Hindu and founder of the Sikh faith, rejected the existence of many gods, insisting instead that there was just one deity worthy of worship. Siddhartha Gautama (the Buddha) also rejected Hinduism, but not by proposing the existence of one god; he rejected belief in God altogether, a position still held in Classical (Theravada) Buddhism. You don't need a degree in mathematics to see fundamental contradictions here. If there are many gods, there cannot be just one. If there is one god, there cannot be many. And if there is no god at all, there can be neither one god nor many.

Take the central Christian belief that Jesus Christ was the Son of God, the promised Jewish Messiah, who died on a cross and rose again. This is nonnegotiable for Christians – without it you don't have Christianity. But modern Judaism insists that Jesus was not the Messiah, just one of many pretenders to that title. The true Messiah, says Orthodox Judaism, is yet to come. This matter gets more complicated with Islam since the Koran declares that Jesus neither died on a cross nor was the Son of God. The Koran describes the latter belief as "blasphemous".[6]

Views on the afterlife are equally contradictory. Hinduism believes in an eternal soul, or *atman*, which resides in every human being (and other living creatures). When we die that soul passes to another physical life. After many such reincarnations this soul, if it is worthy, may escape rebirth in the physical world and return to the ultimate nonphysical reality of Brahman. While people often lump together the Hindu and Buddhist views of the afterlife, this is actually an area of major disagreement between them. Classical Buddhism rejects both the existence of the soul and the goal of returning to Brahman. Extinguishment (*nirvana*) from bodily reality is the hope of Buddhism. The Christian view of the afterlife, with its emphasis on the "resurrection of the body and the life everlasting" (to quote the Apostles' Creed) couldn't be more different from both Buddhism and Hinduism.

Many, many other contradictions could be explored, but in reality you can only insist on the harmony of the great religions (popular pluralism) by ignoring some of their most important beliefs. Here is the important point for a Christian thinking about world religions: the God who produced the Bible could not possibly be the one who produced the Koran (Islamic scriptures), the Tripitaka (Buddhist scriptures) or the Upanishads (Hindu scriptures). The portraits of God, Jesus, ultimate reality and the afterlife offered in these sacred books are so contradictory that, unless God is not altogether truthful, it is just not possible to maintain the popular form of pluralism.

Sophisticated Pluralism

There is a more sophisticated path open to those who want to speak of the universal oneness of religions. Aware of the intractable contradictions between the faiths some theologians have begun to argue that while there are few explicit ideas common to the world religions, there is an implicit *big idea* made apparent by them all.

This grand truth, says the sophisticated pluralist, has little to do with praying to Allah five times a day, or following the Buddha's Eightfold Path or trusting in Jesus' death and resurrection. These are merely human attempts to tap into some deeper spiritual reality. Individual religions do not describe this reality; they merely express a longing to experience it. They are spiritual emblems.

Influential US theologian Marcus Borg has offered a powerful argument along just these lines.[7] Borg dubs his approach to religions "sacramental". By this he means that the importance of religions lies not in their particular claims to truth (their doctrines) but in their capacity to connect believers with the sacredness that lies behind all such claims. Religions mediate spiritual reality without actually possessing that reality themselves.

Borg uses the analogy of Communion or the Lord's Supper (hence the word *sacramental*). The bread and wine convey a sense of Jesus' death and ongoing presence without actually containing those things. In a similar way, he argues, the beliefs and practices of Buddhism, Christianity, Islam and so on mediate an experience of ultimate Reality without truly describing or laying hold of it.

Sophisticated pluralism offers what so many want: a way of thinking about all religions as equally valid. But this form of pluralism delivers far less than it promises. To begin with, pluralists like Marcus Borg never explain how they know that no religion describes a Reality they all mediate. Does the pluralist have access to something no one else does—a true knowledge of this ineffable Reality? If not, how can they say that no religion contains truth in an absolute sense? So far as I can tell, this question is never confronted in the vast literature on pluralism. Pluralists simply affirm their position with something resembling evangelistic zeal.

The presumption of sophisticated pluralism is spectacular. In essence, pluralism insists that although the world religions are entitled to their perceptions of Reality (believing in Christ, Buddha or whatever), the truth of the situation, really only understood by the pluralist, is that this Reality defies their attempts to describe and embrace it. Pluralism, in other words, claims to have discovered a bigger truth that none of the religions has observed before; it then suggests that the smaller truths the religions thought they could see (Jesus' death for sins, for example) are in fact mere symbols and sacraments of sacredness. This is a big call. By describing religions as true in a manner none of them has affirmed before and false in all the ways they have always affirmed, pluralism assumes an intellectual high ground that far exceeds any of the claims of the world religions.

It is true that Christianity, for example, on the basis of Christ's resurrection, makes the grandiose claim that two-thirds of the world's peoples are mistaken in their religious beliefs. But this cannot be any less acceptable than the tiny minority of Western pluralists arguing, without any attempt to substantiate the position, that the entire religious majority of the world is in possession of mere "sacraments" of a Reality they do not themselves understand.

Pluralism is frequently presented as the most bearable way to think about world religions. Marcus Borg is up-front about this. He insists that the idea of millions of non-Christians falling under God's judgment is simply intolerable. Some version of pluralism, then, has to be proposed just to cope with the fact that most people in the world don't belong to a single religious tradition. Pluralism, in other words, is more psychologically satisfying in our modern global context.

I don't think pluralism does avoid unbearableness. As I've just said, pluralism might not consign anyone to hell (since pluralists don't believe in hell), but it does consign virtually every religious tradition (except pluralism) to wholesale error. Remember, while pluralism sees all religions as vehicles of the sacred, it insists that none of them is actually true in the very sense each thinks it is true. The Muslim might think of the Koran as the word of God revealed to Muhammad by the angel Gabriel, but the pluralist knows this idea is merely a vehicle for sacred connection. The Christian might think that Jesus' death and resurrection are the most important events of salvation history, but the pluralist knows these are merely ideas that convey spiritual meaning to the believer. And so on. The serious Muslims and

Christians I know would much rather be accused of being flat-out wrong than damned with the faint and patronising praise of the pluralist.

Even if pluralism were a more bearable way to think about religious truth, is this a compelling basis for determining whether or not something is true? Plenty of intolerable things also happen to be true. The fact that more than 90 percent of the world's wealth is in the hands of less than 10 percent of the world's people is, for me, quite a horrendous thought, but that does not mean the statistic is untrue. Bearableness might provide a *motivation* for adopting a viewpoint like pluralism (we tend to adopt the beliefs we prefer), but it does not provide a rational *justification* for doing so.

Another motivation for embracing some form of pluralism is the fear of intolerance. History is littered with examples of violent intolerance on the part of those who believed their religion to be the only truth. Therefore, say pluralists, it is better to drop talk of absolute truth and view each other's religions as vehicles of the sacred (without actually being true descriptions of the sacred). However, as I have already said, many devoutly religious

---

"Tolerance" has become something of a buzz word for pluralism. In these tense and confusing times, claiming your position as the "tolerant" one seems the sure-fire way to win adherents, without the need for close scrutiny. But Christians should steal this word back. Tolerance comes from the Latin word *tolerare*, meaning "to bear" something harmful or contrary. The ancient Greek equivalent of *tolerare* is *anechomai*, and it appears in Paul's letter to the Ephesians: "Be completely humble and gentle; be patient, bearing (*anechomai*) with one another in love" (Ephesians 4:2). To gently bear another in love is to be truly tolerant.

people (Buddhists, Muslims, Christians and so on) find this more patronising than tolerant. Leaving that aside, surely the solution to intolerance is not to jettison the idea of spiritual truth but to work toward true tolerance.

True tolerance does not involve accepting every viewpoint as true and valid; it involves treating with love and humility someone whose opinions you believe to be untrue and invalid. A tolerant Buddhist, for example, is not one who accepts as true and valid the Hindu idea of the eternal Soul: that would require a denial of the Buddha's doctrine of No-Soul. No, the tolerant Buddhist is one who, while rejecting this particular Hindu belief, nonetheless treats Hindus with kindness and respect. In the same way, being a tolerant Christian does not involve accepting contrary beliefs as valid (as "vehicles of the sacred"); it involves treating with love those whose views we regard as untrue and invalid. True tolerance is the ability to treat with grace those with whom you disagree. And this is a deeply Christian quality, especially since the Lord who is proclaimed in our gospel is the epitome of humility, love and gentleness.

Pluralism promises much more than it delivers. For those who live under God's Word the mission equation of Psalm 96 (and, indeed, of the whole Bible) remains solid and compelling (though it must always be held with humility and tolerance). There is one Lord, to whom all people belong and owe their allegiance, and so the people of the Lord must promote this reality everywhere. Monotheism and mission are intimately related. The existence of just one God makes our mission to the many essential.

Let me now begin to describe that mission as it is revealed in the Scriptures.

CHAPTER 3

Following the "Friend of Sinners"

The Missionary Mind of the Ordinary Christian

> I am not seeking my own good but the good of many, so that they may be saved.
>
> *1 Corinthians 10:33*

You MAY HAVE HEARD the not-quite-true story about two American TV evangelists—let us call them Jimmy A and Jimmy B—who decided it was God's will for them to fly out to my home town of Sydney and set up shop here. They had heard how secular and sinful this city was and wanted to come and save our collective soul.

Unfortunately, twenty minutes short of Kingsford Smith Airport the plane they were travelling in lost all power to its engines and started careering toward the ground. Jimmy A fell to his knees and cried out, "O Lord, you know how much these people need my message: save me!" Jimmy B heard this, got to his knees and pleaded, "Lord, you know how much they need my message: save me!"

The plane crashed 3 km short of the airport. Whom did God save?

Sydney!

I once told a version of this story to a large church on the Gold Coast in Queensland. At the punch line I got nothing but a few nervous smiles and a large murmur throughout the hall. The rest of the sermon was unusually hard going. It turns out that the church I was preaching in was part of the worldwide network of the TV evangelist Jimmy Baker! I've since learnt to do some homework on the places where I speak.

In any case, the story usually "works", in a cheeky sort of way, because it taps into the cringe people feel not just about TV evangelists but about anyone presuming to "save our soul". I was first told the story when I was a travelling evangelist and I have always valued the anecdote as a reminder never to slip into forms of evangelism that are, or could appear, presumptuous and arrogant.

For some Christians this "salvation cringe" is so keenly felt they avoid getting involved in mission in any overt way. It is not that they lack concern for their neighbours; it is just that they do not want to appear too evangelistically zealous. That is too high a price to pay.

One New Testament text provides the perfect rebuke and medicine for those experiencing the salvation cringe. It offers a rebuke because it makes clear that Christians in general—not just apostles and evangelists—are to seek the salvation of their neighbours. It provides the medicine because it reveals that seeking the salvation of others does not involve dying for sins (as Jesus did) or evangelizing the known world (as Paul did). It involves something far less scary, far more manageable and far more basic—a mission mind-set.

The mind-set is stated beautifully in Paul's letter to the Corinthians:

> So whether you eat or drink or whatever you do, do it all for the glory of God. Do not cause anyone to stumble, whether

> Jews, Greeks or the church of God—even as I try to please everyone in every way. For I am not seeking my own good but the good of many, so that they may be saved. Follow my example, as I follow the example of Christ. (1 Corinthians 10:31–11:1)

Notice the logic spelled out here by Paul: just as I (the apostle) follow Jesus in seeking the salvation of others, so you (Corinthians) should follow me in the same task: "Follow my example as I follow the example of Christ."

In the rest of this chapter I want to follow Paul's gospel-logic closely. I will begin with Jesus' mission to save, looking particularly at his friendships with sinners and his death on the cross. Then I will briefly show how Jesus' mission influenced that of the apostle Paul. And, finally (and more importantly for us), I will

It may surprise you to learn that there is a version of the "salvation cringe" among scholars as well. Some historians and biblical experts have argued that neither ancient Judaism nor ancient Christianity was as missionary-minded as was previously thought. If you read their works, it is difficult not to suspect that a scholarly version of the "salvation cringe" has influenced some of their conclusions—Jewish scholars want to protect ancient Jews from appearing too zealous for proselytising; some Christian scholars want to do the same for the early Christians. My own doctoral work took issue with these scholars and tried to demonstrate that both ancient Judaism (to some degree) and Christianity (to quite a large degree) were devoted to the salvation of outsiders. For keen readers the published thesis is *Mission-Commitment in Ancient Judaism and in the Pauline Communities* (WUNT II 159: Tübingen: Mohr Siebeck, 2003), available in most major university and theological college libraries.

explore how we too are to follow the example of the apostle and the Lord in "seeking the good of many, *so that they may be saved*".

Jesus: The Original "Friend of Sinners"

One "evangelist" who could never be made the butt of this chapter's opening joke is Jesus. The "salvation cringe" could never be felt about his ministry—and we should remember, it is his mission that shapes ours.

One of the most striking aspects of Jesus' ministry in its first-century Palestinian setting was his regular socialising with people classed "sinners". "Sinners" were those in Jewish society who lived outside the laws of the Old Testament as interpreted by the rabbis. They were not all prostitutes and thieves—that would be a caricature. They could just as easily be wealthy businessmen who neglected going to synagogue and/or did business with the occupying Romans (tax collectors, for instance). They were, if you like, the "unreligious" in a strictly religious society.

Social interaction with sinners (and with Gentiles) was religiously prohibited in Jesus' day. In particular, you were not to share a meal with such people. In ancient societies, eating and drinking were powerful symbols of fellowship. To share food and drink with people was to identify with and, in a sense, to endorse them. Jesus, however, flaunted these centuries-old customs. He wined and dined with sinners on a regular basis—so much so that the "pious" in his society began to slander him in public. Matthew 11:19 records one such slander: "Here is a glutton and a drunkard, a friend of tax collectors and 'sinners'." Let me remind you of a few more examples from the Gospels:

> While Jesus was having dinner at Levi's house, many tax collectors and "sinners" were eating with him and his disciples, for there were many who followed him. When the teachers of the law who were Pharisees saw him eating with the "sinners" and tax collectors, they asked his disciples: "Why does he eat with tax collectors and 'sinners'?" (Mark 2:15–16)

A woman in that town who lived a sinful life learned that Jesus was eating at the Pharisee's house, so she came there with an alabaster jar of perfume. As she stood behind him at his feet weeping, she began to wet his feet with her tears. Then she wiped them with her hair, kissed them and poured perfume on them.

When the Pharisee who had invited him saw this, he said to himself, "If this man were a prophet, he would know who is touching him and what kind of woman she is—that she is a sinner." (Luke 7:37–39)

Now the tax collectors and "sinners" were all gathering around to hear Jesus. But the Pharisees and the teachers of the law muttered, "This man welcomes sinners and eats with them." (Luke 15:1–2)

Jesus entered Jericho and was passing through. A man was there by the name of Zacchaeus; he was a chief tax collector and was wealthy. He wanted to see who Jesus was, but because he was short he could not see over the crowd. So he ran ahead and climbed a sycamore-fig tree to see him, since Jesus was coming that way.

When Jesus reached the spot, he looked up and said to him, "Zacchaeus, come down immediately. I must stay at your house today." So he came down at once and welcomed him gladly.

All the people saw this and began to mutter, "He has gone to be the guest of a 'sinner'." (Luke 19:1–7)

This last example is especially interesting. Befriending Zacchaeus and delivering a sermon in his home are Jesus' final acts before entering Jerusalem for his last week. This passage is a deliberate climax to Luke's account of Jesus and captures all that his ministry has been about for the last three years.

Imagine being there that day. The most famous teacher in Palestine invites himself to the home of Jericho's archetypal "sinner". Zacchaeus was not only something of a financial tycoon, as a "chief tax collector" he was also deeply involved with the Romans, on whose behalf he collected taxes (the Romans had occupied Palestine since 63 BC). But Zacchaeus is so over-whelmed by this strange acceptance from the one rumoured to be the "Messiah" that right then and there he devotes himself publicly to the path of God. Jesus responds with what are per-haps the climactic words of Luke's Gospel so far:

> Jesus said to him, "Today salvation has come to this house, because this man, too, is a son of Abraham. For the Son of Man came to seek and to save what was lost." (Luke 19:9 – 10)

Jesus' mission is stated perfectly here: "to seek and to save what was lost". Through his preaching Jesus declared that salva-tion, through his death and resurrection (just one week later) he would accomplish that salvation, and through the generosity of his social life he embodied that salvation.

Jesus' friendship with sinners gave people a tangible sign of the welcoming grace of God. His questionable dining habits were not merely an attempt to buck the system of his day; they were an illustration of the fellowship with sinners God so keenly desires. To preempt where I am heading, this is the mission to which we are called. Our entire life, including our social life, should demonstrate the Lord's desire to have fellowship with sinners.

Under God, my own conversion was the result of one person's willingness to embody the mission of the "friend of sinners". My introduction to faith came not through family tradition, Sunday school, church attendance or any other formal means of reli-gious instruction but through the irresistible power of friend-ship and good food. One of the relics of Australia's Christian heritage is the once-a-week Scripture lesson offered in many state high schools around the country. Usually, the person run-ning the lesson was an elderly volunteer from the local church. I took my chances with these harmless old ladies because "non-Scripture" involved doing homework under the supervision of a real teacher. One of these Scripture teachers — Glenda was her name — had the courage one day to invite the entire class to her home for discussions about "God". The invitation would have gone unnoticed, except that she added: "If anyone gets hungry, I'll be making hamburgers, milkshakes and scones."

One Friday afternoon several weeks later I was sitting on a comfy lounge in this woman's home with half a dozen classmates feasting on hamburgers and bracing myself for the God-bit. I had never been to church or even had a religious conversation of length, so this was an entirely new experience. I remember thinking at the time that there was nowhere to run. I had eaten so much of her food I could not have got up out of the couch if I had tried.

As I looked around the room at my friends—all sceptics like me—I was amazed that this woman would open her home (and kitchen) to us. Some of the lads there were among the worst "sinners" in our school: one was a drug user (and seller), one was a class clown and bully, and one was a petty thief with a string of break-and-enters to his credit. We returned the next Friday (with more of our friends) and the next and the next. In fact, we turned up on this woman's doorstep most Friday afternoons for months.

I could not figure Glenda out. She was wealthy and intelligent. She had an exciting social life married to a leading Australian businessman. What was she thinking inviting us for a meal and discussion?

At no point was this teacher pushy or preachy. Her style was completely relaxed and incredibly generous. When her VCR went missing one day she made almost nothing of it, even though she suspected (quite reasonably) it was one of our group. For me, her open, flexible and generous attitude toward us "sinners" was the doorway into a life of faith. As we ate and drank and talked, it was clear this was no mere missionary ploy on her part. She truly cared for us and treated us like friends or, perhaps more accurately, like sons. As a result, over the course of the next year she introduced several of us from the class to the ultimate "friend of sinners", Jesus, which is why this book is dedicated to Glenda.

Paul: The Flexible Apostle

I don't want to jump too quickly from Jesus' mission to ours. Instead, I want to explore briefly how the original "friend of sinners" influenced the mission of Paul, who would later say, "Follow my example, as I follow the example of Christ" (1 Corinthians 11:1).

Paul was not a member of Jesus' original circle of disciples. He was a Jerusalem-trained Pharisee and a slanderer of Jesus and the early Christians. However, when Paul witnessed Jesus raised from the dead, all of his criticisms evaporated. For the next thirty years he devoted himself to proclaiming Jesus as Lord throughout the Roman Empire.

Here is the point of interest: Paul, the one-time Pharisee, became (in)famous in Jewish and Christian circles for his scandalously flexible social conduct. Not only did he preach to pagans, he broke with his Pharisaic customs and ate with them as well. For a first-century Jewish rabbi this was almost unthinkable. Even some of the early Christians found Paul's behaviour problematic. A fascinating insight into this aspect of Paul's ministry can be gleaned from Galatians 2:11 – 21. The apostles Peter and Paul had a rather public argument over the question of eating with pagans. Peter, who should have known better, decided to eat separately from Gentiles. Paul denounced Peter for "not acting in line with the truth of the gospel" (Galatians 2:14). Other Christians continued to criticise Paul, but he could only reply that his flexibility, like that of Jesus, was oriented toward the salvation of outsiders. The point is well made in another passage in 1 Corinthians:

> Though I am free and belong to no one, I have made myself a slave to everyone, to win as many as possible. To the Jews I became like a Jew, to win the Jews. To those under the law I became like one under the law (though I myself am not under the law), so as to win those under the law. To those not having the law I became like one not having the law (though I am not free from God's law but am under Christ's law), so as to win those not having the law. To the weak I became weak, to win

> the weak. I have become all things to all people so that by all
> possible means I might save some. I do all this for the sake of the
> gospel, that I may share in its blessings. (1 Corinthians 9:19 – 23)

This text is fascinating for a couple of reasons. Firstly, the
echo of Jesus' own practice of associating with sinners for their
salvation is strong in this passage. You will recall that by win-
ing and dining with sinners like Zacchaeus, Jesus had, in the
opinion of the Pharisees, acted like someone not obeying the
Jewish law. He did this, as we saw in Luke 19:10, "to seek and
to save what was lost". Here in 1 Corinthians 9:19 – 23 Paul says
he does precisely the same thing in his ministry. With Jews, he
respects the ways of Jews. With Gentiles ("those without the
law") he respects the customs of Gentiles. And with the "weak"
(Christians weak in faith) he respects the frailties of the weak.[8]
He does all this for exactly the same reason as Jesus: "so that by
all possible means I might *save* some".

Paul's approach here is not a mere missionary ploy, an attempt
to get people onside before thumping them with the gospel.
Eating with sinners was for Paul exactly what it had been for
Jesus: an embodiment of the salvation message itself. How could
I preach the gospel, thought Paul, about the welcoming grace
of Christ, without embodying that grace in the way I mix with
Jews, Gentiles and (weak) Christians!

The passage is interesting for another reason. The description
of Paul's flexible mission found here in 1 Corinthians 9:19 – 23
clearly lies behind the apostle's call in 10:31 – 11:1 to follow his
example as he follows the example of Christ. Paul's approach
to his mission (which he inherited from Jesus) is to inform the
mission of all believers. To recall the passage I started with then:

> So whether you eat or drink or whatever you do, do it all for the
> glory of God. Do not cause anyone to stumble, whether Jews,
> Greeks or the church of God – even as I try to please everyone
> in every way. For I am not seeking my own good but the good
> of many, so that they may be saved. Follow my example, as I
> follow the example of Christ. (1 Corinthians 10:31 – 11:1)

The words "So whether you eat or drink" remind us that this paragraph is the conclusion to a discussion that commenced back in 1 Corinthians 8:1: "Now about food sacrificed to idols". For three whole chapters Paul has been discussing one of the thorniest questions to face the first Christians: am I allowed to attend pagan banquets where I will almost certainly end up eating meat offered to idols?

Banquets, Believers and the Mission of Christ

In the ancient Greek world virtually all of the meat sold in marketplaces had been dedicated to a pagan deity. The animals were slaughtered, prayed over by the priests and symbolically presented to a god in the temple. It was then taken to the market to be sold. From the Greek point of view this made their food "blessed"; from the Jewish and Christian point of view it made it tainted, cursed even. It was "demon-meat"!

So, what do you do when a non-Christian/non-Jewish business associate or relative invites you to a banquet in the home or in a local restaurant (of which there were several in Corinth)? There was no BYO meat in the ancient world! Do you accept the invitation and possibly "taint" yourself, or do you decline and keep yourself "pure"? This was a major question and you can understand why Paul would devote three chapters to answering it.

Although the contexts are different, the problem felt by the Corinthian Christians was similar to that raised by the Pharisees against Jesus: "Why does he eat with tax collectors and 'sinners'?" (Mark 2:15 – 16). The issue here is "purity" in one's social life. Can you eat with sinners or dine at pagan banquets and still honour God? Without expounding 1 Corinthians 8 – 10, let me just say that Paul neither instructs the Corinthians to share tainted meals with pagans nor orders them not to. His point is that a Christian's social conduct should be flexible. What is important, says Paul, is not whether you eat or drink but whether you are

Restaurants are not a modern invention. Throughout the Greco-Roman world of Paul's day there were restaurants literally attached to the pagan temples. The temple of Asklepios (a healing god) in Corinth, for instance, seems to have had three dining halls that fronted onto a public courtyard and bathing area. Local Corinthians probably frequented these "restaurants" for personal banquets, birthday parties and wedding feasts. Paul may have had a place like this in mind when he said to the Corinthians: "If anyone with a weak conscience sees you, with all your knowledge, eating in an idol's temple [a temple dining hall], won't they be emboldened to eat what is sacrificed to idols?" (1 Corinthians 8:10).[9]

seeking the good of others — just as Paul does and just as Jesus did. This is what 1 Corinthians 10:31 – 11:1 is about.

Paul insists that our social lives be governed not by "purity rules" but by three simple but profound goals. First, we should live with a desire to bring glory to the one true Lord: "So whether you eat or drink or whatever you do, do it all for the glory of God" (1 Corinthians 10:31). This reminds us of the great mission equation discussed earlier. If the worshipers of the one true God are to promote his glory throughout the world, it makes sense that our social lives — our "eating and drinking" — should be aligned to this reality as well. If God is glorified by your going to such banquets, says Paul, then go; if God will be glorified by your avoiding such banquets, then avoid them. Live for God's honour.

The second and third goals unpack what it means to shape our social life around the glory of God. Paul states the second goal in verses 32 – 33: "Do not cause anyone to stumble, whether Jews, Greeks or the church of God — even as I try to please everyone in every way." Throughout Paul's letters "stumbling" usually means missing out on salvation.[10] This verse, then, is not simply about upsetting people (Paul caused upset just about everywhere he went); it is about acting in a way that puts their salvation at risk. In the context of 1 Corinthians 8 – 10 Paul means that the Corinthians' dining habits must not threaten anyone's experience of salvation – whether Jews, Greeks or the church of God.

To give some concrete ancient examples, Christians must not dine in pagan restaurants in such a way that might lead weaker believers back into idol worship. Along a similar line, believers should not flaunt their dining freedoms in a way that might give Jews a reason to reject Christianity as an "unclean" religion. Nevertheless, attending pagan banquets should not be ruled out lest the Greek majority in Corinth begin to think that Christians are rude, exclusivist or (worse in an ancient context) uncitizenly. It is worth pondering in our modern context whether, humanly speaking, our actions could hinder our neighbour's experience of God's mercy.

What Paul states negatively in verse 32 he states positively in verse 33. Here he offers a third goal of Christian living. Not only are we to avoid jeopardising the salvation of others; we are to actively pursue that salvation: "even as I try to please everyone in every way. For I am not seeking my own good but the good of many, so that they may be saved. Follow my example, as I follow the example of Christ" (1 Corinthians 10:33 – 11:1).

In historical context it is not difficult to imagine how a Christian's flexible social life could contribute to the salvation of friends and neighbours. At the most basic level, Christians who mix with outsiders are visible and can be observed and quizzed by the unbelieving public. The same is true today, isn't it? Those who most regularly get into spiritual conversations with others are usually the ones with a wide circle of nonbelieving friends in the first place. Believers who bring friends and family to church are usually the ones who had dinner with these loved ones the week before.

Then there are the opportunities to talk about Christ. A popular feature of ancient banquets was philosophical discussion.

People would talk about the myths of Zeus at a dinner party just as easily as they would gossip about the latest love affair of some Roman senator. This would virtually guarantee any Christians present an opportunity to answer for their faith in Jesus. It is not much different today. Even the most passing spiritual comment at work, the café or a party will often spark a whole series of comments on the issue. People invariably feel justified in sounding off about "religion", whether or not they know much about it. This can sometimes be annoying but it also provides believers with an opportunity to quiz colleagues and friends about how they arrived at such opinions. Next time you're out with friends who don't believe, make a passing comment about your faith and just watch what happens. A visible (and audible) Christian is one who can be observed and questioned.

I do not want to *instruct* readers to go out and wine and dine with sinners; remember, Paul refrains from offering rules about such things. However, I want to ask you to reflect on Paul's teaching and on Jesus' example. Is your social life oriented toward the good of others—being with them, befriending them, doing good to them and speaking to them about Christ when opportunity invites? In short, does your life illustrate the fellowship with sinners God so keenly desires?

Christ's Photos

Max Lucado, in his classic book *No Wonder They Call Him the Savior*[11] relates the story of Christina, a young woman raised in a town outside Rio de Janeiro in Brazil. Christina had always longed to experience the bright lights and party atmosphere of this famous city but had often been warned off by her mother. Unemployment in the city was high; strip joints and brothels were about the only places offering jobs to young women. Christina didn't listen. One day she packed her bags and secretly took off to the city.

Terrified for what might become of her daughter, Christina's mother set out to find her. She searched the vast city in vain. Fearing the worst, she visited some of Rio's sleaziest establishments. On the walls of these places she pinned photos of herself. On the back of each photo she had written a simple message to her daughter. She returned home, devastated.

Christina eventually ended up employed in a Rio brothel. And one day, as she stumbled down the stairwell, she noticed on the wall a photo of her mum. Taking the image off the wall she discovered her mother's writing on the back. She turned it over and read the words: "Whatever you have done, whatever you have become, please just come home." And she did.

As Lucado points out, the actions of Christina's mother provide a wonderful picture of God's grace. But, for me, the story also offers a kind of allegory for our involvement in the mission of Christ. The "friend of sinners" entered the world in search of his lost ones, and many "Zacchaeuses" were indeed found and saved. But the Lord's mission continues on, long after his return to glory. He has left countless "photos" of himself throughout the world: you and me. Attached to those images is the message of God's welcoming grace toward sinners: "Whatever you have done, whatever you have become, please just come home." By what we say and do we communicate to those around us that the Lord desires the fellowship of sinners. We are the means by which, through God's Spirit, others hear the call to "come home" to the Father. We are Christ's photos.

The "Salvific Mind-set"

All of us are wired differently and have different opportunities to convey God's grace to others. We cannot die for the salvation of others as Jesus did. We probably will not travel the world preaching the gospel as Paul did. We can, however, give ourselves to the same cause: "to seek and to save what was lost". Following the example of Paul and Jesus does not necessarily mean that we do what they did. It means that we live by the same flexible ethos, seeking the good of many so that they may be saved. Every aspect of our lives – including our social lives – can and should be directed toward the glory of God and the salvation of our neighbours.

Paul underlines this point in three words I deliberately overlooked until now: "So whether you eat or drink or *whatever you do*, do it all for the glory of God" (1 Corinthians 10:31, my emphasis). Living for God's glory and the salvation of others applies not only to "eating and drinking" (our social conduct), but also to "whatever you do". What matters most is not whether we go to this or that dinner party, or take up this or that opportunity to speak for Christ. What counts is that our entire existence is informed by the quest to bring honour to God and salvation to others.

Paul is not advocating a specialised adjunct to Christian living called "mission" or "evangelism". He is asking us to put on what (in my more pretentious moments) I call a "salvific mind-set", that is, an outlook on life that cares deeply for the salvation of others.

The Lord is not asking you to be a superstar evangelist who preaches the gospel to everyone you meet (though, if you are wired that way, go for it). Reaching out to your friends and neighbours is a broad task. It is not an optional extra of the Christian life like attending an evangelism course, going on an outreach trip or reading a Christian book on promoting the gospel! It is the orientation of "whatever you do".

This point will become even clearer as we turn to the Bible's specific teaching about our involvement in mission. I hope to show in the remainder of the book that promoting the gospel involves just about every dimension of our existence: our social life (as we have just seen), our prayers, our use of money, our behaviour, our conversations and even our regular church meetings. Far from aggravating the dreaded "salvation cringe", I hope what follows will inspire confidence, creativity and commitment as you seek to follow the "friend of sinners".

We begin with what is perhaps the most basic dimension of promoting the gospel.

CHAPTER 4

The Hidden Mission

Promoting the Gospel with Our Prayers

The harvest is plentiful but the workers are few.
Ask the Lord of the harvest, therefore . . .

Matthew 9:37 – 38

IN THE PREVIOUS CHAPTER I mentioned my Scripture teacher Glenda. She had taught Scripture in the local high school for years with little observable "fruit". She had been faithful in the task but had not witnessed students coming to Christ for almost a decade. That year, everything changed. A citywide movement of prayer had commenced. Her particular group prayed specifically for Sydney's North Shore. They pleaded with the "Lord of the harvest" to open the hearts of many who had not known him before. In particular, they prayed for the school ministries in which several of them were involved.

Within the year Glenda's ministry was booming as she hosted regular evangelistic events in her home. As many as twenty students from the local school eagerly crammed into her lounge room to ask their questions and to hear guest speakers she invited along. At least six of the students from her class of 1982 turned to Christ for the first time. Three of them are now passing on the gospel to others full-time (including the author of this book).

A few years after these strange days, I asked Glenda what she put her "success" down to. Without blinking she answered, "Prayer. We prayed earnestly, regularly and specifically for your school, and the Lord in his grace answered us." As an evangelist who is sometimes tempted to think too highly of skill, style and creativity in evangelism, her words were (and are) a salient reminder that the "harvest" is the Lord's, not mine. The most basic gospel-promoting task, therefore, is not evangelism; it is prayer to the Lord of the harvest.

Compassion and Prayer (Matthew 9:35 – 10:5)

Jesus made a very important statement on this theme:

> Jesus went through all the towns and villages, teaching in their synagogues, proclaiming the good news of the kingdom and healing every disease and sickness. When he saw the crowds, he had compassion on them, because they were harassed and helpless, like sheep without a shepherd. Then he said to his disciples, "The harvest is plentiful but the workers are few. Ask the Lord of the harvest, therefore, to send out workers into his harvest field."
>
> Jesus called his twelve disciples to him and gave them authority to drive out evil spirits and to heal every disease and sickness . . . These twelve Jesus sent out . . . (Matthew 9:35 – 10:5)

This passage is a deliberate hinge in the Gospel of Matthew. It summarises the mission of Jesus so far ("Jesus went through all the towns . . . proclaiming") and introduces for the first time the involvement of Jesus' disciples in that mission, through prayer, preaching and healing. We have here an important passage on mission, one with several key insights into what it means to participate in Jesus' work.

Before the mission of Jesus' disciples is introduced, Matthew provides us with a rare insight into the Lord's emotional stance toward his work: "When he saw the crowds, he had compassion on them, because they were harassed and helpless, like sheep without a shepherd" (Matthew 9:36). There are a number of Greek terms that can be translated into English as "compassion". Matthew has chosen the most evocative to describe Jesus' feeling. *Splanchnizomai* is the verb form of the word "internal organs". An Australian would say, "he was gutted". At the very least, Matthew is saying that Jesus was deeply, inwardly moved by the plight of those "without a shepherd", that is, those without God's Messiah.

I remember watching the evening news during the Kosovo crisis. At one point footage was shown of orphaned Albanian children being piled into an open top truck and driven away, possibly never to see their home towns or relatives again. At one point, the camera zoomed in on one child's desperate face, and I felt physically sick with grief. That is the type of feeling Matthew ascribes to the Lord.

In passing, it is worth reflecting on our own attitude toward the "crowds" living in ignorance or defiance of the Shepherd — that

It probably goes without saying that "without a shepherd" (Matthew 9:36) means without the leadership of the true Messiah. "Shepherd" in the Old Testament was a regular metaphor for leaders and kings (King David, of course, was a nonmetaphorical shepherd). In the prophecy of Micah 5:2 – 4, as in Ezekiel 34:23, 31, the coming Messiah is described as a "shepherd". Matthew quotes Micah's prophecy in reference to Jesus in Matthew 2:6. All of this highlights again the rationale for mission we explored in chapter 1: what moves Jesus in Matthew 9:36 is people's lack of the true Lord (Shepherd). Christological monotheism drives our efforts to reach the world.

blasphemous colleague at work, the materialist down the road, the cynical relative or friend, the ever-mocking journalists in the media. It is easy to look down on such people, to view them with scorn and anger. Righteous anger might be appropriate sometimes, but we would do well to recall Matthew's summation of Jesus' emotional response to the unbelieving masses. Following Jesus in his mission must at least mean sharing something of his compassion.

I also believe that this compassion should wean us off our contemporary Christian dependence on the latest evangelistic program and product. Think about it. Most of the useful evangelistic and church growth systems started as some pastor's empathic effort to understand and reach the wider community with the gospel. Unsurprisingly, such compassionate listening and activity won a hearing and led to great "results" for the Lord.

In times past successes like these would be retold with thankfulness to the Lord, and others would seek to emulate the zeal and compassion of the original pastor. Nowadays, we create products out of the system itself: we put on conferences, write books and develop DVD-based courses. We professionalise and commercialise what started as a simple expression of love for the lost. I am not suggesting we ditch the products (how could I?). I am asking readers to ponder the foundational importance for evangelism of a deep compassion, out of which will flow the right "system" for your own context.

It is directly out of Jesus' compassion that his call to be involved in mission comes:

> Then he said to his disciples, "The harvest is plentiful but the workers are few. Ask the Lord of the harvest, therefore, to send out workers into his harvest field."
>
> He called his twelve disciples to him and gave them authority . . . (Matthew 9:37 – 10:1)

I am very struck by these words. Humanly speaking, the most obvious solution to the problem of a "plentiful harvest" and

The term "workers" in Matthew 9:38 is an agricultural metaphor. It is the regular term for farm labourers. Here it refers specifically to those sent out by Jesus to preach the kingdom. That becomes clear in Matthew 10:10 when Jesus says to the twelve apostles to take "no bag for the journey or extra shirt or sandals or a staff; for workers are worth their keep". As a piece of gospel trivia this term "worker" became one of the most popular titles for missionaries in early Christianity (Romans 16:21; 1 Corinthians 3:9; Philippians 2:25; 4:3; 1 Thessalonians 3:2; 2 Timothy 2:15).

"few workers" would have been straightaway to send out more workers—those who can announce the arrival of the Shepherd. But this is not exactly how it works. Before Jesus "calls" and "sends out" the *twelve* disciples (10:1), he asks *all* disciples to get involved in the harvest in a more basic way (9:37). They are to ask the Lord of the harvest to send out such gospel workers. The vital link between the masses who need to hear the gospel and the "workers" who are sent out to preach the gospel is the whole company of disciples praying for the work of the gospel.

The word translated "ask" in verse 38 is not the usual term for a simple request; it is the more emotive word *deomai*, which means "to beg, plead". The assumption here is that believers will be moved with the compassion of Jesus for the world and so will not simply "ask" God to send out more workers, as one request among many; they will plead with him to do so. God's people understand the world's need for the Shepherd, feel the compassion of Christ toward them and beg the Lord of the harvest to advance the work of the gospel.

Evangelism is grounded in heartfelt prayer. I realise this is a mother's-milk statement, but sometimes I am in danger of treating prayer as if it were mother's milk—something I have grown out of. How many of our churches have spent more time crafting mission statements, devising strategic plans and organising evangelistic programs than pleading with God for success in these activities? I am charging myself here. In my own church we tried to remain conscious of the priority of prayer. Instead of developing a manifold strategy for evangelism, we decided to produce and distribute a seven-paragraph congregational prayer, something that captured our hopes as a congregation and gave focus to our pleas to the Lord and planning in evangelism. We figured that even if our strategies failed, the Lord might still answer our prayers. The irony in our case, unfortunately, is that we probably gave more hours to writing, designing and printing this church prayer than we did over the next year in mission-focused prayer meetings!

Recently my wife read to me from the quarterly magazine of our favourite missionary organization (Church Missionary Society). The article described some of the setbacks experienced over the years by the CMS. After some glory days in the early 1800s CMS started to experience financial troubles. The committee began to consider holding missionaries back from the field – something that would have disturbed the founders of the society no end. Between 1856 and 1872 CMS found itself in debt and without any new missionary candidates. In 1872, however:

> A day of prayer was held – for missionary candidates not money – and it had immediate results. More people offered for service in the next few months than had offered in as many years before. And CMS received, without asking for it, the largest income it had ever received in one year.[12]

The history of CMS remains one of Australia's most exciting missionary stories with over 130 missionaries throughout the world today. In large part, it is a story of earnest prayer.

At the very least, I am saying that when you pray for the work of the gospel, and in particular, for the sending out of more "workers", you are actually promoting the gospel. You are personally seeking the salvation of others in obedience to, and in imitation of, the "friend of sinners".

Prayer and Mission throughout the Bible

The connection between prayer and mission is not peculiar to Jesus' teaching. Intercession for the salvation of the world is a theme that appears throughout the Bible. In fact, the practice began a millennium before Jesus.

As far back as the foundation of the first Jerusalem temple (about 950 BC), prayer was understood to be a means of winning the nations to faith in God. At the grand opening and dedication of the temple, Solomon, the third king of Israel, offered a lengthy and beautiful prayer about the temple's significance in the world (1 Kings 8:22 – 53). Most of the prayer, naturally enough, concerns God's blessings for the Israelites. One paragraph in the middle, however, reveals Solomon's concern for those who do not yet know the glory of the true Lord:

> As for the foreigners who do not belong to your people Israel but have come from a distant land because of your name – for they will hear of your great name and your mighty hand and your outstretched arm – when they come and pray toward this temple, then hear from heaven, your dwelling place. Do whatever the foreigners ask of you, so that all the peoples of the earth may know your name and fear you, as do your own people Israel. (1 Kings 8:41 – 43)

Here is an Old Testament king pleading with God in prayer to help pagans know and fear the Lord just as Israel does. It should not surprise us to learn that many Jews in the ancient world – in the period between the Old Testament and Jesus – saw it as their duty to pray for the salvation of the Gentiles. Jesus, as the ultimate king of God's people, urged his followers to do exactly the same.

Numerous other biblical texts emphasise the role of prayer in God's mission. Two themes can be seen: (1) praying for unbelievers with a view to their salvation; and (2) praying for the ongoing work of those who evangelise unbelievers.

Pleading with God

In the letter to the Romans Paul tells us that it was his practice to plead with God on behalf of people who do not yet follow Jesus (Jews, in this case): "Brothers and sisters, my heart's desire and prayer to God for the Israelites is that they may be saved" (Romans 10:1). I love the thought that Paul, after all the rejection he had experienced from his own people, was still wrestling in prayer, whether in his prison cell or on the road to the next Gentile town, for his beloved fellow Jews who did not yet know his Lord. He was the apostle to the Gentiles, but he worked for the salvation of Israel through his prayers.

In his letter to a long-term missionary colleague, Paul urges Timothy to ensure that the congregations in his care (throughout Ephesus) likewise pray for the unbelieving world:

> I urge, then, first of all, that petitions, prayers, intercession and
> thanksgiving be made for everyone [literally: "all people"] – for

The first-century Jewish teacher and philosopher, Philo of Alexandria, spoke of Israel's calling in the world in terms of prayer for other nations: "a nation destined to be consecrated above all others to offer prayers for ever on behalf of the human race that it may be delivered from evil and participate in what is good" (Philo, *On the Life of Moses* 1.149). Though couched in language appropriate to Philo's Greco-Roman context (he is in northern Egypt, after all), the content of these prayers shows what can only be described as a missionary orientation, dare I say a "salvific mind-set". "Escaping evil" and "sharing in good" can mean nothing other than leaving paganism and adopting the worship of the one true God, the ultimate good in Philo's view.

In another work, Philo says much the same thing about the role of the high priest in Jerusalem:

kings and all those in authority, that we may live peaceful and quiet lives in all godliness and holiness. This is good, and pleases God our Saviour, who wants all people to be saved and to come to a knowledge of the truth. (1 Timothy 2:1–4)

It is important to see the logical connection between verses 1–2 and verses 3–4. Why is it good for Christians to pray for "all people"? Because such prayers please the One who desires "all people" to be saved. In other words, prayers for the unbelieving world fulfil the Saviour God's longing to redeem that world. Praying for those who do not yet believe is actually a way of seeking their salvation. Prayer is not a passive, sideline aspect of evangelistic commitment; it is a fundamental expression of that commitment.

To personalise this, one of my dearest friends, Lucy, spent two years surrounded by committed Christians in her workplace. She was one of the most frequently evangelised people I

Among the other nations the priests are accustomed to offer prayers and sacrifices for their kinsmen and friends and fellow-countrymen only, but the high priest of the Jews makes prayers and gives thanks not only on behalf of the whole human race but also for the parts of nature, earth, water, air, fire. For he holds the world to be, as in very truth it is, his country, and in its behalf he is wont to propitiate the Ruler with supplication and inter-cession, beseeching Him to make His creature a partaker of His own kindly and merciful nature. (Philo, *Special Laws* 1.97)

Whether or not Jews in Israel or the high priest in Jerusa-lem were actually doing what Philo suggests they ought to have been doing, it is reasonable to assume that Philo reflects here a community consciousness on the part of Jews of first-century Alexandria (the largest Jewish community outside Palestine) of their divinely appointed role to pray for the salvation of the Gentile world.[13]

have ever known. For some reason, though, the message did not connect. She liked what she heard; she loved the Christians she mixed with (every day); but she could not bring herself to accept that Jesus died and rose for her. Over those two years many, many "petitions, prayers and intercessions" had been offered to God on her behalf, with no apparent answer. That changed late one night when one of Lucy's friends felt compelled to get up out of bed, get on his knees and pray earnestly for Lucy to come to know the truth. Her friend claims never to have felt this kind of compulsion before or since. That same night, completely unbeknown to the friend, Lucy too was lying in bed pondering all that her friends had been telling her over the last two years.

Suddenly, Lucy explains, a kind of "mental blindfold" was removed and she knew God loved her and that he had sent Jesus to die and rise again for her. In that moment, she thanked the Lord and embraced his gift. Imagine her friend's surprise when the next morning she rang him to say, "I get it. I get it. I understand what God has done for me. I know I'm a Christian!" Lucy's mate nearly fell off his chair. He admits he wept. Many of us did when we found out. Ten or more years later, Lucy and her family continue to grow in the faith.

Those who like church history (I trust I am not the only one) will be interested to know that Ignatius, the third bishop of Antioch and glorious martyr for Christ, urged his fellow believers to pray for the salvation of those around them. In his letter to the Christians of Ephesus, written on the way to his execution in Rome (about AD 110), he writes: "Now for other men pray unceasingly, for there is in them a hope of repentance, that they may find God" (Ignatius, *Ephesians* 10.1). Prayer for an unbelieving world has always been at the core to our mission.

I am not telling you this story for the "spook" factor, nor because I think the Lord operates this way all the time. I am sure he does not. Many of us have been praying for our loved ones for decades with no apparent answer. But Lucy's story crystallises for me, in a dramatic way, that evangelism and prayer are two sides of the one coin. One is public; the other is silent and hidden from view. Both are vital.

As one of the people who was evangelising Lucy I was humbled to know of the hidden prayers of her friends and to observe the wonderfully solo manner of her conversion. Against an occasionally activist church culture, where "busyness", "programming" and "events" are highly valued, I was reminded that the hidden dimension of mission is probably more basic to the achievement of God's purposes than the public dimension. I am all for activism in mission but not at the expense of compassionate, regular prayer for our unbelieving friends, family and world. Such prayers are pleasing to God our Saviour, who wants all people to be saved and to come to know the truth.

Intercession for Others

Intercession on behalf of those who do not yet believe is just one part of the gospel-prayer equation. Equally important – though perhaps not as personally captivating – is prayer specifically on behalf of those who give their time to telling the gospel to others. We have already seen in Matthew 9:37–38 that we are to pray for an increased number of gospel workers. Three further texts in the New Testament urge us to pray for the ongoing success of such workers.

In Ephesians 6:19 Paul urges believers to pray for him as one of those sent out by Christ to preach the gospel:

> Pray also for me, that whenever I speak, words may be given me so that I will fearlessly make known the mystery of the gospel, for which I am an ambassador in chains. Pray that I may declare it fearlessly, as I should. (Ephesians 6:19–20)

Some may think that those engaged in full-time gospel preaching need little ongoing prayer for "words" and "fearlessness". As someone involved in this sort of public ministry, I urge readers never to think that way. If Paul needed such prayers, the rest of us do even more so.

Paul asks the Thessalonians to do the same thing, this time with a focus on praying for the success of the gospel message itself: "As for other matters, brothers and sisters, pray for us that the message of the Lord may spread rapidly and be honoured, just as it was with you" (2 Thessalonians 3:1).

Lifting the Gospel above Our Circumstances

Let me quote one final passage on this theme:

> Devote yourselves to prayer, being watchful and thankful. And pray for us, too, that God may open a door for our message, so that we may proclaim the mystery of Christ, for which I am in chains. Pray that I may proclaim it clearly, as I should. (Colossians 4:2 – 4)

Of all the things Paul urges his churches to pray for, prayer for the work of the gospel is the most common. More than that: of all the things the New Testament mentions as gospel-promoting activities (giving money, speaking of Jesus, and so on) prayer is the one most frequently urged. I do not for a moment want to encourage readers to be silent about their faith: that would be a tragedy and a sure sign of ill health as Christians. But even more tragic, I believe, would be our silence in prayer, the primary evangelistic task of every believer. As British commentator and preacher Dick Lucas affirms:

> It is of great interest that the first duty of the Christians in Colossae was to open their mouths in prayer for the preachers of the gospel whom God had evidently called to this work. It was not, by inference, their first duty themselves to preach.

The fresh and necessary awakening of the churches today to the concept of "every-member ministry," and the mobilization of all Christians to take the gospel to all the world, should not be allowed to tone down this truth.[14]

Why is prayer so critical for mission? The Colossians passage just quoted provides the answer. In prayer we lift the work of the gospel above mere circumstances and into the hands of the One who governs everything. Paul strikes this theme in a wonderful piece of irony in verse 3: "And pray for us, too, that God may open a door for our message, so that we may proclaim the mystery of Christ, for which I am in chains" (Colossians 4:3). An "open door" for the message, even though the chief messenger is locked up "in chains": only prayer could ensure such a beautifully illogical reality! Paul was confident that, through the intercessions of other believers, God's Word would never be constrained by mere circumstances.

So many factors work against the progress of the gospel. There are external matters, such as widespread apathy toward things spiritual or increasing antipathy generated by, among other things, the strident New Atheism of Richard Dawkins, Sam Harris, Christopher Hitchens and others. There are internal matters, such as church politics and disunity. There are personal factors too, like doubt, depression and family strain, things that deflate the evangelistic confidence of congregations and pastors. While there may be a range of practical remedies for these obstacles to gospel work, I am suggesting here that the most practical response is prayer. For, to repeat myself, in prayer we lift the work of the gospel above mere circumstances into the hands of the One who governs all things, the One who can provide an open door where there are currently chains.

The Hidden Mission

I have two "spiritual" memories of my pre-Christian days. The first is of the lovely elderly lady who lived up the road and who babysat me and my brothers when we were kids. Her name was Elsie. I remember she gave me a sticker one day, when I was about nine, which read: "Love never fails". I had no idea this was a quote from 1 Corinthians 13:8, but I stuck it on my bedhead knowing it had something to do with Elsie's God. The words were strangely special to me as I gazed up at them each night over the years.

The other memory is of the Lord's Prayer. Somehow I knew it by heart and used to recite it when I was in trouble (not infrequently): "Our Father who art in heaven, hallowed be Thy name . . ." and so on. I was perplexed, especially after becoming a Christian, as to how I had known a prayer Jesus taught when I had never been to church or Sunday school.

The mystery was solved about ten years later. I was back in my home suburb working as a trainee minister in the local Anglican church. This was the church dear Elsie attended. We had talked plenty of times over the years, especially after I had become a Christian, but I had never thought to ask her about what she had taught me as a child. It was not until I mentioned in a sermon one morning the mystery of my knowing the Lord's Prayer as a youngster that she informed me: "John, I taught you the Lord's Prayer when you were nine. Don't you remember?" The stickers I remembered; learning the Lord's Prayer I did not.

It turns out Elsie, a widow, had been praying for my mum and her three boys ever since my father died when I was nine. Regularly and earnestly she had asked the Lord somehow to bring those Dicksons into his kingdom. Humanly speaking she had little reason to expect that any of us would embrace Christ. Ours was a stable and loving family but, as I said, one devoid of Christian conversations, practices or even friends and relatives. Elsie prayed anyway.

Elsie explained to me that when I became a Christian at fifteen, she just said: "Okay, Lord, that's the first; please bring them all to yourself!" Two years later my brother Jaime came to believe in Christ (and is now in full-time ministry). Again, Elsie just said, "Okay, Lord, that's the second . . ." I haven't seen Elsie for a while but the last time I spoke with her she assured me she was still praying for us all.

Elsie's prayers, I believe, were just as responsible for my Christian faith as my Scripture teacher's evangelistic hamburger events. In fact, it is probably fair to say that my Scripture teacher herself was part of God's answer to Elsie's many pleas on my behalf. More than that: I can now see that Elsie's prayers were being answered in small and hidden ways long before I ended up hearing the gospel as a fifteen-year-old. The strange effect of that little sticker above my head and my frequent renditions of the Lord's Prayer can only be explained, I think, as God's early work in my heart in response to Elsie's requests. Through her prayers God was preparing me to meet the Lord of that prayer I had recited so many times, the One who embodied those strangely appealing words, "Love never fails".

Prayer is the hidden part of our mission. No one but the Lord knew of Elsie's prayers and of the stirrings in my heart (I certainly told no one!). But prayer is also the most basic part of our mission. Observing this reminds us that ultimately the mission is not ours but God's. If the fundamental gospel-promoting activity is hidden from us, it is clear that involvement in God's mission requires faith more than activism, dependence more than programs and humility more than boldness.

As we look around our workplace, home, friends, school, university or suburb, what do we believe to be the "solution" to the problem of so many people not yet appreciating the truth of Christ? The most basic part of the answer must be "prayer" – compassionate petitions to the Lord of the harvest to send out more workers, to give success to such workers and to grant salvation to our friends, family and the world.

Not all of us will feel confident speaking to others about salvation, but all of us can be confident speaking about others to the Saviour himself. Doing so is a fundamental expression of both dependence on God and commitment to his mission; it is a hidden but glorious promotion of the gospel.

CHAPTER 5

Partners for Life

Promoting the Gospel with Our Money

The Lord has commanded that those who preach the gospel should receive their living from the gospel.

1 Corinthians 9:14

WE HAD JUST FINISHED a month of singing and speaking throughout Darwin and around the Northern Territory of Australia. The band I used to sing for—called In the Silence—had enjoyed wonderful opportunities to tell the gospel in song and word in high schools, detention centres, aboriginal stations and the one and only Mindil Beach Market (you have to have been there to appreciate that opportunity). Now we were racing in convoy down the Stuart Highway for similar gospel opportunities a few days later in Melbourne over 3000 km away.

About 100 km from Coober Pedy, two-thirds of the way to our destination, our four ton truck, packed with PA system, lights and our instruments, blew its engine—totally blew its engine. The truck had to be hauled to Adelaide 800 km away.

We had no money. The ten of us (band, crew and spouses) were already struggling from month to month, living partly off random gifts, partly off what churches could afford to pay us for the week-long missions we conducted and partly off album sales. We would have needed an instant No.1 hit to pay for this little disaster.

We were going to have to cancel the next couple of missions —not a big deal in the grand scheme of things, but for the churches that had booked us a year in advance it was probably a bit disappointing. To us it just seemed frustrating and confusing that (humanly speaking) gospel work could be hampered by such small things as engine blow-outs and low bank balances.

The confusion did not last long. After a memorable night jammed into a multi-bed $40 a night motel room, we got a phone call from our manager in Sydney. "Guys," he said, "good news. A friend from church has just given us a gift." Sure enough, Cam—a name we would not forget easily—had written a cheque for the entire amount: for the new engine, the haulage, the mechanics fees, the lot. Within two days we were in Melbourne singing and preaching our hearts out in more schools, universities and prisons.

What seemed like a mess one moment became a happy on-the-road story the next. Any seeming hindrance to the gospel was fully resolved by the beautiful gospel-promoting power of Christian generosity. Cam would be the first to tell you he is not an "evangelist" but, the reality is, his gift to us was the direct means under God of many people hearing and believing the good news over the next months and years of our ministry. From the Lord's perspective, what Cam did that day promoted the gospel every bit as much as what I was doing in front of a microphone each night. We were partners in taking the gospel out to the people.

The word "partner" is exactly the right one to use in this context because, as I want now to explore, the New Testament gives special honour to people like Cam, praising them (and God) for what it describes as "partnership in the gospel".

Partnership at Philippi

In the ten years between the founding of the church in Philippi (AD 50) and the writing of the letter we call "Philippians" there were probably many letters back and forth between the apostle Paul and this beloved Macedonian congregation. This letter is different, though, not only because it survived and is preserved for us to read in the New Testament, but also because it was probably the last the Philippians ever heard from Paul. This time he was writing not "on the road" but from prison in Rome, where he was awaiting his trial before Emperor Nero. What we know – that Paul at the time did not – was that the apostle would be executed under Nero sometime around AD 64.[15]

Living on the Via Egnatia, one of the main roads of the ancient world, the Christians of Philippi would have learnt of Paul's imprisonment and impending trial before just about any other church east of Italy. And their response was instant and inspiring. The Philippians dispatched one of their own revered leaders, Epaphroditus (Philippians 2:25; 4:18), and with him sent a great parcel of gifts for Paul. What the gifts were we do not know: they may have included clothing, bedding, food, parchment for letters and money for provisions and legal expenses.

Imagine how Paul felt that day in about AD 62 when a colleague turned up, having made the two-week journey from Philippi to Rome, bearing gift upon gift from his beloved brothers and sisters in Philippi. We get a sense of how he felt in the heartfelt words with which Paul's returning letter begins:

> I thank my God every time I remember you. In all my prayers
> for all of you, I always pray with joy because of your partnership
> in the gospel from the first day until now. (Philippians 1:3 – 5)

Paul's fondest recollection of the Philippians, the thing that filled him with thanks to God, was their "partnership in the gospel".

The word "partnership" is an excellent translation of the Greek root word in this sentence (*koinôn*) because it conjures up notions of sharing in a business partnership, which is precisely the metaphor Paul wishes to strike. From the "first day" when the Philippians opened their homes to Paul and his missionary team (recorded in Acts 16:11 – 40), right up to "now" when they sent gifts to him in prison, the Philippians have been silent but essential partners in the grand task of promoting the gospel to the world. For the technically minded, Paul's exact phrase is *koinônia eis to euangelion*. The preposition *eis* means "into" or "for" the gospel, similar to Paul's description of himself in Romans 1:1 as "set apart for [*eis*] the gospel." In other words, Paul is saying that the Philippians' "partnership" was not just in the gospel but for the sake of the gospel, that is, for its advancement.

How do we know Paul is speaking principally about *financial* partnership? Partly because of the historical context of the letter just outlined, but also because when Paul returns to the theme of "partnership" in chapter 4, the financial sense is clear (here, the root *koinôn* is rendered "share"):

> Yet it was good of you to share [*koinôn* or *partner*] in my troubles. Moreover, as you Philippians know, in the early days of your acquaintance with the gospel, when I set out from Macedonia, not one church shared [*koinôn* or *partnered*] with me in the matter of giving and receiving, except you only; for even when I was in Thessalonica, you sent me aid more than once when I was in need. Not that I desire your gifts; what I desire is that more be credited to your account. I have received full payment and have more than enough. I am amply supplied, now that I have received from Epaphroditus the gifts you sent. They are a fragrant offering, an acceptable sacrifice, pleasing to God. (Philippians 4:14–18)

When back in chapter 1:5 Paul says, "I thank my God . . . because of your partnership in the gospel from the first day until now," he is recalling the Philippians' wonderful generosity toward him over a twelve-year period: from the moment he first "set out from Macedonia" (4:15) right up to when he received "full payment" from Epaphroditus (4:18).[16]

Types of Financial Partnership

There are plenty of other passages in the New Testament that speak of this monetary aspect of the gospel mission. In fact, by my count, contributing financially to the gospel is second only to prayer as the most frequently urged gospel-promoting activity in the New Testament. I do not believe in ranking issues according to their relative biblical frequency, but the surprise I got when I did the math probably indicates a shortcoming in my perspective on mission. Financial partnership in the gospel is vital.

Several texts speak about the need for full-time gospel workers to be financially supported by the Christian community. You could call this kind of support the *maintenance* of evangelists and missionaries:

> These twelve [apostles] Jesus sent out with the following instructions: "Do not go among the Gentiles or enter any town of the Samaritans. Go rather to the lost sheep of Israel. As you go, preach this message: 'The kingdom of heaven is near.' Heal the sick, raise the dead, cleanse those who have leprosy, drive out demons. Freely you have received, freely give. Do not get any gold or silver or copper to take with you in your belts—no bag for the journey or extra shirt or sandals or a staff; for workers are worth their keep." (Matthew 10:5–10; see also the parallel account in Luke 10:1–7)

> Don't you know that those who serve in the temple get their food from the temple, and that those who serve at the altar share in what is offered on the altar? In the same way, the Lord has commanded [probably referring to Matthew 10:10; Luke 10:7] that those who preach the gospel should receive their living from the gospel. (1 Corinthians 9:13–14)

In addition to this maintenance, the New Testament refers numerous times to the *sending out* of missionaries and evangelists. I do not just mean waving them off at the airport (or seaport in the ancient world); I mean sending them out with everything they need for their evangelistic mission—food, travel expenses, board and even personnel. In the New Testament the technical jargon for this activity is *propempô*, variously translated "send out", "assist" and "help on a journey". British scholar Charles Cranfield describes the significance of this word in the following way: "*Propempô* was used to denote the fulfilment of various services which might be required by a departing traveller, such as the provision of rations, money, means of transport, letters of introduction, and escort for some part of the way."[17] A few of the relevant passages include:

> I plan to do so when I go to Spain. I hope to see you while passing through and to have you assist me on my journey [propempô] there. (Romans 15:24)

> Perhaps I will stay with you awhile, or even spend the winter, so that you can help me on my journey [propempô], wherever I go. (1 Corinthians 16:6)

> Do everything you can to help Zenas the lawyer and Apollos on their way [propempô] and see that they have everything they need. (Titus 3:13)

Coincidentally, as I write these words I am preparing to go out to a church dinner for a young missionary couple who are leaving for a small and gospel-needy country in southern Europe. Our church is committed to supporting them in the long term (maintenance), but the passages I have just quoted challenge me to ensure that we also *send them off* well, with additional financial help for the transition they are about to face. I am challenged to properly *propempô* them!

Giving Honour to the Partners

We could explore numerous other biblical statements on this theme, but for me, the most significant are those in Paul's letter to the Philippians, where financial support of mission work is lauded as partnership for the gospel. We must not think that gospel preachers are the only ones engaged in God's mission to the world. If we are financially supporting the work of the gospel, we are full "partners" in this task. We are not spectators on the sidelines; we are players on the pitch. We might not all be doing the same activity but we are all shooting for the same goal—promoting the gospel for the salvation of others.

Evangelists and financial supporters are both worthy of honour in God's mission to the world. This is a point made beautifully by the ancient scholar and bishop John Chrysostom (AD 347–407), who was dubbed "golden mouth" on account of his extraordinary preaching, being widely regarded as the greatest Bible expositor of the ancient church. Chrysostom was so taken with what Paul says about the Philippians' financial support of evangelism he remarked:

> Great is that which he here [in Philippians 1:5] testifies about the Philippians, and very great; indeed, it is what one might have testified about Apostles and Evangelists. You Philippians did not, because you were entrusted with one city, he says, care for that city only, but you leave nothing undone to be partners of my labours, being everywhere at hand, and working with me, as if taking part in my preaching. (*Homilies on Philippians* 1)

Chrysostom strongly believed in the power of financial support of evangelism and encouraged congregations to come up with innovative ways to do this. In his sermon on "Philip the Evangelist" from Acts 8 (*Homilies on Acts* 18), he urges wealthy landowners in the church to imitate Philip's zeal, not by becoming evangelists themselves but by employing household evangelists who could preach the gospel to every servant, staff member and tenant farmer on their properties. He is forthright about this: you construct buildings, baths and courtyards on your land, he says, so why would you not also spend your wealth bringing the gospel to your estate! It is inspiring stuff and reminds us that there is no end of things that money can do for the kingdom of God. Innovation and generosity are powerful tools in God's hands.

Financially supporting evangelism is not a second-string "unspiritual" contribution to God's mission. It is true partnership in the gospel. Believers must believe this; ministers must affirm it. This activity should be honoured publicly and regularly, just as Paul does when he praises the Philippians' gifts to his mission as "a fragrant offering, an acceptable sacrifice, pleasing to God" (Philippians 4:18). A Jew such as Paul could not have used more extreme language to convey the point. "Fragrant offering" alludes to the pleasing temple sacrifices of Israel, acts at the heart of Old Testament worship (e.g., Exodus 29:18; Leviticus 4:31). Now, says Paul, in the era of the new covenant, money given to the spread of the gospel is an act of high worship.

Doing Some Gospel Sums

The question we must all ask is: are we generously supporting the work of the gospel? I do not mean: are we giving to the local church? (though that is a good place to start). I mean: are we contributing to a particular evangelist, missionary, mission organisation or evangelistic project? Could some evangelist or missionary say of you what the apostle said of his beloved Philippians?

Younger readers might be thinking: *I'll wait until I am earning a bit more before I support gospel work more fully.* Older readers may be thinking: *when I've reduced the mortgage and put the kids through school, I'll be in a position to be more generous.* We all live in different situations and God has blessed us in different ways. Nevertheless, from the biblical perspective it is important that we view the resources we have as gifts from God given to us not only for our own good but also for the good of others. If financial partnership in the gospel is as important as the Scriptures seem to suggest, then we are probably correct to conclude that what we have in our bank account, share portfolio or piggy bank has been given to us by the Lord so that (among other things) others might know the gospel of his grace. We must therefore build generous patterns into our life – at whatever stage we find ourselves.

Some figures from Australia – surely no more or less materialistic than other wealthy, industrialised nations – bring clarity and focus to this discussion. The average Australian household spends $231 per year on all forms of charitable giving. That's less than half a percent (0.4%) of the average household income ($58,656) or just 40¢ in every $100. The wealthier the household, the worse this figure gets. Households in the upper 20 percent income range—households earning $130,000 or more before taxes—spend on average $416 a year on charitable giving. That's just one-third of a percent (0.32%) of household earnings or 32¢ per $100.[18]

On a weekly basis, then, households spend on average just $4.44 on charitable giving. The average household spends more each week just on confectionery ($8.10 on chips, chocolate and ice-cream alone); quite a bit more on pets ($9.18); more again on cigarettes ($11.55); three and a half times more on beer and wine ($15.58); and nearly ten times more on restaurant and takeaway meals ($42.10). Again, these figures are worse among wealthier Australians.

Now, I suspect readers of this book will be trying harder than the average Australian to be generous with their money. Most of my compatriots don't live with the parable of the good Samaritan whispering in their ear. Nevertheless, these "averages" are telling and draw attention to spending patterns we, wherever we live, may never have considered.

In light of the biblical call to promote the gospel with our money, it is worth asking some practical questions. Would I spend as much on the work of evangelism as I would on my CD collection, movie/theatre tickets, sporting events and other weekend outings? Do the missionaries I know get as big a slice of my income as my local restaurants, takeaway joints or café? If not, why not? What possible reason could there be for not matching my expenditure on "luxuries" with expenditure on my "partnership in the gospel"?[19]

It is fantastic that the Lord has blessed us with the resources to enjoy the pleasures of his creation. I am simply pleading with readers to add to this enjoyment the enormous privilege of becoming more active in the financial implications of following the "friend of sinners". Giving money (as well as your time) to evangelistic projects, people and organisations is full and praiseworthy partnership in the gospel. When you financially support the proclamation of the gospel, you are actively seeking to save the lost.

CHAPTER 6

Being the Light of the World

Promoting the Gospel through the Works of the Church

Let your light shine before others, that they may see your good deeds and glorify your Father in heaven.

Matthew 5:16

KATHY WAS JUST SIX YEARS old when her mother became ill with cervical cancer. The burden on the family was immense, made worse by the fact that the family was "quite poor", Kathy tells me. Surgical techniques for this form of cancer were in their infancy in the 1970s. The only operation available was somewhat experimental and therefore expensive. As much as she wanted to live to see her four children grow up, Kathy's mum realised her options were limited.

A knock on the door changed everything. Kathy's family had never been involved with a church and yet somehow the local Baptist congregation had learned of their situation and wanted to help. A representative from the church turned up one day with an extraordinary offer. "If you would allow us," said the stranger at the door, "we as a church would love to pay for the operation."

Naturally, the family accepted. Kathy's mum was soon in hospital and the treatment was underway. The next six months were very difficult, recalls Kathy. The four children were housed separately with friends and relatives around town – Kathy remembers she got to stay with an aunt who could afford ice-cream! The church offered to look after the kids on Sundays, picking them up from their four temporary homes in the morning, taking them to Sunday school and then dropping them back in the afternoon after enjoying lunch with the pastor's family. Thirty or so years later, Kathy has fond memories of these days.

The operation was a success; Kathy's mum recovered well and got to see all her children grow up. Although the family attended church for a while – Kathy's mum even became a Sunday school helper – as the years rolled on, one by one they began to drift away.

But events like these are difficult to forget and the impact of them impossible to predict. In Kathy's case, this Christian kindness somehow lodged itself in her mind. Church was no longer a part of her life, but from age six right up into her thirties she continued to pray to the One she first met through those Baptists. The song "Yes, Jesus Loves Me", which she learnt at Sunday school, remained with her, she says, as a kind of theme tune through life's ups and downs.

And then, about eight years ago, one of Kathy's children started asking questions about Christianity and church. With such beautiful memories of Christian community, Kathy did not hesitate to find a congregation in her area and start attending with her family. Suddenly, her dormant faith was reignited. The Jesus of her memory is today the Lord of her life.

When Kathy tells her story of faith, which she is not shy about doing, she leaves you in no doubt as to what (under God) was the crucial factor in her journey to full faith: the kindness of that Baptist church was "100 percent responsible for my faith", she told me recently. "How that congregation treated my family convinced me there was a God and that he loves me."

Kathy is one of many throughout our churches who will attest to the remarkable and unpredictable power of what you might call the "silent" dimension of the promotion of the gospel: the good works of God's people. This is a theme struck again and again in God's Word.

The "Light of the World" (Matthew 5:14–16)

One passage on this topic is found toward the beginning of the Sermon on the Mount. Jesus declared to his disciples:

> You are the light of the world. A city on a hill cannot be hidden. Neither do people light a lamp and put it under a bowl. Instead they put it on its stand, and it gives light to everyone in the house. In the same way, let your light shine before others, that they may see your good deeds and glorify your Father in heaven. (Matthew 5:14–16)

For Jews in Jesus' day the theme of the "light of the world" was well-known and usually interpreted as a reference to Israel's task of proving to the nations that Yahweh–the God of the Jews reigned over all. The light itself was understood to be the city and people of Jerusalem, the jewel in God's crown. One day, said faithful Jews in this period, all nations would come to the light of Jerusalem and worship God. The thought was based on the Old Testament prophecy of Isaiah 49:6:

> It is too small a thing for you to be my servant
>   to restore the tribes of Jacob
>   and bring back those of Israel I have kept.
> I will also make you a light for the Gentiles,
>   that my salvation may reach to the ends of the earth.
>   (Isaiah 49:6)

In Matthew 5:14 Jesus picks up this traditional idea of a "world-saving light" and applies it to his disciples. Promoting

Let me offer just one example of how this "world-saving light" was interpreted by Jews in the period before Jesus. This will help us to understand how his contemporaries would have "heard" Jesus' teaching in Matthew 5:14 – 16. In the book of Tobit (written around 200 – 165 BC) the Jewish writer declares concerning the city of Jerusalem:

A bright light will shine to all the ends of the earth;
    many nations will come to you from far away,
the inhabitants of the remotest parts of the earth to your
        holy name,
    bearing gifts in their hands for the King of heaven.
Generation after generation will give joyful praise in you,
    the name of the chosen city [Jerusalem] will endure for-
        ever. (Tobit 13:11 NRSV)

The connections between Isaiah 49:6; Tobit 13:11; and Matthew 5:14 – 16 are obvious. Jesus' hearers knew full well that he was completely recasting a traditional Jewish theme. Jesus did a lot of that.

God's salvation to the ends of the earth will not be the task of Jerusalem or its inhabitants; it will be the mission of Jesus' disciples. They are the ones who will give "light to everyone in the house" (Matthew 5:15).

The result of this light, in the words of Matthew 5:16, is that the people of the world will "glorify your Father in heaven". This does not mean that people will simply say: "Gee, thank you, God, for those nice Christians!" The word translated "glorify" is literally "to give glory" (*doxazô*), a biblical expression for paying God the honour due to him. The expression on its own could be interpreted to mean simply that unbelievers will one day be forced to acknowledge God's greatness. However, in context it is

better to understand *doxazô* in the positive sense of people coming to rightly worship God and enjoy his salvation. Jesus is saying
that his disciples will be responsible for leading others into a right
relationship with the one true God. In line with the prophecy
behind Jesus' words (Isaiah 49:6), they will act so that "salvation
may reach to the ends of the earth". This is what it means to be
the "light of the world".[20]

But how does this "light" shine? What will win the world to
the worship of God? Matthew 5:16 makes it clear: "In the same
way, let your light shine before others, that they may see your
good deeds and glorify your Father in heaven." These words are
fascinating and unexpected. The Lord here insists that the world
will be brought to its knees before God through the "good deeds"
of his people. Some have argued that the good deeds of Matthew
5:16 must include the best deed of all, preaching the gospel, since
deeds on their own are mute and unable to convey salvation. I
will discuss the connection between practising good deeds and
preaching the good news in the next chapter. For now I will
simply say that this interpretation does not arise naturally from
the text of Matthew 5.

The phrase "good deeds" in Matthew 5:16 carries the same
meaning it does throughout the New Testament. It means *acts of
kindness/goodness*.[21] In the context of the Sermon on the Mount
(Matthew 5–7), it must principally refer to things like being
meek (5:5), showing mercy (5:7), being a peacemaker (5:9),
valuing marriage (5:27–32), telling the truth (5:37), turning the
other cheek (5:39), loving enemies (5:44), giving to the needy
(6:2) and refusing to judge others (7:1). These are the "good
deeds" that will bring people to glorify our Father in heaven.
Jesus, along with many of his fellow contemporary Jews, taught
that "good deeds" could powerfully affect an unbelieving world.

The Good Deeds of the Christian Community

I want to highlight something that is invisible in the English translation but clear in the Greek text of Matthew 5:14 – 16. It has to do with the frustrating English word "you". In English we have no way of distinguishing between a singular "you" and a plural "you". When I say, "I hope you like my book," you don't know if I mean you individually or readers in general. There used to be a distinction, of course: "thou" was the singular and "you" (or "ye") was the plural. Those of you (plural) who speak another language will know that most cultures have sensibly retained the distinction between the singular and plural.

Anyway, the "you" throughout Matthew 5:14 – 16 is a plural. We might say "y'all" or, as in some parts of Australia, "yous". This might not be pleasing to the ear but it is instinctively grammatical. With apologies to purists, here is a literal rendering of our passage:

Numerous ancient Jewish texts refer to the power of a godly life to attract and convert the Gentiles. For example, the first-century Jewish intellectual, Philo, describes the influence of the biblical Joseph on his Egyptian fellow prisoners:

> They [the prisoners] were rebuked by his wise words and doctrines of philosophy, while the conduct of their teacher effected more than any words. For by setting before them his life of temperance and every virtue, like an original picture of skilled workmanship, he converted even those who seemed to be quite incurable, who as the long-standing distempers of their soul abated reproached themselves for their past and repented. (Philo, *On the Life of Joseph* 86 – 87)

Whether Philo's version of events – which obviously does not appear in Genesis 39 – was a pious tradition of his time

Yous are the light of the world. A city on a hill cannot be hidden. Neither do people light a lamp and put it under a bowl. Instead they put it on its stand, and it gives light to everyone in the house. In the same way, let the light of yous shine before others, that they may see the good deeds of yous and glorify the Father of yous in heaven. (Matthew 5:14–16)

The statement "yous [plural] are the light [singular]" suggests that Jesus has in mind the company of disciples rather than believers individually. As good deeds are done by the Christian community, this light shines and others are drawn into the worship of God. I will talk in the next chapter about the gospel-promoting effect of individual good deeds. Right now I want to stress that the prophecy of a "world-saving light" (Isaiah 49:6) is fulfilled as Christ's community is seen to be living out his teaching – being meek, loving enemies, giving to the needy and so on. The example of Kathy's former Baptist community comes to mind.

or his own invention, the point is that this influential Jewish figure believed that the godly life could convert pagans to the true worship of God. Philo appears to be using this story to encourage his first-century Jewish readership – who, like Joseph, were living in Egypt (Alexandria) – to follow the patriarch's good example. Biblical scholar Scot McKnight, who is generally reluctant to affirm any ancient Jewish interest in mission, nevertheless agrees that the good deeds of Jews in this period had a powerful effect on those around them: "This form of converting Gentiles," he says, "is a consistent feature of the evidence and probably formed the very backbone for the majority of conversions to Judaism."[22]

How Good Deeds Conquered an Empire

Humanly speaking, no one would have thought it possible to bring the nations to the worship of God through simple good deeds. How on earth could "good deeds" change a realm as mighty as the Roman Empire, let alone the whole world? As unlikely as it may have sounded at the time, Jesus' call to be the light of the world was taken seriously by his disciples. They devoted themselves to quite heroic acts of godliness. They loved their enemies, prayed for their persecutors and cared for the poor wherever they found them.

We know that the Jerusalem church set up a large daily food roster for the destitute among them—no fewer than seven Christian leaders were assigned to the management of the program (Acts 6:1−7). The apostle Paul, perhaps the greatest missionary/evangelist ever, was utterly devoted to these kinds of good deeds. In response to a famine that ravaged Palestine between AD 46−48 Paul conducted his own decade-long international aid program earmarked for poverty-stricken Palestinians. Wherever he went, he asked the Gentile churches to contribute whatever they could to the poor in Jerusalem.[23]

Christian "good deeds" continued long after the New Testament era. We know, for instance, that by AD 250 the Christian community in Rome was supporting 1,500 destitute people every day.[24] All around the Mediterranean churches were setting up food programs, hospitals and orphanages. These were available to believers and unbelievers alike. This was an innovation. Historians often point to ancient Israel as the first society to introduce a comprehensive welfare system that cared for the poor and marginalised within the community. Christians inherited this tradition but opened it up to Jew and Gentile, believer and unbeliever, alike.

And the result of all this? Well, within two and a half centuries Christians had gone from being a small band of several hundred Palestinian Jews to the greatest social force in world history. In fact, the influence of Christian good works was so great in the fourth century that Emperor Julian (AD 331 – 363) became fearful that Christianity might take over the world forever by the stealth of good works. He regarded Christianity as a sickness and called it "atheism" (because Christians denied the existence of pagan gods). To one of his pagan officials Emperor Julian wrote these telling words about Christian good deeds:

> We must pay special attention to this point, and by this means effect a cure [for the "sickening" advance of Christianity]. For when it came about that the poor were neglected and overlooked by the [pagan] priests, then I think the impious Galileans [Christians] observed this fact and devoted themselves to philanthropy. And they have gained ascendancy in the worst of their deeds through the credit they win for such practices. For just as those who entice children with a cake, and by throwing it to them two or three times induce them to follow them, and then, when they are far away from their friends cast them on board a ship and sell them as slaves ... by the same method, I say, the Galileans also begin with their so-called love-feast [open meals], or hospitality, or service of tables — for they have many ways of carrying it out and hence call it by many names — and the result is that they have led very many into atheism [i.e., Christianity].[25]

Things got worse for Emperor Julian; Christianity just kept on growing. He wrote to his pagan priests insisting that pagan temples throughout the empire should introduce a welfare system like the one in Christian churches: prison visitation, hospitals, hostels, orphanages and poverty relief programs. In a letter to Arcacius, the (pagan) high priest of Galatia, Julian confirms a massive donation from his own imperial pocket designed to kick-start his welfare program. He wanted to beat the Christians at their own game. The letter is dated AD 362, the year before his death:

> Why do we not observe that it is their [Christians'] benevolence to strangers, their care for the graves of the dead and

the pretended holiness of their lives that have done most to increase atheism? I believe that we ought really and truly to practise every one of these virtues. And it is not enough for you alone to practise them, but so must all the priests in Galatia, without exception. Either shame or persuade them into righteousness or else remove them from their priestly office . . . In every city establish frequent hostels in order that strangers may profit by our benevolence; I do not mean for our own people only, but for others also who are in need of money. I have but now made a plan by which you may be well provided for this; for I have given directions that 30,000 modii of corn [= 175 tons] shall be assigned every year for the whole of Galatia, and 60,000 sextarii of wine [= 33,900 litres]. I order that one-fifth of this be used for the poor who serve the priests, and the remainder be distributed by us to strangers and beggars. For it is disgraceful that, when no Jew ever has to beg [because of the Jewish welfare system], and the impious Galileans support not only their own poor but ours as well, all men see that our people lack aid from us.[26]

Needless to say, Julian's program failed. Without a doctrine of grace in Greco-Roman religion it was difficult to convince people to love the unlovely. Christians, by contrast, had a highly developed idea of God's grace. This was the basis for communities of grace that sought to do good to all and so drew many others into the worship of God. Rodney Stark, professor of the social sciences at Baylor University, concludes his analysis of the rise of Christianity with words that bear out this point:

Therefore, as I conclude this study, I find it necessary to confront what appears to me to be the ultimate factor in the rise of Christianity . . . The simple phrase "For God so loved the world . . ." would have puzzled an educated pagan. And the notion that the gods care how we treat one another would have been dismissed as patently absurd . . . This was the moral climate in which Christianity taught that mercy is one of the primary virtues—that a merciful God requires humans to be merciful . . . This was revolutionary stuff. Indeed, it was the cultural basis for the revitalisation of the Roman world groaning under a host of miseries ... In my judgment, a major way in which Christianity served as a revitalisation movement within the empire was in offering a coherent culture that was entirely stripped of ethnicity. All were welcome without need to dispense with ethnic ties ... Christianity also prompted liberating social relations between the sexes and within the family ... [and] greatly modulated class differences – more than rhetoric was involved when slave and noble greeted one another as brothers in Christ. Finally, what Christianity gave to its converts was nothing less than their humanity. In this sense virtue was its own reward.[27]

Professor Stark has probably underestimated other contributing factors in the expansion of Christianity: for one thing, preaching. Christians not only lived by the motto "God so loved the world", they proclaimed it far and wide. One of the striking things about the early Christian movement was the significant number of evangelists and missionaries who gave themselves to preaching the gospel where it was not yet known.[28] Nevertheless, Stark does helpfully draw attention to an aspect of Christian mission made plain in Matthew 5:14–16 but sometimes played down in modern church life – "good deeds" can win the world to the worship of the true God.

Good deeds must never be thought of as a missionary tactic, a means of getting people onside before hitting them with the gospel ("throwing cakes to children", as Emperor Julian would say). They are the essential fruit of the gospel. Good works must be done for their own sake, in obedience to the Lord. God's grace proclaimed in the gospel finds its essential outcome in the godly life of those who believe the gospel.

Nevertheless, it is precisely because good deeds are an essential fruit of the gospel that they so powerfully promote the gospel. Although we must not find ourselves "doing good" simply as a gospel ploy, there can be no question that Jesus expected unbelievers to observe our acts of love (for the world and for

The statement of Matthew 5:16 has an interesting parallel in Matthew 6:1 – 2: "Be careful not to do your 'acts of righteousness' in front of others, to be seen by them. If you do, you will have no reward from your Father in heaven. So when you give to the needy, do not announce it with trumpets, as the hypocrites do in the synagogues and on the streets, to be honoured by others." The word "honoured" is *doxazô*, the term translated "glorify" in 5:16. In other words, while it is right to do good deeds with a view to moving others to glorify God, it is wrong to do such deeds to move others to glorify oneself.

one another[29]) and through them to be convinced to worship the source of all love: "let your light shine before others, that they may see your good deeds and glorify your Father in heaven" (Matthew 5:16).

When denominations, congregations or home groups ask: "How can we better care for the sick? How can we meet the needs of the poor? What more can we do for the elderly? How can we foster peace?" and so on, they are not only asking questions of obedience; they are also asking questions of mission. They are searching for fresh ways to be, and to convey, the light of God's glory to an unbelieving world.

In emphasising the missionary power of good deeds done by the community of God's people, I am not suggesting that individual acts of mercy and love cannot also win people to faith in Christ. The Scriptures say they can. And that is the topic of the next chapter.

CHAPTER 7

Being Beautiful

Promoting the Gospel through
Christian Behaviour

In every way they will make the teaching about
God our Saviour attractive.

Titus 2:10

TIM WINTON IS AUSTRALIA'S most celebrated novelist today. Author of more than a dozen bestselling books, including *Cloud Street*, *Dirt Music* and *Breath*, and winner of numerous literary prizes, Winton resides on the coast of Western Australia, where he lives out every writer's fantasy—writing, fishing and playing with his family. Winton was interviewed on the popular ABC television show *Enough Rope* with Andrew Denton. The interview was typically Dentonesque—friendly, witty and at times very poignant. At one point, the conversation turned to Winton's well-known Christian faith.

"I want to talk about faith," said Denton. "When you were, I think, about five, a stranger came into your family and affected your family quite profoundly. Is that right?"

Tim Winton went on to tell Denton how his father, a policeman, had been in a terrible accident in the mid-1960s, knocked off his motorcycle by a drunk driver. After weeks in a coma he was allowed home. Winton said he remembers thinking, "He was like an earlier version of my father, a sort of augmented version of my father. He was sort of recognisable, but not really my dad, you know? Everything was busted up and they put him in the chair, and, you know, 'Here's your dad.' And I was horrified."

Winton's father was a big man and Mrs Winton had great difficulty bathing him each day. There was nothing that Tim, five years old at the time, could do to help. News of the family's situation got out into the local community and shortly afterward, Winton recalls, his mother got a knock at the door. "Oh, g'day. My name's Len," said a stranger to Mrs Winton (imagine a thick Aussie accent). "I heard your hubby's a bit crook. Anything I can do?"

Len Thomas was from the local church, Winton explained. This man had heard about the family's difficulties and wanted to help. "He just showed up," continued Winton, "and he used to carry my dad from bed and put him in the bath and he used to bathe him, which in the 1960s in Perth in the suburbs was not the sort of thing you saw every day."

According to Winton, this simple act of kindness from a single Christian had a powerful effect: "It really touched me in that, regardless of theology or anything else, watching a grown man bother, for nothing, to show up and wash a sick man—you know, it really affected me." This "strangely sacrificial act", as he described it, was the doorway into the Christian faith for the whole Winton family.

I have no idea if Len Thomas would have described himself as an evangelist—somewhere along the way someone must have shared the Christian message with the Wintons—but, according to Tim Winton, the thing under God that most profoundly influenced his family's move toward Christ was the sacrificial act of just one of Christ's followers. The New Testament would say a hearty "Amen" to that.

Conversion "without a Word" (1 Peter 3:1 – 2)

The apostle Peter was present when Jesus first uttered the words, "let your light shine before others, that they may see your good deeds and glorify your Father in heaven" (Matthew 5:16). In fact, years later in one of his letters (what we call 1 Peter) the apostle paraphrases the Lord's words:

> Live such good lives among the pagans that, though they accuse you of doing wrong, they may see your good deeds and glorify God. (1 Peter 2:12)

At the beginning of his next chapter Peter goes on to give a specific example of Christians bringing glory to God through "good deeds" among the pagans. He urges Christian wives to win their unbelieving husbands to faith through the power of godly behaviour:

> Wives, in the same way submit yourselves to your own husbands so that, if any of them do not believe the word, they may be won over without words by the behaviour of their wives, when they see the purity and reverence of your lives. (1 Peter 3:1 – 2)

Leaving to one side the issue of marital "submission", Peter's teaching in 1 Peter 3:1 – 2 is quite extraordinary: unbelievers can be won to the faith simply by observing Christian behaviour.[30] Peter goes out of his way to underline this point by adding the phrase "without words", which in Greek is literally "without a word" (*aneu logou*). Wives can win over their husbands to faith in the gospel without even speaking of the gospel. If this were not in our Bibles, I suspect some of us would caution believers who thought they could win people to Christ "without a word" simply "through behaviour".

Does this mean that people can start believing in Christ without hearing the gospel at all? No. As the apostle Paul makes clear, "faith comes from hearing the message" (Romans 10:17). First Peter 3:1 shows us that the gospel's role in conversion is more complex than we sometimes realise. It is not enough simply to affirm that people are won to faith *only* through the hearing of the gospel. Let me explain.

Leaving aside the important theological observation that all conversion is ultimately the enlightening work of the Holy Spirit, let me try and account for conversion from the human side of the equation, which is what Paul and Peter are talking about in the above texts.

Humanly speaking, hearing the gospel is the necessary and sufficient cause of faith in Christ. It is *necessary* inasmuch as people cannot put their faith in Jesus without first learning the gospel about him. It is *sufficient* in that the gospel can bring people to faith all on its own—it needs no other factor (other than the work of the Holy Spirit). However, none of this means that hearing the gospel is the *only* cause of faith, or even that it is always the *primary* cause of faith. Other factors (on the human side of the equation) will frequently play a minor or major role in winning people over to the One revealed in the gospel.

Tim Winton, as I said earlier, must have heard the gospel message somewhere along the line: he could not have placed his faith in someone he had not learned about. But this does not for a moment mean that other factors were not also, or perhaps even primarily, responsible for his acceptance of Jesus. Winton insists that it was the sacrificial behaviour of Len Thomas that most influenced his family's move toward Christ. In light of what the apostle says in 1 Peter 3:1–2, this seems a perfectly valid way to describe matters.

My friend Kathy (from the previous chapter) must also have learnt the gospel message—at a Baptist Sunday school; how could it be otherwise? But, again, this does not call into question Kathy's unequivocal statement that Christian kindness was "100 percent responsible" for her acceptance of the Lord she learnt about in Sunday school.

A closer look at 1 Peter 3:1–2 supports the idea that the gospel is the necessary and sufficient cause of faith without always being the only or primary cause of faith. Peter describes non-Christian husbands as those who "do not believe the word" (1 Peter 3:1). Literally, this is "those who disobey the word". This tells us two things: first, that Peter thinks of Christian conversion, almost by definition, as acceptance of the gospel word and, second, that Peter assumes these husbands have already heard something of the word – how else could they be disobeying it?[31] Peter, then, is not suggesting that faith in Christ can come about without hearing the gospel and having it explained. He is simply saying that humanly speaking, the thing which is going to win these husbands over to the gospel is the behaviour of their loved ones. The gospel "word" remains the necessary and sufficient cause of faith but, in this case, it is not the primary cause. That accolade belongs to the "behaviour of the wives".

A friend of mine is a Senior Lecturer at the University of Sydney and, until recently, was something of a sceptic. Working in an academic environment Bruce felt he had to keep the Christian faith at a respectable distance. Unfortunately for him, Bruce was married to Brenda, a deeply godly believer. For the last twenty years Bruce has been able to observe the difference Christianity makes in one's life. Slowly but surely – aided, Bruce tells me, by a timely health scare – his intellectual arguments could not withstand the power of the Christianity he observed every day in the home. He eventually gave his life to Christ, to Brenda's great joy. Numerous factors have contributed to Bruce's newfound faith – among them Brenda's prayers and the occasional half-coherent sermon – but toward the top of the list for Bruce was the transparently good life of his beloved wife.

Is 1 Peter 3:1 – 2 a "Let Off"?

It probably goes without saying that 1 Peter 3:1 – 2 cannot be used as an excuse never to talk about our faith with unbelievers. As I have said more than once, there are clear New Testament passages urging us all to speak up for Christ when we can. In just a few paragraphs Peter will write, "Always be prepared to give an answer to everyone who asks you to give the reason for the hope that you have. But do this with gentleness and respect" (1 Peter 3:15).

Peter's words in 1 Peter 3:1 – 2 are not intended as a "let off" for those who are simply too shy to speak of Christ. They are meant to be an encouragement to those who find themselves in situations in which speaking about the faith is difficult or inappropriate. The marriage relationship (the specific context of Peter's words) is a classic example. Over the years I have heard many Christian spouses say of their unbelieving partners, "I just can't talk about Christ at home. As soon as I do my husband/wife just clams up; he/she doesn't want to hear about him from me!"

The parent-child relationship is similar. Many teenagers (and quite a few adults) have said to me over the years, "I can hardly mention my faith to my mum and dad without them thinking I am presuming to teach them." The reverse is true as well: Christian parents sometimes find that their grown-up children are no longer willing to hear their "preaching". A similar observation could be made about the teacher-student and the employee-employer relationships. It may be inappropriate for teachers to share the gospel with students; it may be difficult for students to tell the gospel to teachers. Likewise, employers may in some contexts feel rightly awkward about using their position to speak to workers about Jesus; employees may find it difficult to get their bosses to listen to what they say about matters of faith.

It would be tempting to say to Christians in each of these contexts: "Don't be ashamed! Declare Christ regardless of the situation, whatever the outcome." But this would be unwise and unbiblical. Apart from potentially leading to a lack of "gentleness and respect" in mission (1 Peter 3:15), such advice ignores Peter's clear statement that Christian behaviour *without a word* can win people over to Christ.

Peter's words should be read for what they are: an assurance to Christian wives – and to all who find themselves in contexts where speaking about the Lord is difficult or inappropriate – that the Lord of the harvest can win over our loved ones without a word (from you) by the power of a godly life. It is nothing other than the application of the teaching of Jesus: "let your light shine before others, that they may see your good deeds and glorify your Father in heaven" (Matthew 5:16). For a "talker" like me, one who is tempted to think that conversion is the domain of the evangelist alone, this is an important lesson to learn. How I live from day to day can also win people over to faith in the gospel.

Several other passages in the New Testament speak about the effect of Christian behaviour on those who do not yet believe.[32] But I want to conclude with one that makes explicit the connection between Christian behaviour and gospel preaching.

Making the Gospel Beautiful (Titus 2:1 – 10)

To the leader of the church on Crete (Titus) the apostle Paul emphasises just how important Christian behaviour is for the work of the gospel. He begins by explaining that the good life can halt criticism of God's Word. He ends up saying that godliness can actually promote God's Word:

> You [Titus], however, must teach [the Christians on Crete] what is appropriate to sound doctrine. Teach the older men to be temperate, worthy of respect, self-controlled, and sound in faith, in love and in endurance.
>
> Likewise, teach the older women to be reverent in the way they live, not to be slanderers or addicted to much wine, but to teach what is good. Then they can urge the younger women to love their husbands and children, to be self-controlled and pure, to be busy at home, to be kind, and to be subject to their husbands, *so that no one will malign the word of God.*
>
> Similarly, encourage the young men to be self-controlled. In everything set them an example by doing what is good. In your teaching show integrity, seriousness and soundness of

speech that cannot be condemned, *so that those who oppose you may be ashamed because they have nothing bad to say about us.*

Teach slaves to be subject to their masters in everything, to try to please them, not to talk back to them, and not to steal from them, but to show that they can be fully trusted, *so that in every way they will make the teaching about God our Saviour attractive.* (Titus 2:1 – 10, emphasis added)

Paul first states his point in negative terms. Godly behaviour can silence those who "malign" God's Word (verse 5) and embarrass those who "oppose" the preachers of the Word (verse 8).

Sometimes godliness is the only defence. Sadly, I have an ever-growing collection of media articles in my file marked "Criticism of Christianity". Here are just a few of the headlines:

"Christianity is fine, but please don't mention the church."
"Faith in churches dropping, survey shows."
"Man of God with a heart of stone."
"In politicians we trust, but not the church."

Add to this the shrill criticisms of the so-called New Atheists: Richard Dawkins, Sam Harris, Christopher Hitchens and others. Hitchens has some particularly pointed things to say about the damage done to society by religion, and by Christianity in particular:

We believe with certainty that an ethical life can be lived without religion. And we know for a fact that the corollary holds true – that religion has caused innumerable people not just to conduct themselves no better than others, but to award themselves permission to behave in ways that would make a brothel-keeper or an ethnic cleanser to raise an eyebrow.[33]

The subtitle of Hitchens' *God Is Not Great* says it all: *How Religion Poisons Everything.* Of course, there are things we can argue in response to this line of attack. First, we can and should concede that it is partly, though disturbingly, true that Christians have done awful things through history.

Second, we point out the great good done in the name of Christ through the centuries: the establishment of welfare for all, the end of slavery in Britain, the civil rights movement in the US and the fact that most nongovernment social services in Western countries – overwhelmingly in Australia – are organised through Christian agencies. Hitchens is deafeningly quiet about such matters.

Third, we could also point out rather large elephant in the atheist's room. There have only been a few formally atheistic regimes in the history of the world – Stalin's, Mao's and Pol Pot's – and they were not exactly moral improvements.

All of that said, I doubt such an apologetic will win over the likes of Hitchens, Harris and Dawkins. In the end, the only way to dispel the story that Christianity has been imperialistic, arrogant and harmful is to offer a powerful counternarrative in our lives, day by day committing ourselves to Jesus' vision of a kingdom marked by meekness, peace-making and love. It might be right occasionally to fire off a letter to the editor defending the church from some unfair criticism in the media, but, ultimately, I suspect the only true defence is the one Paul urges in Titus 2:5 and 8. We must live out God's Word and so outlive the criticisms.

An analogy comes to mind. As a parent I am conscious that my reputation in some ways is tied up with my children's behaviour. How they act reflects not only on them as individuals but also on me as their father. For instance, if I am out shopping in the supermarket and one of the kids decides to throw a tantrum in aisle 7, I know that every other parent in the aisle is looking at me thinking: "Oh, what a bad parent!" If, however, we are out on the football pitch and my lad scores two goals in a row, as he did just last weekend (truly), I know the other parents are thinking: "Boy, that John Dickson must be a good player to have a boy who can play like that!" My children somehow carry my reputation with them.

My point, of course, is that in naming us his children our heavenly Father has entrusted his reputation – his public image in the world – to you and me. How we act, as a group and as individuals, often affects how people think of God. We have all met people whose image of God and his gospel has been damaged by the actions of believers. Humanly speaking, the only way to challenge such an impression is to bear the fruit of the gospel, a life of good deeds.

What Paul puts defensively in Titus 2:5 and 8 he states positively in verses 9 – 10. Christians (in context, "slaves") are to live humble, honest and trustworthy lives, "so that in every way they will make the teaching about God our Saviour attractive". Good works not only defend the Word of God, they promote it.

Paul has a particular word of God in mind here. He describes it as "the teaching about God our Saviour". The word translated "teaching" here refers to a specific Christian teaching (*didaskalia*) rather than Christian teaching in general. A clearer translation might be "the *doctrine* of God our Saviour" (RSV). Paul is concerned in this passage that the particular news about God as Saviour – the "gospel", in other words – is promoted by the lives of Christians. According to Paul, humility, honesty and trustworthiness can make the gospel "attractive" to those who do not yet believe.

The word translated "attractive" in verse 10 is *kosmeô*, from which came the English word *cosmetic*. The word means exactly what you would expect, "to beautify." It's a lovely idea. The gospel is beautiful on its own, of course – the news that Christ died for sins and rose as Lord is just stunning – but it can be beautified, says Paul. The good lives of believers can enhance the gospel's appearance in the minds of those who hear it.

The connection between godliness and evangelism is clear. There were several preachers on the island of Crete dedicated to the task of preaching the gospel. Titus was one, and in Titus 1:9 – 14 Paul has already reminded him of the importance of declaring the truth in an unbelieving world. Other preachers on the island included Zenas, Apollos, Artemas and Tychicus (Titus 3:12 – 13).[34] The thought behind Titus 2:10, then, is that as these preachers declare the doctrine about the Saviour, the Christian community generally is to provide an "apologetic" in the godly life, silencing criticisms and wooing the population of the island to the beauty of the gospel.

As the preachers speak of God's generosity, believers are to embody that generosity in their care for the poor. As the preachers declare God's forgiveness, believers are to display that mercy in their dealings with those who oppose them. As the preachers announce Christ as the Truth, believers are to be marked by honesty and trustworthiness in their daily affairs. As they do this, the message will be "beautified" and people will be drawn to the Saviour revealed in the gospel. Understood in this way, good deeds are anything but "mute". So long as the gospel is being spread widely throughout our communities, the godly life of ordinary Christians will promote the gospel whether or not they are the ones doing the evangelism. Emphasising the power of good deeds, therefore, in no way undermines the centrality of the gospel in our mission. Both are about promoting the news of Christ to those who do not believe.

My wife and I have some dear friends who provide a clear example of the way good deeds and gospel proclamation combine to draw people to Christ (whether or not the deeds and the proclamation are done by the same people). Some years ago Kim and Christian were faced with every parent's worst nightmare. Their daughter Sophie, two years old at the time, was diagnosed with leukemia. And so began the regular visits to the hospital, the endless tests and anxious months and years of waiting. The birth of their second child at just this time brought extra challenges.

Kim and Christian were not believers and never attended church. Kim did, however, go to the church playgroup—where local mums brought their toddlers to the church hall for an hour or two of "social time", playing and singing. The "Christian component" of the group was low-key. Kim recalls the group was "very social and, from my perspective at the time, not at all linked to the church building just next door!" Nevertheless, everyone knew the group was run by Christian mothers, and these women worked hard at creating a warm and caring environment for those who might otherwise feel awkward about coming to a church group.

But this Christian "atmosphere" became palpable when little Sophie fell ill. Suddenly, a food roster was set up, as people from the playgroup and church dropped off regular meals to Kim and Christian. Others phoned to see how they were doing and to offer assistance. Kim remembers a woman she did not know arriving at the door one day with a bunch of flowers—"She wanted to let us know that her Bible study group was praying for us and to see if we needed any help." Kim met others on different occasions who, "on finding out who I was, told me of their prayers for us and Sophie, which to me showed a level of concern and involvement which went 'above and beyond' a normal person's level of interest in our problems".

One of Kim's great supporters during this difficult time was Lisa, the playgroup coordinator. On occasion, Lisa had offered to pray for little Sophie at her bedside. "At the time I was quite taken aback," says Kim, "but each time was filled with peace and hope." The gospel effect of all this on both Kim and Christian was real: "The prayers and support we felt from that group really made us want to find out what it was about them that made them do that, go out of their way to help us in our time of need." Christian adds, "It has been so powerful to witness exceptional behaviour and to want to find out where it comes from."

The opportunity to find out more came one evening when Lisa invited Kim to an evangelistic talk by Frank Retief, a visiting minister from South Africa. "I'm sure I would never have gone," remembers Kim, "had she (Lisa) not taken me." Lisa's (and others') love and concern over the months had given Kim not only an interest in the Christian message but also a hunch that it might be relevant. Kim listened to Retief's words that night with a heart wide open: "Towards the end of his talk—it may even have been during a prayer at the end—I started to shake and to cry fairly uncontrollably." In that moment, the Lord made himself real to Kim and she embraced him with all her heart.

Christian too – who joked that I should call him "non-Christian" up to this point – embraced Christ soon afterward. He had been somewhat sceptical about Christianity. His French humanist tradition, I remember, had left him with numerous questions about God and about the validity of religious belief. Observing "exceptional behaviour", however, together with learning the gospel in a sensitive and intelligent way, confronted his doubts with the reality of Christ.

Kim and Christian – now both very much Christians – give thanks to the Lord for all he has taught them and for the fact that Sophie has been in remission now for well over seven years, which is usually the "all clear" sign. For me, what God has done in their lives is living proof of the way good deeds and gospel proclamation often combine to draw people to Christ, whether or not those doing the deeds are also the ones doing the proclamation. They are a reminder to me of the responsibility we all have to "make the teaching about God our Saviour attractive" (Titus 2:10).

Where to from Here?

So far in this book I have tried to demonstrate that seeking the salvation of others involves more than our lips. As I said in the introduction, perhaps the best kept secret of Christian mission is that the Bible lists a whole range of activities that promote Christ to the world and draw others toward him. These, as we have seen, include financial support for the work of the gospel, prayer for the lost and for those who preach and, of course, good works that beautify the news of Christ and win others to the worship of the Father. These are not background, ancillary contributions to God's mission; they are full expressions of a devotion to the mission of the "friend of sinners".

In all of this I have also tried to show that emphasising the range of missionary activities in no way diminishes the centrality of the gospel in God's plan of salvation. The phrase *promoting the gospel* is intended to remind us that all of these activities have as their goal the advancement of the news of Christ, the gospel, the necessary and sufficient cause of conversion. This is particularly clear in Titus 2:9–10.

The importance of the gospel in God's mission comes into special focus in the next few chapters as we explore what the Bible says about using our "lips" to promote the gospel. To recall what I said earlier, speaking about the faith is the wonderful icing on the cake of mission. It may not be the main part of the day-to-day mission of the typical believer, but, when tasted, it is definitely the sweetest. First, of course, I must unpack what is meant by the "gospel".

CHAPTER 8

What Is the Gospel?

The Message We Promote

> I want to remind you of the gospel I preached to
> you, which you received and on which you have
> taken your stand . . .
>
> *1 Corinthians 15:1*

SOMEHOW I HAVE MANAGED to write the bulk of a book subtitled *Promoting the Gospel* without stopping to ask: what exactly is the content of the gospel? (I will more than make up for this over-sight by the inordinate length of this chapter!)

At one level, this is perfectly understandable. Almost by defi-nition, Christians know the gospel. It is, after all, the thing on which believers stand, as Paul says in the text quoted above. The gospel is the foundation of Christian belief. Why would we need to recheck the foundation?

Having said that, "gospel" is one of those words that is so basic, so fundamental to Christian life that it can be taken for granted. It can become the term for just about anything at all in the Christian faith. "Gospel" can become so full of the meaning *I* want to put into it that it can be emptied of meaning altogether. Like the word "love" in popular music, "gospel" can mean everything and nothing at the same time. I've heard people describe congregations as "gospel churches", and ministers as "gospel men", when all they really mean is "Bible-based" or "we like them".

But "gospel" does not refer to everything taught in the Bible. It has a specific content. This is why in 1 Corinthians 15:1 Paul can talk about "reminding" the Corinthians of the message he had "preached" to them (five years earlier), the message they "received" and on which they had taken their stand. In the verses that follow (15:3–6) Paul offers a brief summary of that gospel message (that's his "reminder"). We'll explore this in a moment. For now, I just want to underline what might be obvious: the gospel has a particular content. It does not include all of the themes raised in 1 Corinthians: *unity* in chapter 3, *church discipline* in chapter 5, *Christian marriage* in chapter 7, *food sacrificed to idols* in chapters 8–10, *spiritual gifts* in chapter 12–14 and so on. It refers only to the message on which all this other stuff is based. Put crudely but no less accurately, while all of 1 Corinthians *assumes* and *applies* the gospel, only 1 Corinthians 15:3–6 articulates the gospel (in highly brief form).

Let's begin this exploration of the gospel with some important background.

The Kingdom of God: The Theme of the Gospel

In the ancient world the noun "gospel" (*euangelion*) and its verb "telling the gospel" (*euangelizomai*) were media terms. They always referred to the announcement of happy or important events. News of military victories, national achievements, weddings, births and, in one ancient text, the bargain price of anchovies at the marketplace were all called "gospels". The modern media term "newsflash" probably comes closest in meaning to the ancient word *gospel*.[35]

The most well-known "gospels" proclaimed in the ancient world were those announcing the emperors' achievements. The caesars' ascensions, conquests and political deeds were all the subject of the gospels of the empire. "Gospel" was very much an imperial term in the period of the New Testament. One famous example comes from an inscription found in Priene in southwestern Turkey. It dates from just a few years before Jesus (9 BC to be precise). The inscription describes how one of the governors in Asia Minor (modern Turkey) decided that the birthday of Emperor Augustus (23 September 63 BC) should mark the beginning of a whole new calendar and dating system (much the same as Jesus' birth would later determine the Christian calendar). In this context the inscription tells how Augustus' arrival in the world occasioned "gospels" about his wonderful imperial deeds:

> Augustus has made war to cease and put everything in peaceful order; and, whereas the birthday of our god (the emperor) signalled the beginning of gospels [*euangelion*] for the world because of him, Paulus Fabius Maximus, benefactor of the province, has discovered a way to honor Augustus that was hitherto unknown among the Greeks, namely to reckon time from the date of his birth.[36]

When the first Christians came along saying they had a new gospel about a new lord, their claims would have sounded like a challenge to Rome. And, in a sense, they were.

I am not suggesting that Christians simply borrowed the pagan idea of an imperial "gospel" and used it for their own newsflash. Far from it. "Gospel" language was already known to God's people (Israel) centuries before the Roman Empire. The Old Testament had foretold a day when the kingship of Israel's God would be revealed to all and proclaimed throughout the world as a "gospel". The prophet Isaiah, centuries before Jesus, spoke these famous words:

> How beautiful on the mountains
>   are the feet of those who *bring good news* [literally: *telling a gospel*],
> who proclaim peace,

> who *bring good tidings* [literally: *telling a gospel*],
> who proclaim salvation,
> who say to Zion,
> "Your God reigns!" (Isaiah 52:7, my emphasis)

The precise content of this promised gospel is: "Your God reigns." The word "reign" here is the verb form of the word for "king" (literally, "reign as king"). Ever since Isaiah spoke these words (which are echoed in Isaiah 40:9 and 61:1), God's people had longed for the arrival of the messenger with "beautiful feet" who would announce the unveiling of God's kingdom.[37] Those feet, of course, belonged to none other than Jesus, the Messiah with the good news or gospel everyone had been waiting for:

> After John was put in prison, Jesus went into Galilee, proclaiming the good news of God. "The time has come," he said. "The kingdom of God has come near. Repent and believe the good news!" (Mark 1:14–15)

Here, as in Isaiah, the main theme of the gospel is God's kingdom. The same idea is captured in Matthew's summary of the Lord's preaching: he "went throughout Galilee, teaching in their synagogues, proclaiming the good news of the kingdom, and healing every disease and sickness among the people" (Matthew 4:23). This way of speaking about Jesus' ministry came straight from the Lord's own lips: "And this gospel of the kingdom will be preached in the whole world as a testimony to all nations, and then the end will come" (Matthew 24:14).

At the heart of the gospel message (in the Old and New Testaments) is the idea of God's rule as king, in other words, his kingdom. When the first Christians proclaimed this gospel of the kingdom, they were not copying the "gospel" of the Roman kingdom; they were exposing it as a fraud. It was God, not any human king, who ruled over all. This is the central theme of the Christian gospel.

The core theme of the gospel points us back to where this book began. In chapter 1 I asked: what is the single most important idea driving our mission to the world? I suggested that the answer has to do with monotheism (one God) or, more correctly, Christological monotheism – the lordship of the one true God through his Messiah. We are involved fundamentally in a reality mission, calling men and women to return to the One to whom they belong. To recall what I described as the "mission equation": if there is one Lord to whom all people belong and owe their allegiance, the people of the Lord must promote this reality everywhere. The core reason for our gospel mission corresponds to the core theme of the gospel itself: God through his Messiah reigns as king over all.

To put it in simple and practical terms, the goal of gospel preaching – and of gospel promoting – is to help our neighbours realise and submit to God's kingship or lordship over their lives. In Appendix 2 ("A Modern Retelling of the Gospel") I'll offer an example of how this might be done in a modern context.

The Deeds of the Messiah: The Content of the Gospel

But the gospel is not the announcement of a mere idea. Simply saying to your friends, "Hey, God is the king; accept it!" is not what the New Testament means by telling the gospel. Ancient Greco-Roman gospels proclaimed not simply the idea of Roman imperial authority but the actual deeds of the Roman emperors. In the same way, the Christian gospel does not just announce the concept "God reigns"; it outlines exactly how that reign has been revealed to the world. To preempt the conclusion of this chapter, the core content of the gospel is the work of God's anointed king, Jesus. Through his birth, miracles, teaching, death and resurrection God's kingdom has been manifested (and will be consummated upon his return). Telling the "gospel", then, involves recounting the deeds of the Messiah Jesus. In this rest of this chapter I am going to try to demonstrate that authentic "gospel telling" will always recount the broad narrative of Christ's life (as told in the books we call the Gospels).

Although the word *gospel* (in noun and verb) appears well over a hundred times in the New Testament, biblical writers rarely stop to remind readers what the content of the gospel is.[38] This is presumably because the bulk of the New Testament was written for Christians. The details of the gospel could be assumed, just as they are in many of the books, sermons and songs in the modern church. Those few New Testament passages that do stop to outline the gospel are therefore all the more crucial. They keep us from merely assuming the substance of the gospel. They prevent us from filling the word with whatever meaning our brand of Christianity wishes to emphasise. These important texts preserve for us the core content of our message to the world. Let's explore them in detail.

A Bullet-Point Summary of the Gospel: 1 Corinthians 15:3 – 5

I have already referred to this passage a couple of times in this chapter. In 1 Corinthians 15:1 – 6 Paul reminds the Corinthians of the gospel he preached to them about five years earlier. He doesn't expound the message fully; instead, he offers a summary designed to recall the major elements of the message.

Scholars universally regard the verses I am about to quote as the earliest formal "creed" in Christianity. A creed is a pithy statement of what someone believes. Some of you may say the Apostles' Creed in church. This was originally set down in the second century and then expanded in subsequent centuries. The creed found in 1 Corinthians 15 was probably composed and passed on to Paul as early as AD 34, just a few years after Jesus' resurrection.[39] Paul used the creed as a kind of bullet-point summary of the gospel. He handed it on to his congregations as a pithy reminder of the founding message. In 1 Corinthians 15 Paul quotes something everyone in his readership knew well. I have indented the lines of the creed:

Now, brothers and sisters, I want to remind you of the gospel I preached to you, which you received and on which you have taken your stand. By this gospel you are saved, if you hold firmly to the word I preached to you. Otherwise, you have believed in vain. For what I received I passed on to you as of first importance:

that Christ died for our sins according to the Scriptures,
that he was buried,
that he was raised on the third day according to the
    Scriptures,
and that he appeared to Cephas, and then to the Twelve.
After that, he appeared to more than five hundred of the brothers and sisters at the same time, most of whom are still living, though some have fallen asleep. Then he appeared to James, then to all the apostles, and last of all he appeared to me also, as to one abnormally born. (1 Corinthians 15:1–8)

Needless to say, the gospel Paul recalls in this passage is all about Jesus, his death (in accordance with the Old Testament Scriptures), his burial, his resurrection (again, in accordance with the Scriptures) and his appearances to Peter and the twelve disciples. Paul then adds a reference to some other appearances he knows about—to the five hundred brothers and sisters, to James the brother of Jesus, to all the apostles together and then to Paul himself—but these lines were not part of the original creed itself.

There are really five parts to Paul's summary—this could easily provide a good modern outline of the gospel:

1. Jesus' identity as the Christ
2. Jesus' saving death
3. Jesus' burial
4. Jesus' resurrection
5. Jesus' appearance to witnesses

So, there it is; that's an outline of the gospel, according to the apostles. It's probably worth asking ourselves: how does this compare with our own ideas about the content of the gospel?

Some might be thinking: but where is the idea of the *kingdom* so central to ancient understandings of the gospel? The answer is simple: it is present in the first word of the creed, "Christ". Unfortunately, "Christ" is frequently used today as a kind of surname, as if "Jesus Christ" was his full name, and his mum and dad were Mr and Mrs Christ! But "Christ" is a title. It refers, of course, to God's anointed king. The Greek word *christos* translates as "anointed one" (in Hebrew, "Messiah"). When the creed states "*Christ* died for our sins", it doesn't mean a man named Christ died; it means that God's promised Messiah–the king of God's kingdom–died. The theme of the kingdom is always present in the title Christ.

Most of this creed focuses on the events surrounding Jesus' death and resurrection, the material covered in the last quarter of any of the Gospels. The title "Christ", however, captures all that the Gospels say about Jesus leading up to his death–his birth, his miracles and his teaching. These were the things that led the disciples to the affirmation: "You are the Messiah" (Mark 8:29). The same confession of Jesus as the Christ/Messiah appears in the middle of each of the other Gospels: Matthew 16:16; Luke 9:20; John 11:27.

It is true that authentic gospel preaching always focuses on Jesus' death and resurrection; the books we call the Gospels do the same. It is equally true, however, that people could never have arrived at the conclusion that the crucified Jesus was actually the promised Messiah, the Christ, without knowing something of his earthly credentials. This, of course, is why the Gospels begin the way they do, with story after story about Jesus' authority in word and deed. Hence, gospel preaching must outline *something* of Jesus' messianic credentials. As renowned New Testament scholar Martin Hengel insists: "In the ancient world it was impossible to proclaim as Son of God and redeemer of the world a man who had died on the cross . . . without giving a clear account of his activity."[40]

What I am saying is that the title "Christ" at the beginning of Paul's gospel creed is intended to recall Jesus' credentials as Messiah. It is only against this backdrop that the heart of the gospel message—the passion and resurrection of this Messiah—makes sense. Paul's evangelistic sermon in Acts 13:13–39, which we'll look at in a moment, confirms that Paul's preaching indeed included some of the pre-passion events that demonstrated Jesus' status as Messiah: mentioned there are Jesus' royal birth, the preaching of John the Baptist introducing Jesus' ministry, Jesus' journey from Galilee to Jerusalem, his rejection among the Jews of the holy city, his trial by the Sanhedrin and the need to involve Pontius Pilate.

To put this in practical terms, one of the goals of gospel preaching—and of gospel promoting—is to help our neighbours acknowledge that Jesus is God's Messiah. Whether or not we use the Jewish term "Messiah/Christ" is probably secondary. What is important

---

Paul's gospel preaching actually included an account of the Last Supper (not just the crucifixion itself). This is confirmed just a few chapters earlier in 1 Corinthians, when the apostle reminds his readers of something else he "passed on" to them five years earlier:

> For I received from the Lord what I also passed on to you: The Lord Jesus, on the night he was betrayed, took bread, and when he had given thanks, he broke it and said, "This is my body, which is for you; do this in remembrance of me." In the same way, after supper he took the cup, saying, "This cup is the new covenant in my blood; do this, whenever you drink it, in remembrance of me." (1 Corinthians 11:23–25)

These words are virtually identical to the Last Supper scene found in Luke's Gospel. They confirm that the larger passion narrative (together with its atonement theology) formed an important part of Paul's gospel preaching. It is this entire narrative that the words "died for our sins according to the Scriptures" (1 Corinthians 15:3) are intended to recall.

is that our friends and family come to realise that Jesus as the One whom God has made Lord in his kingdom. This acknowledgment is impossible, though, without some clear idea of the deeds and words by which Jesus outlined what his lordship involves.

The second item in Paul's gospel creed is that the Christ "died for our sins according to the Scriptures". This recalls the two major themes of the passion narratives in the Gospels. From the Last Supper to the crucifixion the Gospel writers underline (1) that Jesus' death was in full accordance with the Old Testament and (2) that his death atoned for sins. The crucifixion scene itself, for instance, is saturated with allusions to the Jewish Scriptures.[41] Again, the narrative of the Last Supper describes Jesus' death as the fulfilment of the long-awaited new covenant promised in Jeremiah 31:31 – 34. This covenant was to usher in the "forgiveness of sins" (Matthew 26:26 – 28). Jesus' atoning death, as foretold in the Scriptures, is clear throughout the passion narrative.

Simply put, one of the goals of gospel preaching – and of gospel promoting – is to help those around us acknowledge their sinfulness and trust in Jesus' death as the means of their salvation. This means that judgment must be part of the gospel (as Paul confirms in Romans 2:16). The kingdom of God is coming upon the world precisely to overthrow all that is contrary to God's purposes. This includes all who have rebelled (sinned) against the Creator's ways.

But in advance of this "kingdom upheaval" God has provided a way for rebels to be forgiven so that despite their sins they may become members of the kingdom now. The kingdom's openness to the undeserving is possible only because the judgment coming on the world has fallen in advance on Jesus. His atoning death, just as much as his messianic credentials, belongs to the gospel of the kingdom.

The third element of Paul's gospel reminder may seem irrelevant at first: "that he was buried" (1 Corinthians 15:4). When was the last time you thought of telling your unbelieving friends about Jesus' burial? And, yet, the burial was a significant part of the early telling of the gospel. In fact, the Gospels devote almost as much space to the burial scene as they do to the crucifixion scene (see Mark 15:40–16:3). This does not mean that the burial is as important as Jesus' death. It simply underscores that the entire passion-resurrection narrative (from Last Supper to appearances) was included in what the first Christians called the "gospel".

Interestingly, the burial of Jesus also rates a mention in Paul's evangelistic address in Pisidian Antioch (Acts 13:13–39). Nothing profound is made of the point; it is just stated by way of fact. It belongs in a gospel presentation simply because it is a basic part of the sequence of the passion-resurrection narrative. This is instructive. The gospel is not only theology—a message about atonement and lordship—it is *news of events*. It is an account of what happened.

To flag where I am going with all this: there is no such thing as a gospel presentation that does not recount (in broad terms, at least) the narrative of Jesus' life. This brings us to perhaps the climactic element of the gospel-creed.

The gospel includes, of course, the news that the Christ "was raised on the third day according to the Scriptures" (1 Corinthians 15:4). This formed the punch line, you could say, of the Christian newsflash. The One established as God's Messiah was not defeated by death; he was raised in victory.

For us today the burial has some apologetic significance: it demonstrates—against the tide of sceptical scholarship—that the resurrection was a real bodily event. The disciples did not just experience a vision of a spiritual Jesus; they saw an actual resurrected and glorified Jesus. This, however, is not the point of the burial narrative in its ancient context. Jews in this region and period would never have thought to invent a notion so "postmodern" as a visionary resurrection. "Resurrection" for ancient Jews meant dead body comes back to life. A story of a tomb was not needed to underline this.

It is not clear whether "according to the Scriptures" refers to "on the third day" or simply "he was raised". Either way, the statement underlines one of the key themes of the resurrection narratives of the Gospels: the fulfilment of Scripture.[42] Jesus' rising from the dead marks him out as the eternal Lord of the world – just as the Scriptures foretold!

Whether or not our friends explore the intricacies of the Old Testament background, Christian faith is simply not possible without a clear idea of Jesus' bodily resurrection and what it implies. Indeed, according to Romans 10:9, trusting that God raised Jesus to be my Lord is the primary content of saving faith: "If you declare with your mouth, 'Jesus is Lord,' and believe in your heart that God raised him from the dead, you will be saved."

The last line of Paul's gospel creed recalls the events described in the closing chapters of all four Gospels: "he appeared to Cephas, and then to the Twelve" (1 Corinthians 15:5). In the Gospels, as here, Peter's experience of the risen Jesus is singled out for special mention (Mark 16:7; Luke 24:34; John 21). Moreover, in Luke's Gospel the reference to Peter's experience is followed immediately, as here, by the account of Jesus appearing to all twelve disciples (Luke 24:33 – 43).[43] Paul's gospel creed looks very much like it was crafted to follow this narrative sequence exactly.

The mention of these appearances probably has significance beyond simply being part of the official narrative of Christ's life. Peter and the Twelve were the guarantors of the entire message. Christianity has always claimed to be more than a religious truth revealed in the head of a prophet and transcribed in a holy book to be accepted in "blind faith". The Christian gospel – like the gospels about the Roman emperors – was a news report about significant public events observed by many witnesses. The earliest Christians never said simply, "Here's the message: see if this rings true for you," or "Try our doctrines and see if they improve your life." Believers always said, "Look, these things happened in Palestine recently and a whole bunch of witnesses saw them with their own eyes."[44]

Reminding our friends and relatives today that the message of Christ is not a historical myth like the story of Troy or Santa Claus but one based on eyewitness testimony will go a long way to dispelling the popular excuse: "That might be true for you but it is not for me!" The nature of the Christian gospel is such that, if it is untrue, it is untrue for everyone, and if it is true, it is true for everyone. I have tried to reflect this apologetic angle in Appendix 2 ("A Modern Retelling of the Gospel").

Summing up what we learn from the bullet-point summary of the gospel in 1 Corinthians 15:3–5: the news on which believers are to take their stand concerns (1) the sin-atoning death, (2) the burial, (3) the resurrection, (4) and the appearances (5) of the one authenticated by God to be Messiah/Lord. The connection between Paul's gospel and the books we call the Gospels is obvious. Matthew, Mark, Luke and John all demonstrate Jesus' messianic credentials before emphasising his atoning death and glorious resurrection. The preached gospel and the written Gospel are virtually identical. This becomes clearer as we explore other New Testament texts.

A Bookend Summary of the Gospel: Romans 1:3–4

In the epistle to the Romans Paul writes to a congregation he has never personally met. Before he engages in the wonderful arguments of the letter itself, he underlines for his readers the content of his evangelistic preaching. He wants to assure them that his message is the traditional one, the one long accepted as the true gospel. In introducing his gospel Paul quotes what most scholars regard as another early creed:[45]

> Paul, a servant of Christ Jesus, called to be an apostle and set apart for the gospel of God—the gospel he promised beforehand through his prophets in the Holy Scriptures regarding his Son,

who as to his earthly life
> was a descendant of David,
and who through the Spirit of holiness
> was appointed the Son of God in power,
> by his resurrection from the dead:
> Jesus Christ our Lord. (Romans 1:1 – 4)[46]

Paul introduces his summary of the gospel by stressing its connection with the Old Testament: "the gospel he promised beforehand through his prophets" (verse 2). As in 1 Corinthians 15:3 – 5, the content of the gospel is "according to the Scriptures". This theme reminds us of the strong emphasis on scriptural fulfilment that marks the introductions of all four Gospels.[47]

The content of the gospel is twofold, according to verses 3 – 4: (1) Jesus was born a royal descendant of King David, and (2) he was raised from the dead as God's great Son. Both of these realities – his royal descent and resurrection from the dead – demonstrate him to be the promised Messiah; he is "Christ our Lord" (verse 4).

The first half of the gospel creed, then, presents Jesus as the fulfilment of the promise to David that one of his sons would rule forever:

> I will raise up your offspring to succeed you, who will come from your own body, and I will establish his kingdom . . . and I will establish the throne of his kingdom forever. I will be his father, and he will be my son. (2 Samuel 7:12 – 14)

The connection between the gospel and God's kingdom is clear once again. The theme of the kingdom finds definitive expression in Jesus, the king of God's kingdom.

The second half of the creed emphasises that Jesus' kingship is more than a mere earthly and temporal dynasty. By birth Jesus was seen to be David's royal son; by his resurrection he was established as the glorious Son in full possession of the Spirit-life of God's kingdom. It is important to understand that resurrection and Spirit are fundamental themes of God's future kingdom. According to the Old and New Testaments, the coming kingdom would usher in resurrection life for all of God's people. This life would be animated and sustained by the Spirit himself.[48] By saying that Jesus "through the Spirit of holiness was appointed the Son of God in power by his resurrection from the dead", this creed makes clear that Jesus has entered into the full life of the kingdom of God, which we too will one day share.

You probably noticed that the two parts of Paul's gospel summary correspond exactly to the first and last parts of the books we call the Gospels. These begin with Jesus' credentials as the Messiah (in David's line) and end with an account of his powerful resurrection. The point is especially clear in the Gospels of Matthew and Luke, which devote the first few chapters of their accounts (complete with genealogies) to proving Jesus' identity as the long-awaited "son of David".[49]

The brief summary of the gospel here in Romans 1 recalls the starting point and end point of the narrative of Christ. This doesn't mean that Jesus' atoning death is less important in this creed than it is in 1 Corinthians 15:3–5. Romans 1:3–4 is not intended to be a bullet-point summary of the gospel; it is what you might call a "bookend" summary. By mentioning the first and last events of the story (birth and resurrection), this gospel creed captures the entire narrative. All that Jesus said and did between his birth in David's line and exaltation as God's true Son is implied in this ancient outline of the gospel. As New Testament scholar Peter Stuhlmacher says:

> Verses 3 and 4 contain the history of Christ told in the Gospels in short form, and emphasise that the entire way of Jesus, from his birth to his exaltation, stands under the sign of the promises of God.[50]

Put simply, recounting the whole story of Jesus in a way that demonstrates he is God's appointed Lord, which is exactly what the four Gospels do, is what telling the gospel involves.

The Bible's Shortest Summary of the Gospel: 2 Timothy 2:8

The "bookend" way of summarising the gospel is not unique to Romans. The third explicit New Testament outline of the gospel refers to exactly the same two items, though in reverse order. To his long-term apprentice Timothy, the apostle Paul recalls the heart of his message:

> Remember
>   Jesus Christ,
> raised from the dead,
> descended from David.
> This is my gospel,
> for which I am suffering even to the point of being chained like
>   a criminal. (2 Timothy 2:8 – 9)[51]

Again, the emphasis of Paul's gospel is on Jesus' status as the "Christ", the king of God's kingdom. In support of this Paul refers to Jesus' royal descent and resurrection from the dead. As in Romans 1:3 – 4 Paul is not overlooking the events in between Jesus' birth and exaltation. He includes them. By referring to the first and last events of Jesus' life Paul refers to them all. I don't mean to sound like a broken record but for Paul the gospel is the news of Jesus' royal birth, authoritative teaching and miracles, sacrificial death and burial, glorious resurrection and appearances to witnesses. It is the whole story of the Messiah establishing him as Lord, Judge and Saviour in God's kingdom.

The Gospel and the Gospels

Some of us might feel uncomfortable with the gospel summaries of 2 Timothy 2:8 and Romans 1:3 – 4. We may find ourselves asking: Where are the gospel themes of sin and judgment? Where is the affirmation of forgiveness and atonement? Where is the doctrine of grace and the call for repentance and faith?

The answer is simple: they are located within the story of Christ. The gospel themes of sin and judgment are frequently found on Jesus' lips (Matthew 7:22 – 23; 16:27; 19:28; 25:31 – 33; Luke 13:23 – 27; John 5:22 – 30). Moreover, in Romans 2:16 Paul refers to the theme of judgment as part and parcel of his gospel: "This will take place on the day when God judges everyone's secrets through Jesus Christ, as my gospel declares." The idea that God has set a day when he will judge the world through the Messiah Jesus comes not from a personal revelation to Paul, nor from the apostle's Jewish background, but directly from the teaching of Jesus on this subject. Even this aspect of Paul's gospel derives from the traditions found in the Gospels.

What of the themes of forgiveness and atonement? They too are found throughout the Gospels' highly theological passion narratives (Matthew 26:27 – 29; Mark 14:32 – 36; Luke 23:39 – 46). And the doctrine of grace is found in almost all of the Gospels' reports about Jesus' dealings with "sinners" (beautifully embodied, for instance, in Luke 7:36 – 50; 15:1 – 32; 18:9 – 14; 19:1 – 10). The call for repentance and faith – which characterises all true gospel preaching – is heard every time we come across the Gospels' refrain "follow me" (Mark 1:17; 2:14; Luke 18:22; John 1:43). The gospel (message) and the Gospels (books) are one.

The gospel message is not a set of theological ideas that can be detached from the events that gave these ideas definitive expression. Nor is the gospel a simple narrative devoid of theological content. One without the other is not the gospel. To recount Jesus' words and deeds without explaining their significance for our salvation is not what the Bible means by "telling the gospel". Then again, to explain the doctrines of salvation without recounting the broad events of Jesus' life as contained in the Gospels is not telling the gospel either. The gospel message is the grand news about how God's coming kingdom has been glimpsed and opened up to a sinful world in the birth, teaching, miracles, death, and resurrection of God's Son, the Messiah, who will one day return to overthrow evil and consummate the kingdom for eternity. This is the content of the Gospels; this is the content of the gospel message. This is the news the first Christians took into an empire of false (imperial) gospels. It is also the news we are to promote to our friends and neighbours.

Two passages in the Gospels confirm this connection between "gospel" and the books of the same name ("Gospel" with a capital "G").

The opening line of Mark couldn't have put it more clearly: "The beginning of the good news [gospel] about Jesus the Messiah" (Mark 1:1). Just like 1 Corinthians 15:3–5; Romans 1:3–4; and 2 Timothy 2:8, the opening line of Mark's book tells us that the gospel is all about Jesus and, in particular, about how he is the Messiah (Christ).

More can be said. Mark 1:1 is not simply a statement of a theme; it is obviously the introduction to all that follows. By commencing his book with the words "the beginning of the good news [gospel]", Mark makes clear that his account of Jesus' life is the gospel message itself. One does not find the gospel sprinkled here and there in Mark's narrative; Mark's narrative *is* the gospel.

A passage later in Mark suggests the same thing. The gospel includes all of the individual episodes that make up the narrative of the Messiah's life. In Mark 14 Jesus is anointed with perfume by an anonymous woman.[52] While some complain about the waste, Jesus praises her:

> She poured perfume on my body beforehand to prepare for my burial. Truly I tell you, wherever the gospel is preached throughout the world, what she has done will also be told, in memory of her. (Mark 14:8–9; Matthew 26:12–13 has similar words)

It is possible Jesus simply meant that wherever Christians meet in the world this woman's deed would be talked about. The natural meaning, however, is that this episode from Jesus' life will henceforth be *part* of the gospel message itself. This woman's

act of devotion is so significant — particularly in the way it antici-
pates Jesus' death and burial — that it was to be included among
the events that announce the arrival of God's kingdom. It is part
of the gospel.[53] The fact that at least three of the Gospels recount
this event is testimony to how seriously the first disciples took
Jesus' words.[54]

As with Mark 1:1 we are left with the clear impression here in
Mark 14:9 (and Matthew 26:13) that telling the "gospel" involves
recounting the saving deeds of God's Messiah, including individual episodes like the anointing. This is precisely what we observed
in 1 Corinthians 15:3 – 5; Romans 1:3 – 4; and 2 Timothy 2:8.
The gospel and the Gospels are one.

To put this in practical terms, our responsibility as Christians
is to promote the entire story of Jesus, showing the world that
in his life, teaching, death and resurrection God has revealed
himself to us and graciously opened up his kingdom to those
deserving judgment.

The First Gospel Messages

The book of Acts records the earliest evangelistic adventures from
Jerusalem to Rome. While the author (Luke) probably didn't
intend to leave us with a "theology of evangelism", his summaries of what the apostles announced to unbelievers in their travels
provide us with a reliable insight into the content of the apostolic
gospel. The passages require little comment since, basically, they
bear out what I have been saying about the gospel and the Gospels.

The first sermon, given by Peter on the day of Pentecost,
sounds like a plot summary of any one of the Gospels:

> People of Israel, listen to this: Jesus of Nazareth was a man
> accredited by God to you by miracles, wonders and signs,
> which God did among you through him, as you yourselves
> know. This man was handed over to you by God's deliber-
> ate plan and foreknowledge; and you, with the help of wicked
> men, put him to death by nailing him to the cross. But God

raised him from the dead, freeing him from the agony of death, because it was impossible for death to keep its hold on him. David said about him:

> "I saw the Lord always before me.
>> Because he is at my right hand,
>> I will not be shaken.
> Therefore my heart is glad and my tongue rejoices;
>> my body also will rest in hope,
> because you will not abandon me to the realm of the dead,
>> you will not let your Holy One see decay.
> You have made known to me the paths of life;
>> you will fill me with joy in your presence."

Brothers and sisters, we all know that the patriarch David died and was buried, and his tomb is here to this day. But he was a prophet and knew that God had promised him on oath that he would place one of his descendants on his throne. Seeing what was to come, he spoke of the resurrection of the Messiah, that he was not abandoned to the realm of the dead, nor did his body see decay. God has raised this Jesus to life, and we are all witnesses of the fact. Exalted to the right hand of God, he has received from the Father the promised Holy Spirit and has poured out what you now see and hear. For David did not ascend to heaven, and yet he said,

> "The Lord said to my Lord:
>> 'Sit at my right hand
> until I make your enemies
>> a footstool for your feet.'"

Therefore let all Israel be assured of this: God has made this Jesus, whom you crucified, both Lord and Messiah. (Acts 2:22–36)

Obviously, Luke provides us with only a short summary of Peter's message (the words recorded here would take less than three minutes to preach). But it is more than enough to see that the gospel is the news about Jesus' descent from David, miraculous deeds, death on the cross, resurrection from the dead, appearances to witnesses and lordship over God's kingdom. In other words, it is the message contained in the Gospels.

Peter's second sermon, following the healing of the crippled beggar, covers the same territory, this time emphasising the forgiveness of sins:

> People of Israel, why does this surprise you? Why do you stare at us as if by our own power or godliness we had made this man walk? The God of Abraham, Isaac and Jacob, the God of our fathers, has glorified his servant Jesus. You handed him over to be killed, and you disowned him before Pilate, though he had decided to let him go. You disowned the Holy and Righteous One and asked that a murderer be released to you. You killed the author of life, but God raised him from the dead. We are witnesses of this. By faith in the name of Jesus, this man whom you see and know was made strong. It is Jesus' name and the faith that comes through him that has completely healed him, as you can all see.
>
> Now, brothers and sisters, I know that you acted in ignorance, as did your leaders. But this is how God fulfilled what he had foretold through all the prophets, saying that his Messiah would suffer. Repent, then, and turn to God, so that your sins may be wiped out, that times of refreshing may come from the Lord, and that he may send the Messiah, who has been appointed for you – even Jesus. Heaven must receive him until the time comes for God to restore everything, as he promised long ago through his holy prophets. (Acts 3:12 – 21)

Importantly, Peter here adds a reference to God's intention to "restore everything" (verse 21). This means the consummation of God's kingdom, when God will overthrow evil and restore creation (including our bodies) to its proper order.

Again, Peter's proclamation to the Gentile centurion, Cornelius, focuses on the saving events of the Messiah's life, death and resurrection:

> I now realise how true it is that God does not show favouritism but accepts those from every nation who fear him and do what is right. You know the message God sent to the people of

Israel, announcing the good news [literally: telling the gospel] of peace through Jesus Christ, who is Lord of all. You know what has happened throughout the province of Judea, beginning in Galilee after the baptism that John preached—how God anointed Jesus of Nazareth with the Holy Spirit and power, and how he went around doing good and healing all who were under the power of the devil, because God was with him.

We are witnesses of everything he did in the country of the Jews and in Jerusalem. They killed him by hanging him on a cross, but God raised him from the dead on the third day and caused him to be seen. He was not seen by all the people, but by witnesses whom God had already chosen—by us who ate and drank with him after he rose from the dead. He commanded us to preach to the people and to testify that he is the one whom God appointed as judge of the living and the dead. All the prophets testify about him that everyone who believes in him receives forgiveness of sins through his name. (Acts 10:34–43)

The mention of John the Baptist in verse 37 may sound out of place. When was the last time you thought of mentioning him in a conversation with your friends and neighbours? But the detail is significant precisely because it is part of the authoritative narrative about Christ (as told by all four Gospels). It is part of the gospel—fully told.

Verse 42 above highlights something else I said earlier. The Messiah's role in the final judgment was a common theme of Jesus' own teaching (Matthew 7:22–23; 16:27; 19:28; 25:31–33; Luke 13:23–27; John 5:22–30). It was also part of Paul's own gospel (Romans 2:16). It is therefore very much part of our gospel today. After all, it is from God's judgment that Jesus' death saves us.

The similarities between Peter's sermons and that of the apostle Paul in Pisidian Antioch are striking. After a brief account of the history of Israel leading up to King David, Paul continues:

From this man's descendants God has brought to Israel the Saviour Jesus, as he promised. Before the coming of Jesus, John preached repentance and baptism to all the people of Israel. As

John was completing his work, he said: "Who do you suppose I am? I am not the one you are looking for. But there is someone coming after me whose sandals I am not worthy to untie."

Brothers and sisters from the children of Abraham and you God-fearing Gentiles, it is to us that this message of salvation has been sent. The people of Jerusalem and their rulers did not recognise Jesus, yet in condemning him they fulfilled the words of the prophets that are read every Sabbath. Though they found no proper ground for a death sentence, they asked Pilate to have him executed. When they had carried out all that was written about him, they took him down from the cross and laid him in a tomb. But God raised him from the dead, and for many days he was seen by those who had travelled with him from Galilee to Jerusalem. They are now his witnesses to our people.

We tell you the good news [literally: telling the gospel]: What God promised our ancestors he has fulfilled for us, their children, by raising up Jesus. As it is written in the second Psalm:

> "You are my Son;
> today I have become your Father."

God raised him from the dead so that he will never be subject to decay. As God has said,

> "I will give you the holy and sure blessings promised to David."

So it is also stated elsewhere:

> "You will not let your Holy One see decay."

Now when David had served God's purpose in his own generation, he fell asleep; he was buried with his ancestors and his body decayed. But the one whom God raised from the dead did not see decay.

Therefore, my brothers and sisters, I want you to know that through Jesus the forgiveness of sins is proclaimed to you. Through him everyone who believes is set free from every sin, a justification you were not able to obtain under the law of Moses. (Acts 13:23–39)

Several things are worth observing. First, the sermon is virtually a plot summary of the narrative of the Gospels (particularly that of Luke). According to verse 25, Paul even included the words of John the Baptist in his gospel presentation (cf. Luke 3:16).

Second, the connections between this speech and the gospel creeds in Romans 1:3 – 4 and 2 Timothy 2:8 are obvious. Both the creeds and this speech underline Jesus' messiahship by referring to his descent from King David and his resurrection from the dead.

Third, Paul refers here to two themes that appear again and again in his letters: "forgiveness of sins" and "justification by faith" (Acts 13:38 – 39).[55] In his epistles the apostle rarely stops to locate these gospel themes within the larger gospel narrative of the Messiah's life, death and resurrection. Presumably this is because his letters are not only "occasional" in nature but they address Christians specifically whose knowledge of the Jesus-narrative could be assumed. Paul, after all, had passed it on to them. When addressing unbelievers, however (as here in Acts 13), Paul would not – could not – speak about sin, atonement and forgiveness without placing these themes within the events that gave these ideas definitive expression. As I said earlier, just as there can be no telling of the gospel that excludes the doctrines of salvation, there can be no telling of the gospel that overlooks the narrative of the Saviour's life. The gospel message and the Gospel books are one.

Attentive readers might be wondering whether Paul's speech in the Athenian Areopagus (Acts 17:22 – 31) provides an exception to the pattern of gospel preaching I have been describing. Here, Christ's resurrection and future judgment appear only at the conclusion of a rather philosophical critique of idol worship; indeed, the risen judge is not even named. Jesus is the climax of the talk, but he is not its substance. This may be the exception that proves the rule. But, actually, I think the peculiar apologetic setting of the speech easily accounts for Paul's (atypical) approach. According to verses 18 – 21, the speech itself was an answer to Epicurean and Stoic objections to the message Paul had been preaching "in the marketplace day by day" (verse 17).

So, what had Paul been preaching before he got into trouble with these local intellectuals? Luke tells us Paul had been "preaching the good news about Jesus and the resurrection". In other words, before finding himself in the philosophically charged context of the Areopagus, Paul's typical preaching focused on the very things outlined (as we have seen) in Acts 13:23–39—namely, the life of Jesus climaxing in his resurrection. It is probably accurate to describe Acts 17:22–31 not as a presentation of the gospel proper but as a defence of the gospel against the particular criticisms of pagan philosophers.

To these observations we can add the many "summary statements" about gospel preaching scattered throughout the book of Acts. These reveal in brief form how Luke understood the content of the apostolic gospel. I will simply quote them:

> Day after day, in the temple courts and from house to house, they never stopped teaching and proclaiming the good news [literally: telling the gospel] that Jesus is the Messiah. (Acts 5:42)

> Philip went down to a city in Samaria and proclaimed the Messiah there. (8:5)

> But when they believed Philip as he proclaimed the good news [literally: told the gospel] of the kingdom of God and the name of Jesus Christ, they were baptised, both men and women. (8:12)

> Saul spent several days with the disciples in Damascus. At once he began to preach in the synagogues that Jesus is the Son of God. (9:19–20)

> Yet Saul grew more and more powerful and baffled the Jews living in Damascus by proving that Jesus is the Messiah. (9:22)

> As was his custom, Paul went into the synagogue, and on three Sabbath days he reasoned with them from the Scriptures,

explaining and proving that the Messiah had to suffer and rise from the dead. "This Jesus I am proclaiming to you is the Messiah," he said. (17:2–3)

When Silas and Timothy came from Macedonia, Paul devoted himself exclusively to preaching, testifying to the Jews that Jesus was the Messiah. (18:5)

For he [Apollos] vigorously refuted the Jews in public debate, proving from the Scriptures that Jesus was the Messiah. (18:28)

"In the name of Jesus, whom Paul preaches, I command you to come out." (19:13)

I have declared to both Jews and Greeks that they must turn to God in repentance and have faith in our Lord Jesus. (20:21)

However, I consider my life worth nothing to me; my only aim is to finish the race and complete the task the Lord Jesus has given me—the task of testifying to the good news [gospel] of God's grace. Now I know that none of you among whom I have gone about preaching the kingdom will ever see me again. (20:24–25)

For two whole years Paul stayed there in his own rented house and welcomed all who came to see him. He proclaimed the kingdom of God and taught about the Lord Jesus Christ—with all boldness and without hindrance. (28:30–31)

God's kingdom as glimpsed in the person of Jesus, God's Messiah, is the core content of the gospel in all of these summaries. This in no way sidelines the themes of sin, judgment and forgiveness; it simply places these doctrines of "grace" (20:24) within the narrative of Christ's revelation of God's kingdom.

New Testament historian Martin Hengel states well the relationship between the Gospels and the gospel, between the deeds of the Messiah and the message of salvation:

It is not a matter of chance that in his letters Paul sometimes refers by way of allusion to the narration of stories about Jesus. These allusions presuppose that the readers know more

(1 Corinthians 11:23ff; 15:3ff; Romans 1:3; 15:8; Philippians 2:6–11; Galatians 4:4 etc.). We must assume that in his mission preaching – which fades right into the background in his letters – Paul also of course told stories about Jesus, and primarily the passion story, the account of the crucifixion of Jesus ... These isolated references are therefore all the more important ... According to the earliest Christians the saving event was "history", which comprised not only the death and resurrection of Jesus as the specific event lying at the heart of salvation, but also his activity and the authentication of the apostles by the risen Jesus.[56]

"Gospel" in the Early Church

Historically minded readers may be interested in a final point about the connection between gospel and the Gospels; others may want to advance straight to the conclusion! Not surprisingly, Christians in the period immediately after the writing of the New Testament (that is, in the second and third centuries) used the term "gospel" in precisely the manner shown above – to refer to the news about Jesus as recounted in the Gospels. This is significant. As our earliest interpreters of Christian Scripture, the early "church fathers", as they are called, often draw our attention to nuances and emphases in the New Testament to which modern Christians have become blind. I read the writings of the early church for the same reason I read modern biblical commentaries: to get a second opinion about various New Testament passages from people who know the Greek language and culture better than I do.

The first piece of evidence from the early church is the title of the Gospels themselves. Have you ever stopped to wonder why we call these four books at the front of the New Testament "the Gospels"? The reason is simple: all of our earliest manuscript copies of these documents carry the heading "The Gospel according to ... (Matthew, Mark, etc.)". We don't know exactly when these titles were added to the manuscripts, but it cannot have been any later than the early second century and may even have occurred when the books were first produced and circulated (in the first century).[57] What we can say is that the Christians who first passed on these precious documents used the title "Gospel according to . . ." for the simple reason that these writings contained the message preached by the apostles. To the early church, the written Gospels were the gospel.[58]

Underlining this point is the fact that some of the earliest church fathers insisted that the Gospel of Mark and the Gospel of Luke (neither of which had been penned by an apostle) contained the very gospel message preached by Peter and Paul respectively. Papias was the bishop of Hierapolis (AD 60–130) and a disciple of those who knew the apostle John. Papias informs us of something he was told by his own teachers. Mark had been the apostle Peter's personal assistant. After the apostle's death Mark put into writing all that he could recall of Peter's teaching, being careful "to leave out nothing of what he had heard and to make no false statements". The result was what we call the Gospel according to Mark.[59]

Similarly, Irenaeus (AD 120–200), a leading Christian of the second century, believed that the Gospel of Luke was the written record of the apostle Paul's public preaching: "Luke, who was Paul's follower, set down in a book the gospel which he preached."[60] Whether or not we accept the claims of Irenaeus and Papias, my point is this: these leaders of the early church understood the Gospels to contain the apostolic gospel.

In the same vein, Eusebius (AD 260–340), bishop of Caesarea, writes about the role of evangelists in the period immediately following the apostles. He describes their task as twofold: "to preach to all who had not yet heard the word of the faith, and to pass on the writing of the divine Gospels".[61] In other words, to share the gospel was to establish people in the material contained in the Gospels.

Conclusion: What Is the Gospel?

So, what is the gospel? Let me try to summarise what we have learned from the gospel creeds in the epistles, the gospel messages in the book of Acts and the evidence of the Gospels themselves.

The core theme of the gospel is the kingdom of God, the establishment of his rightful kingship over the world, which will one day be fully disclosed in a new creation. This kingdom was glimpsed in and established by the birth, miracles, teaching, death and resurrection of God's Messiah Jesus, who will return to consummate the kingdom. The core content of the gospel therefore goes something like this:

- Jesus' royal birth secured his claim to the eternal throne promised to King David.
- Jesus' miracles pointed to the presence of God's kingdom in the person of his Messiah.
- Jesus' teaching sounded the invitation of the kingdom and laid down its demands.
- Jesus' sacrificial death atoned for the sins of those who would otherwise be condemned at the consummation of the kingdom.
- Jesus' resurrection establishes him as the Son whom God has appointed Judge of the world and Lord of the coming kingdom.

Recounting the saving achievements of our Lord from birth to exaltation is what telling the gospel is. This does not mean that every gospel presentation must include every element mentioned above, but it does mean that the immediate goal of evangelism is to introduce people to the Jesus whom the Gospels describe in these terms. Appendix 2 ("A Modern Retelling of the Gospel") contains an attempt to do just this in a contemporary context.

I realise this chapter has been content-heavy — a chapter about the content of the gospel could hardly be otherwise. One simple thing to take away from all this, however, is that the Christian faith is founded on the message proclaimed in the four books at the beginning of our New Testament. Whatever excellent gospel tracts, training courses and books hit the modern mission market, the Gospels ought to remain the key to our promotion of the gospel. They provide the surest account of the content of the gospel. Their presentation of the Saviour offers a rich source of motivation for our own involvement in the work of the gospel. And, all these years later, they still provide unbelievers with the clearest account of what it is Christians believe and do. When friends and family ask to read something that captures the substance of our faith we, like the ancient evangelists just mentioned, could do no better than "pass on the writing of the divine Gospels".[62]

None of this is because these writings are more "inspired" than the rest of God's Word; it is simply because the Gospels are singularly designed to recount the founding message of the faith (which, of course, is why they were put at the front of the New Testament in the first place). All of the Scriptures point to the gospel and apply the gospel, but only the Gospels *recount* the gospel in all its fullness. The Gospels and the gospel are one.

It has been a long time coming, but I want to turn now to the ways in which we promote this gospel *with our lips*.

CHAPTER 9

The Few and the Many

Evangelists and the Local Church

So Christ himself gave . . . the evangelists.
Ephesians 4:11

IN THE YEAR OR SO after they became Christians, some teenage lads I know decided to use their school holidays for the cause of Christ. For years they had attended government Sport and Recreation Camps, where they spent their time chasing girls, picking fights and sneaking out of their cabins at night. Not anymore. Now they were planning to convert the entire camp population. To assist them in their mission they packed the usual camp essentials as well as an entire suitcase full of Bibles, Christian tracts and "Jesus Saves" stickers.

It was a thrilling seven days for this bunch of young believers armed with prayer, teenage abandon and, of course, the "holy bag" (as they called it). By the end of the week, "Jesus Saves" was plastered on every wall of the campsite, not a single Bible or tract remained, and the lads found themselves conducting daily Bible discussions during free-time with about fifteen other teenage campers, many of whom embraced Christ for the first time.

There was every indication these young men would grow up to pursue a ministry of evangelism. Several of them are now full-time evangelists. One of them is the author of this book.

Another friend of mine, Chester, is one of the most risk-taking Christians I know. I remember Chester once caught a taxi from Sydney central to the north side of the city. The whole way he was trying to think of a way to start up a conversation about Christ with his driver – this was typical for Chester. Everything he said, however, failed. The man seemed completely uninterested.

Fifteen minutes later they arrived at Chester's destination just underneath the northern end of the famous Harbour Bridge. The driver seemed quite taken with the bridge as he looked up out of his window at the enormous structure. "Beautiful bridge, isn't it?" said Chester. "Best bridge in the world," the driver replied enthusiastically. Suddenly, Chester remembered the gospel tract in his top pocket – the well-known "Bridge to Life". "Do you mind," asked Chester, in a manner only he could get away with, "if I tell you about the best bridge I know about?" I kid you not: for the next fifteen minutes Chester led that man through a careful presentation of Christ as the bridge between God and man. The driver soaked up Chester's every word and thoughtfully took the tract away with him. I suspect Chester could write a book entitled *101 Crazy Ways to Tell Others about Jesus*. I for one would buy it.

It would be easy to present examples like these as typical of what God expects of every believer – innovation, zeal and pro-activity in outlining the gospel to others. But this would not be appropriate. At a pragmatic level, it is obvious that not all of us are wired like Chester or those young lads. There is no shame in that. The existence of evangelists like these should not make us feel guilty that our own gospel opportunities are less frequent or less daring or less comprehensive; it should be a cause of rejoicing.

More importantly, God's Word does not teach that every Christian is an evangelist. Yes, we must all be open about Christ, answering for our faith whenever opportunity invites – and let me personally urge readers to take whatever opportunities the

Lord provides. But this is not what Chester and these lads were (and are) doing on a near daily basis. Some of God's people go beyond the passing, conversational "bites" about the gospel hopefully common to us all. They pursue a focused ministry of outlining the whole gospel to others. They are the evangelists.

In this chapter, I want to explore the speaking role of the few. In particular, I want to show that the New Testament envisages a special place in our congregations for "evangelists", people given to the church by Christ for the express purpose of articulating the gospel to those who do not yet believe. Once we have studied the role of the evangelist, we will explore the privilege and responsibility all Christians have to promote Christ with their lips.

The Word "Evangelist"

An entire volume could be written about the biblical and practical significance of the evangelist, but since I want this book to address all believers, not just evangelists, I have made this chapter much briefer than the topic deserves.[63]

You may already know that the word "evangelist" (*euangelistçs*) is simply the word "gospel" (*euangelion*) with a new ending. The word literally means *gospeller*, that is, *one who announces the gospel*. The term seems to have been coined by the first Christians (it appears nowhere else in Greek literature before the New Testament) as a shorthand way of referring to those in the church who took on the task of proclaiming the life, death and resurrection of God's Messiah (the gospel) to those for whom this message was *still news*.

The term *evangelist* appears only in Paul's late letters (Ephesians 4:11; 2 Timothy 4:5) and in the even later book of Acts (21:8). Before this period (before, say, AD 60) evangelists went by various other labels, including "workers", "co-workers", "servants", "brothers/colleagues" and even "apostles". In contrast to the modern figure of the "itinerant evangelist", many of these

I have sometimes heard it said that because all of Christian preaching/teaching is based on the gospel, the term "evangelist" applies equally to congregational teachers. The evidence is against this. First, there is the obvious point that evangelists and teachers are listed as separate functions in Ephesians 4:11. More importantly, central to the meaning of the word *euangelion* (and therefore to *euangelistçs*) is the idea of "news". That is how "gospel" is consistently used throughout Greco-Roman literature of the period. The New Testament follows the pattern. "Gospel" does not refer to everything that is preached and believed by Christians. It refers to the *founding* message, the "news", of Christ's life, death and resurrection. "Evangelist" must therefore refer someone who lays down this message to those for whom it is still news.[64]

New Testament "gospellers" appear to have been connected either with a single congregation or with a small cluster of congregations in a geographical region. Let me race through the New Testament evidence and then draw out some practical implications.

Evangelists in the New Testament

First, there is an unnamed "brother" in 2 Corinthians 8:18, who, although currently travelling with Paul to Jerusalem, is a delegate of the churches of Macedonia (Philippi, Thessalonica and perhaps other towns). Paul describes him as "praised by all the churches for his service to the gospel" (probably a reference to gospel preaching). In context, "all the churches" refers simply to the Macedonian churches, of which there were just a handful, meeting in towns smaller in size and population than the average modern suburb. This guy, whoever he was, was a kind of district evangelist.

While we are in Macedonia I should mention the three named "gospellers" active in the city of Philippi, a town of fewer than 15,000 people in Paul's day. Euodia, Syntyche and Clement (Philippians 4:2 – 3), all residents of Philippi, are referred to by Paul as his "co-workers", a term usually reserved for fellow missionaries. These are said to have contended with Paul "in the cause of the gospel", which, as commentators point out, probably refers to active involvement in proclaiming the gospel.[65] These three were small-town evangelists.

Moving over to Turkey we find Epaphras, who evangelised the Colossians (Colossians 1:7) and whose field of ministry eventually expanded to include a little triangle of towns 30 km apart in southeastern Turkey (Colossians 4:12 – 13). Like the anonymous brother in 2 Corinthians 8:18, Epaphras seems to have been a district evangelist.

In Rome, from where Paul penned the letter to the Philippians, there seems to have been a whole bunch of local church evangelists. From an imperial prison the apostle advises his beloved Philippians:

> And because of my chains, most of the brothers and sisters have become confident in the Lord and dare all the more to proclaim the gospel without fear.
>
> It is true that some preach Christ out of envy and rivalry, but others out of goodwill. The latter do so out of love, knowing that I am put here for the defense of the gospel. The former preach Christ out of selfish ambition, not sincerely, supposing that they can stir up trouble for me while I am in chains. (Philippians 1:14 – 17)

The situation Paul describes is exciting. Despite the apostle's imprisonment—in fact, because of it—a good number of Christians have been emboldened to preach Christ throughout Rome. Some of these preachers were doing so in a manner that was stirring up trouble for Paul while in prison (perhaps they were publicly distancing themselves from him in their preaching). Others, however, were acting with true motives. Paul doesn't mind, so long as the gospel is preached.

Who are these preaching "brothers" ("and sisters" – though it is one word in Greek)? Some insist they are the rank-and-file believers of Rome. After all, the expression "the brother(s)" (*ho adelphos* in Greek) occurs twenty times in Paul's letters with the clear meaning *fellow believer*. However, things are not so simple. One of the other standard dictionary definitions of *ho adelphos* is "colleague, associate".[66] And, while statistics alone cannot always decide such matters, it is worth noting that the label "the brother(s)" in Paul's letters refers to *missionary colleagues* specifically on at least twenty-four occasions.[67] Given the formal way Paul describes the activity of the "brothers" ("and sisters") of Philippians 1:14 – 17, "colleagues" seems to me to be the more natural sense of the term in this text.

"The brothers" ("and sisters") pop up again at the end of the letter (Philippians 4:21 – 22). Here, Paul sends greetings to the

Even if one were to interpret Philippians 1:14 – 17 as referring to ordinary believers rather than missionary colleagues, it is still not clear whether this would mean believers today are to imitate this example, since Paul says nothing to the Philippians about imitating the example of these Roman "brothers" ("and sisters"), and there is nothing anywhere else in the letter asking the Philippians to evangelise. Philippians 1:14 – 17 offers a description not a prescription.

To offer a comparison, should believers today sell all their possessions and give the proceeds to the church as the Jerusalem Christians did in Acts 2:44 – 45 (and as some cults have insisted upon through the centuries)? Most of us, I think, would say no. Such a passage is descriptive of what believers did at one particular time, but it is not necessarily prescriptive for what believers should do all the time.

Philippians from two sets of people in Rome: first from "the brothers" and then from "all the saints". Since "saints" is Paul's default term for believers in general, it is clear that "the brothers" in this verse, as in 1:14, are his missionary colleagues. Other (more technical) arguments can be mounted,[68] but the main point for now is that Rome appears to have been blessed in Paul's day with an abundance of local evangelists.

Briefly, we can add a few more evangelists to our list. Philip, who had previously evangelised Samaria and the famous Ethiopian eunuch (Acts 8), is described in Acts 21:8 as "Philip the evangelist". Interestingly, Luke gives him this title in connection with his settled ministry in Caesarea on the Palestinian coast. Philip seems to have been both a travelling and a stationary evangelist.

Then there is Timothy, who, in the context of his local ministry in the city of Ephesus, is urged: "do the work of an evangelist: discharge all the duties of your ministry" (2 Timothy 4:5).

Another example of the descriptive/prescriptive problem is found in Luke 9:60, where Jesus commands a would-be disciple: "Let the dead bury their own dead, but you go and proclaim the kingdom of God." If we take this text to mean all believers should preach the gospel, what do we do with those other passages in which Jesus tells his disciples not to spread the word about him (Matthew 8:4; Mark 7:36; Luke 8:56)? In any case, Luke 9:60 probably does not refer to a rank-and-file disciple. The fact that this passage falls between the sending of the two missionaries into Samaria (9:51–56) and the sending of the seventy-two missionaries into Israel (10:1–24) suggests that the words of Luke 9:60 are directed toward a would-be missionary, not a typical disciple.

I have heard this statement interpreted as though Timothy were not really an evangelist but should assume the role anyway. The implication then was that all Christians should do the work of the evangelist. Apart from the fact that the Pastoral Epistles, as 1 Timothy, 2 Timothy and Titus are called, were written for Christian leaders (pastors), there is nothing in the Greek text to suggest that Timothy was not an evangelist. Actually, a brief study of Timothy's role alongside Paul shows that he was an evangelist par excellence.[69] This is why Paul adds here, "discharge all the duties of your ministry". What Timothy had been doing for years as an itinerant evangelist he was now to carry on in a local context; he was not only to teach believers and appoint elders, he was to keep evangelizing the unbelievers of Ephesus.

While we are in Ephesus, here is one final text in which Paul describes evangelists as "gifts" from Jesus to the church:

> This is why it says: "When he [Christ] ascended on high, he took captives and gave gifts to his people" . . . So Christ himself gave the apostles, the prophets, the evangelists, the pastors and teachers, to equip his people for works of service, so that the body of Christ may be built up. (Ephesians 4:8 – 12)

Whether the evangelists mentioned here are travelling or stationary is impossible to tell since Paul's words appear to concern the body of Christ generally rather than the church of Ephesus in particular. Two things are clear, though. First, only *some* Christians are evangelists, since the way the sentence is constructed in Greek it is clear "the apostles", "the prophets" and "the evangelists" are separate groups of workers. In saying this I do not want to discourage the rest of us from doing what we can to tell the gospel to others. Each of us should speak of Jesus as our personalities, abilities and opportunities allow, confident that, as we do, God's Spirit will work through us.

During my years as a local church minister there were few things I enjoyed more than watching members of my congregation share the gospel with their friends and family (and even with complete strangers). My point here, though, is that while I hope and pray that all believers will speak of the Lord whenever they can, I do not have any justification for pressing them all into the role of an evangelist. That is simply not how the Scriptures talk about the issue. It would be akin to my urging every Christian to become a Bible study leader or Christian aid worker simply on the grounds that the Scriptures urge all of us to be devoted to God's Word (Colossians 3:16) and ever-mindful of the poor (James 2:14–17).

Second, evangelists are among Christ's gifts to the church (along with prophets and pastors) "to equip his people for works of service, so that the body of Christ may be built up". This does not mean that evangelists prepare other Christians to be evangelists, any more than it means apostles prepare us to be apostles, and prophets prepare us to be prophets. Paul's point is simple: when all of these various ministries are functioning throughout the church, God's people are properly equipped to serve and grow. The evangelist's role in all this is obvious. He or she evangelises the lost so that they might become part of the body of Christ in the first place.

My observation throughout this section is simple: as part of the call for all of us to promote the gospel, it is clear from God's Word that some in our congregations will devote themselves specifically to the task of outlining the gospel to the wider community. These are our "gospellers", our evangelists.

Picking the Evangelist Today

Of course, the obvious question is: how do you determine who the evangelists are? It is sometimes put to me that because there is no real way of discerning evangelists, we might as well urge and train all Christians to be evangelists and just see what eventuates. I appreciate the sentiment, but it seems to me we would never consider urging everyone in our churches to become Bible study group leaders, Sunday school teachers, hospital or nursing home

Eusebius of Caesarea, the famous bishop and church chronicler (AD 260 – 340), reports the activity of evangelists in the early second century, a generation after the apostles:

> Many of those then disciples, smitten in the soul by the divine Logos with an ardent passion for the love of wisdom, first fulfilled the Saviour's command and distributed their property to the needy, then, starting on their journey, took up the work of evangelists and were zealous to preach to all who had not yet heard the word of the faith, and to transmit the writing of the divine Gospels. (Eusebius, *Ecclesiastical History* 3.37.2)

In another passage he mentions one evangelist by name, Pantaenus (died AD 190), and tragically suggests that such evangelists were a dying breed:

visitors and so on. Why would we do it for evangelists? It is not difficult to find suitable people for these other ministries. With a little thought and planning the same can be true for evangelists.

Let me offer four tips for picking the evangelist. Two are simple guesses; the others are grounded in the Bible itself.

First, I assume that evangelists will be marked by a keen desire to tell the gospel to others. It makes sense to me that, if Christ has given individuals to the church for a focused ministry of evangelism, and if he has appropriately fitted them out for the task, such people will want to perform the role. Of course, every Christian should be zealous for the salvation of others. But some, as I am sure you will know, are especially keen to talk to others about Jesus. Think through your Christian friends right now; I am confident you will be able to name several who stand out for their passion to tell the gospel to others. Perhaps it is you![70]

Second, I assume that most evangelists will relate well to those who do not yet believe. This is guesswork on my part.

He [Pantaenus] showed such zeal in his warm disposition for the divine word that he was appointed as a herald for the gospel of Christ to the heathen in the East, and was sent to India. For indeed there were *until then* many evangelists of the word who had forethought to use inspired zeal on the apostolic model for the increase and the building up of the divine word. (Eusebius, *Ecclesiastical History* 5.10.2; emphasis mine)

The words "until then" are a sad hint that by the time Eusebius wrote, there were few taking up the mantle of the evangelist. Eusebius wrote in the comfortable Christian era following the conversion of Emperor Constantine. His perspective, therefore, seems to be one of establishment rather than gospel entrepreneurialism. Perhaps there is a salutary lesson here for us who live in so-called Christian nations. May we never think of evangelists as a thing of the past!

But it seems reasonable to me that those given to the church for the express purpose of communicating the gospel to those who do not believe will feel relaxed with them, enjoy befriending them, understand them and so on. In some ways, this is no different from determining a Sunday school teacher or Bible study leader by observing (or predicting) how well the person relates to the respective audience. Do you relate well to those outside the church? Can you think of others in your church who do? Perhaps these are Christ's evangelists.

Third, and importantly, an evangelist will be a mature Christian. Like anyone who performs a ministry in the church—a Bible study leader, for instance—those in the church who play a focused role in evangelism (through door-knocking, conducting evangelistic courses, etc.) must display the kinds of qualities Paul expected of any leader—self-control, honesty and commitment to the truth, and they should not be recent converts (1 Timothy 3:1–10).

I am not saying that new Christians must fit the description of a mature Christian before they share the gospel with their friends and neighbours. Not at all. Here, I am talking about the particular function of the evangelist as observed in the Bible. An evangelist is not just any Christian who talks about Jesus, any more than a "teacher" (a Bible study leader, for instance) is any Christian who chats to fellow believers about the Bible. The role of the evangelist is just that—a role. As such, it is important that a designated evangelist be a mature Christian.

Finally, and perhaps most obviously, an evangelist will be clear with the gospel. I do not just mean clear about what the gospel is—hopefully, that will be all of us. I am talking about clarity in outlining the gospel. This point arises directly from

Whether an evangelist is also necessarily someone with a track-record for converting people, I am not sure. Laying the emphasis on a spiritual knack for turning people to Christ assumes that the power of conversion resides in some human behaviour or skill. I prefer to think of it differently. It is interesting that in the various lists of spiritual gifts in the New Testament (Romans 12:3–8; 1 Corinthians 12:1–11, 27–31; and Ephesians 4:8–12), a gift of "evangelism" is not mentioned. The gift of the evangelist is mentioned in Ephesians 4:11, but here the "gift" is not an ability given to an individual but an individual given to the community of believers. The evangelist is the gift.

I am not sure how significant this observation is and I do not want to belabour the point. I just want to flag a slight hesitation I have with the idea that evangelists have spiritual powers to bring about conversion. The power resides in the gospel itself, and so I prefer simply to emphasise the evangelist's ability to be clear (which may indeed be a spiritual gift).

the word "evangelist" itself. A "gospeller" (*euangelistçs*) must be particularly able to explain the message plainly. I am not talking about having a gift of the gab or even being an extrovert – clarity does not always go with these. I am talking specifically about an ability to take the truths of the gospel and make them plain to others (key here will be an ability to talk about Christ without jargon, in the everyday language of those who don't believe). This presupposes that Christians are talking and listening to each other – over morning tea, at church functions, during Bible studies or whatever. Assuming we do, I am sure that those with a knack for clarity will be obvious to most of us. Gospel clarity, I believe, is the main predictor of the evangelist.

A friend of mine provides a good example of how all four of these "tips" can come together to reveal a local church evangelist. Tim is a thirty-something boat builder and a follower of Jesus for as long as he can remember. Over the years he had helped out with all sorts of ministries – youth group, Bible studies, holiday programs and so on. He was a proven and godly Christian. In addition, it was clear Tim had a deep concern for and an excellent rapport with his friends and neighbours outside the church. I don't think he had personally led anyone to Christ, but he was the kind of guy who was always getting into conversations about the faith and was frequently bringing friends to church.

On a hunch that he was just the sort of guy to lead people through the gospel message, Tim's church invited him to sit in on a short course for "seekers" run in the minister's home over five weeks. Tim was there to learn the ropes, to read passages from the Bible and to offer the occasional personal perspective on believing in Christ. Everything he did over the weeks was crystal clear. He was not a preacher or especially extroverted – Tim is a decidedly laid-back Australian. But when he spoke of Christ, he had a knack for keeping it simple, avoiding jargon and addressing his words directly to his hearers.

When Tim felt comfortable with the course material, he gave it a go himself. Soon he had a lounge room full of his own sceptics, spectators and searchers. He did brilliantly, casually taking people through the life, death and resurrection of Jesus and winsomely urging people to accept the Lord. And some did. As a result of his first couple of enquirer courses, Tim ended up with a sizeable home group of new and almost Christians to follow up. He did so diligently throughout the rest of the year, grounding them in the truths of the gospel. This boat builder was clearly a "gospeller" as well.

Congregations or clusters of congregations would do well to consider employing focused evangelists in their midst. Theological colleges could assist by providing a specialist training stream for those who appear most useful in this regard. Perhaps most importantly, we should all be on the lookout for people in our local churches (perhaps even ourselves) who can be trained and utilised for a focused evangelistic ministry in our local area. Like my friend Tim they could be trained in apologetics as well as in some modern evangelistic tools. They could then be set loose in our midst.

Well, that covers (too briefly) the speaking role of the few. In the next two chapters I want to explore at length the way God's Word encourages all Christians to keep Christ on our lips. We begin with a type of gospel proclamation that is rarely considered.

CHAPTER 10

Heralds Together

Promoting the Gospel through
Our Public Praise

> . . . that you may declare the praises of him who
> called you out of darkness into his wonderful
> light.
>
> *1 Peter 2:9*

NIKKI GEMMELL, AUTHOR OF THE acclaimed and controversial *The Bride Stripped Bare*, is perhaps an unlikely convert to mainstream Christianity. Ever since her parents divorced when she was ten years old, the ritual of church attendance disappeared from her life and other things took priority. In a *Sunday Life* magazine article she described her twenties as "too busy, too hungry, too grasping" for any commitment to Christ or the church.[71] A career in journalism and writing and a desire to "live it up" were her main goals. After a time as a presenter on Australia's "grooviest" radio station, Triple J, she moved to London, where she read the news for the BBC and worked on her now celebrated novels. It was there that she found Christ.

While in London she and her husband "discovered the solace of Evensong" at a local Church of England. The combination of prayers, Scripture readings, psalms and choral music was a long way from Triple J, but the effect on the couple was significant. "It completely stilled me," she remembers, "and brought me to an experience of calm." Later she was invited to another, more contemporary, church in London's famous Notting Hill. This service too was to have a lasting influence. "We went along because an Aussie friend was having a child christened there," she explains, "and we were so taken, we've gone there ever since." Gemmell, now a keen sermon note-taker and part of the welcoming roster at church, is refreshingly open about her newfound faith and is enjoying the opportunity to instil it in her young boys.

Nikki Gemmell's story is one of many I have heard over the years that emphasise the unusual "effect" of a simple church service on one's journey to faith. I used to brush aside stories like this, preferring to hear (and retell) the testimonies of people who attended special evangelistic events – the sort of thing I preached at regularly – where the straight-shooting, twenty-minute gospel presentation was the "star" of the mission story. But neither the Evensong service Gemmell attended nor the christening service she was so taken with was intentionally evangelistic. Both, however, exerted an influence for the gospel in her life and that of her husband. The humble church service was a powerful promotion of the news of Christ.

There is a temptation to view our regular services as only vaguely related to the proclamation of the gospel. Some view church services as mere "in-drag" as opposed to true "outreach", that is, going out into the "marketplace" with the gospel. Do not get me wrong: I am all for "marketplace" evangelism and have greatly enjoyed my involvement in business lunches, pub nights and various other innovative "outreach" events over the years. My point is: the Bible accords a significant place to the normal gathering of God's people as a means of declaring God's truth to the world. Research by sociology professor Rodney Stark shows that one of the key reasons evangelical churches grow is that their members simply "invite their neighbours to church".[72] Nikki Gemmell's story is far from unusual.

Without at all wanting to discourage innovative "outreach", in this chapter I want to explore what seems to me a much-neglected aspect of the biblical idea of proclamation: the gathered public worship of God's people.[73] What we do in church once a week is (among other things) a promotion of the gospel.

From the Psalms to the Synagogues

As far back as the psalms of ancient Israel, the gathered worship of God was understood, in part, to be a declaration of God's power and mercy within earshot of those who do not believe. Consider the famous Psalm 96, discussed in chapter 1:

> Sing to the LORD a new song;
>   sing to the LORD, all the earth.
> Sing to the LORD, praise his name;
>   proclaim his salvation day after day.
> Declare his glory among the nations,
>   his marvellous deeds among all peoples.
> For great is the LORD and most worthy of praise;
>   he is to be feared above all gods.
> For all the gods of the nations are idols,
>   but the LORD made the heavens.
> Splendour and majesty are before him;
>   strength and glory are in his sanctuary.
> Ascribe to the LORD, all you families of nations,
>   ascribe to the LORD glory and strength.
> Ascribe to the LORD the glory due his name;
>   bring an offering and come into his courts.
> Worship the LORD in the splendour of his holiness;
>   tremble before him, all the earth. (Psalm 96:1 – 9)

This is one of several psalms in the Bible where the singing of God's praises (which is what the psalms were designed for) is described as a declaration of God's "marvellous deeds" within earshot of outsiders (see also Psalms 57:9 – 11; 66:1 – 8; 108:1 – 5). Psalm 96 is particularly interesting because idol-worshiping

Gentiles—the "families of nations"—are addressed directly in this song. They are invited to come into God's courts and join in the worship of the one true God. Psalm 117:1 issues the same invitation: "Praise the LORD, all you nations; extol him, all you peoples."

Ancient Jerusalem was a bustling international city and Jewish synagogues were scattered throughout the Mediterranean. It is not difficult, then, to close your eyes and imagine crowds of pagans listening to songs of praise like these and beginning to feel themselves addressed by words such as "Great is the LORD and most worthy of praise; he is to be feared above all gods." Recall King Solomon's prayer at the dedication for the temple. He longed that Gentiles would come to Jerusalem and join in Israel's praise (1 Kings 8:41–43). The second Jerusalem temple (the one standing in Jesus' day) had a court specially built for the Gentiles. It is often said that this was intended to keep Gentiles separate from Jews, but that is only part of the story. The "Court of the Gentiles", as it was called, was principally designed to allow pagans to learn and take part in Israel's praise of the one true God. Jesus in fact denounced the temple authorities of his day in Mark 11:17 for creating a "den of robbers" out of what was meant to be a "house of prayer for all nations".

It may surprise you to know that many Jews in the period between the Old and New Testaments took seriously the idea of public worship as an act of mission. They knew full well that the collective praise of God in the synagogue or the temple was one of God's ways of convincing Gentiles to bow their knee to the Lord. In some cases the Jews had great success. We know that numerous synagogues in the first century attracted great crowds of pagans wanting to know more about the God of the Jews. Josephus, a Jewish aristocrat and Pharisee of the first century, tells us that in Antioch, the capital of ancient Syria and third largest city in the Roman Empire, synagogue services attracted considerable crowds of pagans, and some of these were getting converted or, as Josephus describes it, "incorporated":

The Jewish colony in Antioch grew in numbers . . . They were constantly attracting to their religious ceremonies multitudes of Greeks, and these the Jews had in some measure incorporated with themselves.[74]

On occasion this Jewish "incorporation"—not to speak of "mission"—was a little too successful for the authorities. In AD 19, while Jesus was still a young carpenter in faraway Galilee, the sizable Jewish community of Rome was expelled *en masse* from the city by order of Emperor Tiberius. Why? Four separate sources say it had something to do with the way the Jews were infecting the Romans with their ways. The Roman consul and historian Cassius Dio provides the bluntest account: "As the Jews had flocked to Rome in great numbers and were converting many of the natives to their ways, he banished most of them."[75] Exactly how Jews were converting Romans is not explained (though I think we can rule out anything like a preaching campaign), but if Josephus's statement about Jews in Antioch is anything to go by ("they were constantly attracting to their religious ceremonies multitudes of Greeks"), we are probably on good historical ground to assume that invitations to synagogue services and other festivals played a significant role.

From the psalm singing of ancient Israel to the synagogue services of Jesus' day, public praise of the one true God was believed to serve a missionary function. This was not the purpose of the gatherings—I am not suggesting these were Jewish "seeker services"—but it was considered an important by-product of the corporate praise of God.

Not surprisingly, the New Testament echoes this theme: Christian gatherings, by their nature, are a means of proclaiming the splendour of God within earshot of outsiders.

Declaring God's Praise: 1 Peter 2:9

The apostle Peter, who grew up participating in the public praises of the Capernaum synagogue, urges his largely Gentile readership to continue that tradition:

> But you are a chosen people, a royal priesthood, a holy nation,
> God's special possession, that you may declare the praises of
> him who called you out of darkness into his wonderful light.
> (1 Peter 2:9)

Most commentators detect a missionary dimension in the words "declare the praises". The theme of promoting the gospel looms large in the middle chapters of 1 Peter. In 2:12 the apostle urges believers to live such good lives that their pagans neighbours will end up giving glory to God (compare Matthew 5:14 – 16). In 3:1 Peter drives this point home by urging wives to win their unbelieving husbands to faith through godly conduct (as we saw in chapter 7). Then, just a few paragraphs later in 3:15, he calls on us "to give an answer to everyone who asks you to give the reason for the hope that you have" (a statement we'll explore in the next chapter). Given the missionary thrust of these chapters it seems likely that Peter is thinking of some kind

The word "declare" in verse 9 (*exangellô*) is not a missionary term like *euangelizomai* ("tell the gospel"), which Peter uses elsewhere in the letter with its normal missionary meaning (1:12, 25; 4:6). *Exangellô* is straight out of the book of Psalms, where (in the ancient Greek translation of the Old Testament, the Septuagint) it is a default term for "declaring" things in public worship (Psalms 9:11 – 14; 56:4 – 13; 71:14 – 18; 73:28; 79:13; 107:21 – 22; 119:12 – 14).[76] Just as importantly, the plural "praises" (*aretai*) in "declare the praises" occurs only four other times in the Bible, where it always refers to the glorious deeds/qualities of God proclaimed by God's people in their public worship (Isaiah 42:8, 12; 43:21; 63:7) and where it translates the Hebrew plural *tehilim*, "praises"/"glories". This word is the Hebrew title of the book of Psalms, Israel's book of praises.

of evangelism in the words of 1 Peter 2:9: "declare the praises of him who called you out of darkness".

But what type of evangelism is Peter talking about? I once assumed (and taught) that the apostle was talking about *personal* evangelism. I interpreted the phrase "declare the praises" to mean something like *tell the gospel to your friends and family*. I now think that was probably a bit hasty. The expression "declare the praises" is a *liturgical* one (to use an old-fashioned but useful term); it comes straight out of the Old Testament's description of Israel's public praise, with its creeds, prayers and ever-present psalm singing.

When we remember that the biblical Judaism of Peter's day already thought of its public praise as beneficial to outsiders, it seems far more likely that the apostle is talking in 1 Peter 2:9 not so much about conversational evangelism but about the evangelism that goes on when God's people gather to celebrate in word and song the saving wonders of the Lord. It's the same thing we see in Psalms 57, 66, 96 and 108. Peter's words are strongly evangelistic without actually having anything to do with what we call personal evangelism.

This kind of evangelism has been dubbed by Edmund Clowney, former president of Westminster Theological Seminary, as "doxological evangelism" — that is, proclaiming the gospel through our declarations of God's *doxa* or "glory". Reflecting on this in *Worship by the Book*, Tim Keller of New York's Redeemer Presbyterian Church writes:

> Israel was called to make God known to unbelieving nations (Ps 105:1) by singing his praises (Ps 105:2). The temple was to be the center of a "world-winning worship." The people of God not only worship before the Lord but also before the nations (cf. Isa 2:1 – 4; 56:6 – 8; Ps 47:1; 100:1 – 5; 102:18; 117). God is to be praised before all nations, and *as* he is praised by his people, the nations are summoned and called to join in song. This pattern does not essentially change in the New Testament, where Peter tells a Gentile church to "declare the praises" of

him who called us out of darkness. The term cannot merely refer to preaching but must also refer to gathered worship.[77]

This interpretation is confirmed by the fact that Peter's description of Christians here in 1 Peter 2:9 deliberately rewords Isaiah 43:20–21, a passage all about Israel's temple worship (or the failure thereof). Let me put both passages side-by-side:

Isaiah 43:20–23	1 Peter 2:9
. . . my people, my chosen, the people I formed for myself that they may proclaim my praise. Yet you have not called on me, Jacob . . . nor honoured me with your sacrifices.	But you are a chosen people, a royal priesthood, a holy nation, God's special possession, that you may declare the praises of him who called you out of darkness into his wonderful light.

Israel's public worship had failed, says Isaiah. But it has been redeemed and transformed, says Peter centuries later, in the new "praises" of the new people of God. The Christian community fulfils Israel's temple service. This point is especially clear when we notice that Peter has been describing the Christian community as the new Jewish temple for most of chapter 2. In 1 Peter 2:5, for instance, he described believers as "living stones", who are "being built into a spiritual house to be a holy priesthood, offering spiritual sacrifices acceptable to God through Jesus Christ". The allusions to Israel's temple worship are obvious.

Of course, the *sacrificial* dimension of the ancient temple service is gone—it has been fulfilled in the death and resurrection of Jesus. But sacrifice was only one part of the temple's purpose, as the passage from Isaiah above reminds us. The temple was as much a venue for "praise"—for psalm singing, public prayer, creeds and Scripture reading—as it was a place for atonement. The book of Psalms, remember, was designed for the prayers and praise in the temple (the Hebrew name for the book is *Tehilim*, "praises"). These spoken dimensions of Israel's temple service have not been done away with at all; they continue on in the gatherings of Christ's people. Through our readings, preaching, creeds and "psalms, hymns and songs from the Spirit" (Ephesians 5:19; Colossians 3:16), we do now what, according to Isaiah and Peter, Israel failed to do: we "declare the praises" of God.

So strong is this connection between ancient temple worship and the Christian community today that Peter can even talk about believers "offering spiritual sacrifices acceptable to God through Jesus Christ" (1 Peter 2:5). This is temple language again. What are these new "spiritual sacrifices"? The answer comes four verses later: we "declare the praises of him who called us out of darkness and into his wonderful light". While, in one sense, the temple sacrifices are fulfilled and replaced by Jesus' atoning death, in another sense they are reflected or, perhaps better, refracted in the ongoing "sacrifice" of our praise.

Peter wasn't the only one to think of praise as a sacrifice. The book of Hebrews uses a similar expression to refer to the activity of the new people of God: "Through Jesus, therefore, let us continually offer to God a sacrifice of praise – the fruit of lips that openly profess his name" (Hebrews 13:15).

Declaring God's praises together – in our readings, creeds, preaching, psalms, hymns and spiritual songs – is one of our central acts of worship as the people of God (though, of course, worship means much more than what goes on in church; see Romans 12:1). As Peter says, you have been chosen "*that* you may declare the praises" of God.[78] One reason for the central importance of praise is God's sheer worthiness; we need no other reason for viewing praise as a high and holy activity. But, given the strong mission theme in 1 Peter, combined with the equally strong Jewish biblical tradition of doxological evangelism, we are probably right to detect a secondary reason for the great importance of public praise. Through it, we announce God's mercy and power to those who overhear us, who have not yet been called out of darkness into his wonderful light.

The Triumphal Entry: Luke 19:28–40

In Luke 19 there is a delightful case study of how public praise can also function as a proclamation to outsiders. As Jesus entered Jerusalem on the first Palm Sunday, we are told:

> The whole crowd of disciples began joyfully to praise God in loud voices for all the miracles they had seen:
>
> > *"Blessed is the king who comes in the name of the Lord!"*
> > *"Peace in heaven and glory in the highest!"*
>
> Some of the Pharisees in the crowd said to Jesus, "Teacher, rebuke your disciples!"
> "I tell you," he replied, "if they keep quiet, the stones will cry out." (Luke 19:37–40)

In this case, public praise was not exactly *effective* evangelism —the Pharisees ask for the volume to be turned down—but it was evangelism nonetheless. The Pharisees knew exactly what was being declared in these joyful chants: Jesus is the Messiah, the promised King of peace. Later on, according to the Gospel of Matthew, the children imitate the crowds and likewise declare the gospel through joyful praise:

> But when the chief priests and the teachers of the law saw the wonderful things he did and the children shouting in the temple courts, "Hosanna to the Son of David," they were indignant.
> "Do you hear what these children are saying?" they asked him.
> "Yes," replied Jesus, "have you never read,
>
> > *"'From the lips of children and infants*
> > *you have ordained praise'?" (Matthew 21:15–16)*

Passages like these illustrate just how natural it was for biblical writers to see corporate praise as public proclamation, as a type of evangelism. This doesn't mean that all gospel proclamation is "praise" but it does mean that all true praise has the potential to be gospel proclamation, for in it we recount the wonders of Jesus' life, teachings, miracles, death, resurrection and return.

Of course, all of this assumes that unbelievers are present at our celebrations in the first place. Short of setting up a PA system outside the building, it might be difficult for some of us to envisage unbelievers overhearing anything of our church services.

There are all sorts of reasons some of our churches have visitors – location, architecture, demographics and so on – but, in my experience, the most significant factor is the quality of the church service. By "quality" I do not mean the professionalism of the leader or the standard of technology and music. I mean the degree to which the congregation revels in its experience of praising God and encouraging one another. I would go as far as to say that, over time, the number of visitors in our church services is directly proportionate to the level of enthusiasm felt by those who regularly attend.

This is not rocket science. If I am not personally inspired by what goes on in my regular church service, there is little chance I am going to invite friends and family to come and share the experience. Nor am I likely to talk about church in daily conversation. If, however, I am thrilled, challenged, rebuked and uplifted by the prayers, songs, creeds, readings and sermons I hear on a Sunday, there is every chance I will feel confident mentioning church in conversation and inviting friends to join me there one Sunday.

I was speaking to a brand-new Christian who told me about a cocktail party he went to recently. Some of Henry's friends were a little perplexed by his "finding religion". One of them said, "Why on earth would you go to church?" Henry threw it straight back at him: "Come with me on Sunday and you can see for yourself!" That is a believer who enjoys his church service! And why wouldn't he? It was a church service that hooked him in the first place.

Henry had not attended church since the enforced chapel services of his Catholic school days. But one day his wife, Sandra, decided she wanted to take the kids to Sunday school – she had been invited to the church by a local school mum. Sandra went and loved it and within a few months found herself trusting in

Christ. Naturally, she asked Henry to come along. Reluctantly, he did, and to his surprise he too loved the experience. He couldn't put his finger on it but something about the singing and the prayers and the preaching (and the people) captivated him. He says it was an hour of depth and solace in an otherwise full and frantic life.

Henry came back again and again. He soon found himself joining in with the songs and the prayers and finding that he really meant it. Christ had become real to him. Henry and Sandra have not looked back. They are among the most regular members of my church and remain eager to throw down the challenge to their friends and family: "Come with me on Sunday and you can see for yourself!"

The services Henry and Sandra were so taken with were not evangelistic events; they were regular services designed for the praise of God and the strengthening of believers. There were Bible readings, songs, prayers, creeds and preaching—all the things that have always been part of church gatherings. Henry and Sandra were eavesdroppers, as it were. And this, I think, is part of the power of services like these. Visitors to church can easily feel threatened if they suspect the whole event is pitched at them. But when they feel the freedom simply to observe what Christians do—praying to the Lord, giving thanks to him, listening to his Word—visitors are often more at ease, less defensive and more open to the things they hear. They are more attentive to our "praises" of him who called us out of darkness into his marvellous light.

I still think there is a place for the evangelistic church service and even for the so-called seeker service. I also think it is important to consider making small adjustments to our gatherings to make them more comprehensible to the uninitiated. However, I want to stress in the strongest terms that visitor-focused services are not an evangelistic necessity. Normal church meetings conducted exceptionally well will not only inspire the regulars; they will draw in visitors and, through the powerful vehicle of our corporate praise, promote the gospel to them.

The burden is on us – whether we are laypeople or leaders – to do everything we can to enhance what goes on in our services and to invite our friends and family to eavesdrop on what we do.

Conversion in Church: 1 Corinthians 14:23 – 26

A passage penned by the apostle Paul provides a concrete example of a visitor overhearing our public worship and, as a result, turning to the Lord. In 1 Corinthians 14:23 – 26 Paul stresses the missionary significance of normative, intelligible, congregational declarations. He asks us to imagine an "unbeliever" walking into church:

> So if the whole church comes together and everyone speaks in [uninterpreted] tongues, and inquirers or unbelievers come in, will they not say that you are out of your mind? But if an unbeliever or inquirer comes in while everyone is prophesying, they are convicted of sin and are brought under judgment by all, as the secrets of their hearts are laid bare. So he will fall down and worship God, exclaiming, "God is really among you!"
>
> What then shall we say, brothers and sisters? When you come together, each of you has a hymn, or a word of instruction, a revelation, a tongue or an interpretation. Everything must be done so that the church may be built up. (1 Corinthians 14:23 – 26)

When tongues are left uninterpreted, says Paul, unbelievers visiting the church will think Christians are insane. If, however, everyone is "prophesying" (an intelligible form of speech), visitors will be able to understand what we are on about and so will "fall down and worship God" (verse 25).

There is great debate about what exactly Paul means by "prophesying". Believe it or not, entire PhDs and numerous scholarly books have been written on the topic.[79] My own view, for what it's worth, is that "prophesying" here in 1 Corinthians 14 is Paul's catch-all term for any type of intelligible speech uttered by members of the congregation during public worship. It includes everything listed by Paul at the conclusion of his discussion: "What then shall we say, brothers and sisters? When you come together, each of you has a hymn, or a word of instruction, a revelation, a tongue or an interpretation. Everything must be done so that the church may be built up" (verse 26). My larger point remains regardless of whether you agree with my understanding of prophecy, but let me spend a moment unpacking the argument.

Three clues in the New Testament give some indication of what "prophesying" might broadly include. In Acts 2 the corporate praise of God among the first believers is described as a form of prophecy. You may remember that when the Spirit was first given at Pentecost, believers began to magnify the Lord in foreign languages. Unbelievers visiting Jerusalem from the countries round about overheard these praises—doxological evangelism again—and exclaimed: "We hear them declaring the wonders of God in our own tongues!" (Acts 2:11). When the apostle Peter stood up to explain this strange event, he equated these Spirit-enabled declarations with "prophecy":

> This is what was spoken by the prophet Joel:
>
>> "In the last days, God says,
>>   I will pour out my Spirit on all people.
>> Your sons and daughters will prophesy,
>>   your young men will see visions,
>>   your old men will dream dreams.
>> Even on my servants, both men and women,
>>   I will pour out my Spirit in those days,
>>   and they will prophesy." (Acts 2:16–18)

For Peter, "declaring the wonders of God" in a comprehensible manner is a type of "prophesying". As the first outpouring of the Spirit upon the church and therefore the beginning of Christian prophecy, I believe Acts 2 provides a helpful starting point for understanding the Spirit's work of "prophecy" in 1 Corinthians 14. Intelligible declarations about God's greatness in the

context of the gathered people of God are a form of "prophecy".
As an aside, I think the Pentecost event of Acts 2 informs the
entire argument of 1 Corinthians 14. The themes of the giving
of the Spirit, prophesying, intelligibility and public witness loom
large in both Acts 2 and 1 Corinthians 14. It would, I think, be
surprising if the Pentecost event – which was a definitive moment
in early Christianity – did not somehow inform Paul's teaching
about the role of the Spirit in the Christian community.

The second clue is in 1 Corinthians 14 itself. In verses
3–4 Paul says, "Those who prophesy speak to people for their
strengthening, encouragement and comfort. Those who speak in
a tongue [which is not interpreted] edify themselves, but those
who prophesy edify the church". At the very least, we can say
from this that "prophesying" is an intelligible form of speech in
church that contributes to the strengthening, encouragement
and comfort of the congregation. Broad, I know, but clarifying
nonetheless, especially given the "heat" associated with discussion about prophecy.

The third clue is in the final verse of the passage we've been
looking at. Having explained what can happen when a visitor
overhears the congregation prophesying, Paul wraps up his argument by referring to all sorts of speaking in church. And "prophesying" is conspicuous by its absence:

> What then shall we say, brothers and sisters? When you come
> together, each of you has a hymn, or a word of instruction, a
> revelation, a tongue or an interpretation. Everything must be
> done so that the church may be built up. (1 Corinthians 14:26)

Why is there no mention of "prophecy" here in Paul's conclusion, when for the last twenty-five verses straight he has been
insisting that this form of speech is the key to the building up
or strengthening of the church? I think the answer is simple:
any appropriate "hymn", "word of instruction", "revelation" or
"tongue" (interpreted) functions as prophecy. In other words,
"prophesying" is Paul's catch-all term for any of the congrega-

tional declarations (sung or spoken) intended for the strengthening of the church. I suspect this is why Paul can speak of an unbeliever overhearing *"everyone . . .* prophesying" (14:24) – we do all say something in the church service, whether in songs or prayers or creeds or whatever. We all prophesy.

As I said earlier, my larger point remains regardless of how one understands "prophesying": the intelligible words of the congregation (not just the preachers) during the church service can have evangelistic significance, according to Paul. Notice that the congregational speech referred to by Paul is not *pitched* at the visiting unbeliever; this is not an evangelistic service. Paul simply describes an outsider walking into a church service and overhearing what believers are saying (and/or singing). This is enough, says Paul, to convince such a visitor to worship God with us.

Conclusion

In light of Psalm 96, 1 Peter 2:9 and 1 Corinthians 14:23 – 26, we have to conclude that what happens in church can, by its very nature, be a powerful promotion of the gospel. Our songs, our creeds, our prayers, our sermons, our testimonies and perhaps even the "weekly notices" are all announcements of the wonders of God. As such, they not only inspire the regulars; they can also help visitors realise what believing in Christ is all about.

At heart, I am an evangelistic preacher and writer; these are my skills and passions. But I can honestly say that in the years I worked as a local church pastor, I saw as many visitors join God's people through the regular Sunday service as I did through my more deliberate evangelistic preaching and programs. It was a humbling experience for an evangelist. I am more than ever convinced that getting our church praise right, by which I mean making it gospel-focused, heartfelt and intelligible to all, is a vital expression of our commitment to promoting the gospel.

A dear friend was, until moving to the UK, a TV news producer. Emma was a groovy young mum and, when I met her, an outright atheist. In fact, in one of our first deep conversations she said to me, "Look, I'm an atheist, I was raised an atheist, so don't bother trying to convert me, will you!"

Emma came to the baptism of the child of mutual friends (Kim and Christian mentioned in chapter 7). The baptism itself was simply part of the regular Sunday service. It was sandwiched between prayers, Bible readings, songs of praise, a sermon and the weekly notices. Emma could count on two fingers the number of church services she had been to over the years, but she left the service "struck by the spiritual feeling of it all". She came back the next week, and the next, and the next. Each week she said the same thing: "Look, I'm not at all religious, but boy I like this stuff!" Eventually, Emma was invited to an evangelistic course—a five-week walk-through of the life of Jesus. She came. Within weeks this "atheist" was a passionate and vocal follower of Christ.

It was delightfully ironic, as she herself would point out, that something she would have once disparaged—the humble church service—was, under God, the very means of opening her mind to the gospel and drawing her irresistibly to faith in Christ.

The church services Emma went to were not pitched at atheists or unchurched people in general. They were normal services of praise and encouragement. And that is my point: when we gather to declare the wonders of God we are engaged in promoting God's glory to the world.

CHAPTER 11

The Apt Reply

Promoting the Gospel in Daily Conversation

> Always be prepared to give an answer to every-
> one who asks you to give the reason for the hope
> that you have.
>
> *1 Peter 3:15*

AMERICAN AIRLINES PILOT ANGELO KEANE (not his real name) had just returned from a week-long mission trip in Costa Rica. He was fired up for action. Many of us know this feeling. Going to the frontline, as it were, and seeing lives transformed by the gospel is enough to inspire even the most evangelistically reluctant Christian to get more involved in seeking the salvation of others. Captain Keane was anything but reluctant.[80]

Back at work, Angelo had wondered how he might apply his evangelistic zeal to his work life. He had an idea—a rather innovative one. As Flight 34 took off from Los Angeles headed for JFK Airport in New York, the captain welcomed the passengers over the PA and then announced: "Ladies and gentlemen, would the Christians on board today please identify themselves by raising their hands." I cannot imagine what I would have done. Anyway, Keane then urged the rest of the passengers to use the four-hour flight time to discuss Christianity with those who had identified themselves. He added that he would be keen to discuss the faith with any who were interested.

The response was not what he had hoped for. Passenger Amanda Nelligan recalls that in the course of his announcement Captain Keane called non-Christians "crazy" for not believing in Christ. His words, she said, "felt like a threat". The reaction of others was similar. In the wake of September 11 people were worried this might be a veiled warning: become a Christian now because I'm in charge of the plane! Fearing the worst, several on board even tried to call relatives from their mobile phones before crew members assured them everything was going to be fine.

Of course, everything was fine. Angelo Keane just wanted his passengers (a captive audience) to know about Jesus and was willing to do whatever he could to achieve that. American Airlines spokesman Tim Wagner later said Captain Keane's announcement "falls along the lines of a personal level of sharing that may not be appropriate for one of our employees to do while on the job". One of my best mates is a Qantas captain and a Christian and he says this is quite an understatement!

Captain Keane's keenness to speak to others about Jesus and to urge other believers to do the same raises a question many of us ask. Some ask out of zeal, others out of fear: when and how does the Lord expect me to speak to others about him? I have already given two answers to this question: some of us are evangelists and will declare the gospel in a focused way; all of us are heralds of God's glory through our songs, prayers, readings and creeds in public praise.

What further encouragement does God's Word offer us as we seek to talk about Christ with those who do not yet know him? Two passages in the New Testament offer wonderful instruction on this theme. You probably won't be surprised to learn that the approach of our American Airlines friend is not part of the package. Let me quote the texts, then reflect on the truths they contain.

1 Peter 3:13–16	Colossians 4:2–6
Who is going to harm you if you are eager to do good? But even if you should suffer for what is right, you are blessed. "Do not fear their threats; do not be frightened." But in your hearts revere [literally, "set apart"] Christ as Lord. Always be prepared to give an answer to everyone who asks you to give the reason for the hope that you have. But do this with gentleness and respect, keeping a clear conscience, so that those who speak maliciously against your good behaviour in Christ may be ashamed of their slander.	Devote yourselves to prayer, being watchful and thankful. And pray for us, too, that God may open a door for our message, so that we may proclaim the mystery of Christ, for which I am in chains. Pray that I may proclaim it clearly, as I should. Be wise in the way you act toward outsiders; make the most of every opportunity. Let your conversation be always full of grace, seasoned with salt, so that you may know how to answer everyone.

The apostle Peter's "be prepared to give an answer to everyone" sounds very much like the apostle Paul's "know how to answer everyone". It is as if the two of them got together on this issue to make sure they told their congregations the same thing: be ready and willing to answer those who do not yet believe. Curiously, another famous teacher from the first century, Rabbi Eleazar ben Arak, taught his Jewish disciples something similar: "Be constant in the learning of Torah (God's Word). And know how to answer an unbeliever" (Mishnah, 'Abot 2:14). The teaching of Peter and Paul may well have been a basic part of Jewish instruction in this period. It is not enough simply to know the truth; one must also embrace the privilege of explaining and defending the truth to those who don't believe. The fact that 1 Peter 3:15 and Colossians 4:5 are the only texts in the New Testament (that I can find) clearly urging believers in general to speak to unbelievers about the faith makes them precious passages indeed. Fortunately, they are rich with insights about how, when and why to speak up for the Lord.

A Responsibility for All Christians

First, both texts noted above make clear that all believers have a responsibility to answer for the faith. Unlike the exhortation "do the work of an evangelist" (2 Timothy 4:5), which is plainly directed to an evangelist and church leader (Timothy), our two

---

There is another text that is sometimes thought to instruct believers to speak about their faith with others. Ephesians 6:15 in the Contemporary English Version reads: "Your desire to tell the good news about peace should be like shoes on your feet." I quote this particular translation because it brings to the fore what some have tried to find in the text – an exhortation to proclaim the gospel. The reality is, the Greek says something quite different, as all other major translations bear out.

Literally, the sentence reads: "and having shod the feet with preparation/stability of the gospel of peace". The idea here is simply that if the gospel of peace is your footwear, you will be able to stand in readiness (or stability) for the fight. This is the sense found in all of the standard translations, the New International Version, Today's New International Version, English Standard Version, Revised Standard Version and so on. The thought is reiterated in verse 17 – "Take the helmet of salvation and the sword of the Spirit, which is the word of God." Holding fast to God's Word, the gospel of peace, is the key to withstanding and overcoming the powers of darkness. Gospel preaching is not in view.[81]

passages are written to congregations as a whole. The instructions of 1 Peter 3:15 and Colossians 4:6 apply to Christians generally, not to evangelists in particular. Both apostles clearly expected believers of all kinds to be ready and willing to speak up for Christ to those who inquire about the faith.

Paul goes further in the Colossians passage and creates a comparison between his own speech as a preaching apostle and the everyday speech of believers generally. He deliberately elevates conversational answers to the status of missionary activity. I need to get technical for a moment but hopefully it will be worth it.

Paul begins his paragraph by asking the Colossians to get involved in *his* mission by praying for him: "And pray for us, too, that God may open a door for our message" (Colossians 4:3–4). Only then does he go on in verses 5–6 to urge the Colossians to give attention to their *own* mission among those who don't yet believe. In verse 5 he asks them to live godly lives toward those who don't believe, and in verse 6 he asks them to employ their lips. What is fascinating, in terms of the connection between Paul's mission and ours, is that there is a play on words in verses 3 and 6. The words "message" in verse 3 and "conversation" in verse 6 are exactly the same in Greek (*logos*). Here is a literal translation:

Paul's "word": *an obligation to proclaim Christ*	[3](pray) that God may open for us a door for the *Word* . . . [4]so that I may make it clear as I ought to proclaim it
Congregational "word": *an obligation to answer questions*	[6]let your *word* be always in grace, seasoned with salt, so that you may know how you ought to answer each one

Paul is trading on the flexibility of the Greek noun *logos* to strike a comparison between the apostolic word of the gospel and the congregational word of everyday conversation.[82]

Paul strengthens this comparison by using another neat parallel in verses 4 and 6. In describing his own missionary duty as an apostle, he literally says, "I ought to proclaim" (verse 4). In describing the missionary duty of every Christian he literally says, "you ought to answer" (verse 6). The effect of this symmetry (which is obvious in Greek[83]) is to create a thematic parallel between Paul's obligation to proclaim the gospel word and the congregation's duty to answer with the words of their everyday conversation. What bold proclamation is to evangelists, gracious answers are to believers in general. Both are activities with missionary significance. The well-known British preacher and commentator, Dick Lucas, captures the thought perfectly:

> Just as there is an "ought" about the apostle's speaking, so there is an "ought" about theirs. But a comparison between the two final phrases in each half of the section shows a difference in emphasis that is of some significance. They are to pray for the apostle that he might make the gospel known as he ought to speak. He in turns gives them sound advice so that they may know how they ought to answer everyone. We may describe this difference by saying that while the apostle looks for many opportunities for direct evangelism and teaching, the typical Christian in Colossae is to look for many opportunities for responsive evangelism. If this distinction is a correct one, it immediately commends itself by its sanity and realism.[84]

Not all of us will proclaim the gospel as Paul did, but all of us will answer for the gospel whenever opportunity allows. And, God willing, sometimes those answers will blossom into perfectly natural opportunities to explain the whole gospel to someone. When that happens, don't rush off to find an evangelist! Say what you know of Christ's life, death and resurrection. Taste for yourself the sweet "icing on the cake of mission".

A Range of Answers to a Range of Questions

Although the English word "answer" is used in both Colossians 4:6 and 1 Peter 3:15, Paul and Peter used different Greek terms to convey their ideas. These two words remind us of the range of answers we might be called upon to give to those who do not believe.

In Colossians 4:6 Paul uses the Greek word *apokrinomai*, which refers to a simple "reply". The term does not necessarily mean a reply to an explicit question (though that is typically its meaning); it can refer to a response to a comment. Hence, *apokrinomai* in this passage is a kind of catch-all term for any statement we might offer in response to a query or statement from nonbelievers. A work colleague might ask: "Why do you go to church?" A family member might declare: "Oh, religion isn't relevant for me." What you offer in reply is the "answer" Paul has in mind.

This doesn't mean we have to wait for others to say something about Christ before we respond with an answer! The Lord will bless whatever statements about the faith, prompted or unprompted, you can muster given your opportunities, abilities and personality. I would simply say that *as a minimum* all believers are to be willing to answer for Christ whenever opportunity invites.

Peter uses a different word. The term is *apologia*, which means a *defence* in response to some criticism or accusation. In context, the apostle is probably thinking of the criticisms levelled against Christians for their good works. The paragraph begins: "Who is going to harm you if you are eager to do good? But even if you should suffer for what is right, you are blessed" (1 Peter 3:13–14). Verse 16, furthermore, refers to those who "speak maliciously against your good behaviour". Christians in this era were often criticised (and worse) for their particular way of life. For instance, rejecting idol worship was regarded as civic treachery, since devotion to the gods was believed to provide

Why are we to answer for our "hope", when we might have expected Peter to use the word "faith" instead? Did the apostle really expect people outside the church to raise questions or criticisms about Christian eschatology, about our future hope? Is the apostle urging us to talk in public specifically about the second coming, the final resurrection and so on? Probably not. "Hope" in Peter's letter is a default term for what today we might call our Christian faith (see 1:3; 1:21). Here in 3:15, then, Peter just means: be ready to defend yourself whenever your Christian devotion (your hope) is called into question.

protection for the city. Again, shunning orgies and drunken banquets was viewed as prudish and antisocial. As Peter says in the next chapter, "They [unbelievers] are surprised that you do not join them in their reckless, wild living, and they heap abuse on you" (4:4). Peter expects believers to cop such abuse on the chin and to pluck up the courage to defend themselves against anyone who questions "the reason for the hope that you have" (3:15).

Today, a great range of criticisms of Christian faith and practice will require an *apologia*. Biblical views on sexuality are frequently criticised in the media and queried by our friends. The conduct and statements of church leaders (past and present) are occasionally scrutinised and judged hypocritical. Faith in God is sometimes characterised as mindless in an age of science or groundless in view of the world's suffering. Are we willing to stand up for the faith in such settings? Peter says, "Always be prepared to give an answer to everyone."

It is in this context that I think we should all consider putting ourselves through some kind of apologetic/evangelistic training—something that helps us bring the gospel to bear on people's modern questions. My experience with one particular program of evangelism (mentioned in the Introduction) has not put me off all of them. My only qualification is that the emphasis of this training should be on *conversational* explanations of the faith, not ones involving monologues. As I have said before, most of our opportunities to answer for Christ will come in passing conversations, not in one-off gospel presentations. That is simply the reality, and not preparing for it will be limiting. Outlining the whole gospel may be the norm for gospel workers, but it will be preciously rare for most of us. More common by far will be the brief opportunities to respond to the range of contemporary comments, criticisms and questions about Christianity.

Allegiance to Christ: The Basis of Our Speaking

The context of Peter's exhortation implies that answering for the faith is a matter of allegiance to Christ as the true Lord:

> But even if you should suffer for what is right, you are blessed. "Do not fear their threats; do not be frightened." But in your hearts revere Christ as Lord. Always be prepared to give an answer . . . (1 Peter 3:14–15)

In the original language verse 15 is a single sentence: "But in your hearts revere Christ as Lord, always being prepared to give an answer . . ." The logic is simple. When you suffer for living out your faith, do not fear the power that frightens and motivates most of the citizens of the Roman Empire (the emperor and his cronies); instead, remember who the real Emperor is and live and speak up accordingly. The command "revere [or 'set apart'] Christ as Lord" might seem a strange thing to say to those who already believe in Christ, until we realise that the title "lord" (*kyrios*) was the typical first-century way of referring to the Roman emperor. Immediately, then, Peter's statement takes on daring force. Believers are to associate the title *kyrios* not with the name "Nero" (emperor at the time: AD 54–68) but with "Christ".

Actually, Peter's description of Jesus Christ goes way beyond anything that could be said of the emperor. The words "Do not fear their threats; do not be frightened. But in your hearts revere Christ as Lord" (1 Peter 3:14–15) are a deliberate paraphrase of Isaiah 8:12–13, which reads: "Do not fear what they fear, and do not dread it. The LORD Almighty is the one you are to regard as holy." Isaiah's phrase "regard as holy" is literally "set apart", exactly the same expression (translated here as "revere") used by Peter in connection with Jesus. This is quite extraordinary. What is said of the Lord Almighty in the Old Testament is said of Jesus here in the New Testament; he is the universal Lord who is to be revered above all others. Peter not only has a kind of imperial Christology; he has a divine Christology as well.

All of this amounts to a powerful call to shore up our allegiance to Jesus as the one true Lord—to fear him and no one else. And it is precisely in this attitude of renewed loyalty to Christ that the rationale to answer for the faith is found. When we know who is really in charge—not the emperor and his officials but the Lord Jesus Christ—we will stand ready to give our defence in his name.

There are all sorts of reasons modern Christians feel coy about mentioning their faith to others: fear of being labelled "fanatical" or "fundamentalist", a craving to fit in with friends and colleagues, personal shyness, a mild insecurity about the credibility of Christianity, a fear of saying something theologically incorrect or socially inept, an overly negative impression of how unbelievers perceive Christianity and so on. This last one appears to be common. Somehow, many of us have come to believe that most non-Christians think most Christians are weird.

This corporate inferiority complex is a novelty in the history of Christianity and even today is found only in the West: Asian, African or Middle Eastern Christians are blissfully unaware that they are meant to feel embarrassed about following the Lord of the universe! It is true that the Western media occasionally portrays Christians in an "oddball" light (it does this with all sorts of things it doesn't understand). But in reality the world's view of Christianity is usually far less negative than we suppose.

A common result of this sense of inferiority is a tendency to keep quiet about our faith, to keep it under the radar. When in the company of Christians, of course, we all talk freely and unconsciously about God, prayer, church, Bible, faith, Jesus and so on. These words are not forced; they are a natural part of our real world. However, when in the company of those who do not share our faith, suddenly all such talk disappears. We push our natural faith-speak below the level of our ordinary conversations, almost never allowing it to bubble to the surface.

But such intentional quietness is unnatural and forced, and it requires serious reconsideration. While I would not advocate strategically forcing God-words back into daily conversation, I would propose that we decide to allow our faith to rise back to the surface where it belongs. We should let what is real within us find verbal expression without, regardless of who is listening. In this context, I have always been struck by what an Australian colleague of mine, Stephen Abbott, author of *Everyday Evangelism*, calls "God-talk". God-talk is brief, casual, passing references to the faith in everyday conversation. It is not necessarily designed to initiate conversations about Christianity; it is simply part of being a relaxed and natural Christian. It is a refusal to participate in the corporate inferiority complex that plagues many in our churches.

Examples of God-talk are endless. You might add "God bless" as you say goodbye to friends and colleagues—just as you might when with Christians. In conversation you might make a passing reference to "a friend from church", just as you might refer to a friend "from work" or "from the gym" or wherever. To someone who confides in you about a problem you might respond, "I'll remember to pray for you about that!" I have been surprised over the years just how thankful people are when I have said this. Again, in talking about your travels and ambitions you might add the caveat "God willing" (as advised in James 4:15). I am not suggesting here that you should introduce any of these particular expressions into your daily conversation. I am simply illustrating what it might mean to allow your faith vocabulary to rise to the surface regardless of whose company you are in.

Whatever the causes of Christian coyness, the antidote is a renewed vision of Christ's lordship over all: as Peter says, setting apart Christ as Lord. Our bosses, professors, parents, friends, politicians and the media do not rule heaven or earth. Jesus owns the room. If for just a moment we could lift the curtain of heaven and see "the glory of God, and Jesus standing at the right hand of God" (Acts 7:55), all causes of Christian embarrassment would vanish in an instant. We would see things as they really are, with God and his Messiah at the helm. One day, this curtain will be lifted for everyone to see, and until then we are to live as those who know what lies behind the veil.

So, next time you are handed an opportunity at work, home or elsewhere to give an answer for the faith, take a deep breath, remind yourself who really owns the room and speak up. You may not instantly transform into the articulate evangelist, but you will become the best version of yourself. And that is all the Lord asks of you.

In an attitude of fresh allegiance to Christ as *kyrios*, we must never hide our faith and must always be willing to answer for Christ whenever opportunity invites. Loyalty to Jesus motivates openness about him. As we saw in chapter 1, the universal lordship of God through his Messiah (Psalm 96; Matthew 28:18 – 19) – *Christological monotheism*, in other words – provides the fundamental rationale and motivation for lifting our voices in his honour throughout the world.

The Importance of the Manner of Our Reply

It is fascinating that in both Colossians 4:6 and 1 Peter 3:15 the emphasis falls not on the content of our replies – which will depend on the particular question or comment we are responding to—but on their manner. Notice how both apostles are very concerned with *how* we answer our neighbours.

In Colossians 4:6 Paul insists that our speech "be always full of grace, seasoned with salt". The first expression, "full of grace", doesn't mean brimming with the doctrine of grace—that would be to stretch Paul's words too far. It simply means that the generosity of God (his grace) must shape the character of our conversation. We are to speak *graciously*.

Some have taken the second phrase, "seasoned with salt", to mean "spicy" or *interesting* speech. In addition to being gracious, then, we would have to be intriguing or captivating. I think this is mistaken. It is unlikely Paul would call upon all his readers to display what basically amounts to a personality trait. All of us can be gracious, but how many of us can be interesting? In any case, there is no "and" between these two descriptions of Christian speech. This suggests that "full of grace" and "seasoned with salt" refer to the same thing, not two separate things. The salt we are to add to our speech is grace. Put simply, we are to season our words with graciousness.

In different words Peter says much the same thing: "Always be prepared to give an answer . . . But do this with gentleness and respect." Given that the answer Peter calls on us to give is the defence-type, we might have expected him to insist on boldness of speech. Instead, he qualifies his call to defend the faith by emphasising that believers must be courteous in replying to critics. This is good advice. When you're defending yourself, it is tempting to get hotheaded and impatient and resort to insulting your critic's point of view (or is that just me?). Instead, Peter says we are to speak in a godly fashion.

"Gentleness" here does not imply weakness or reticence. It denotes the absence of all arrogance or pushiness. To be gentle, in biblical usage, is to moderate one's power for the sake of others. Even when you can think of a slam-dunk reply that would crush your unbelieving critic, Peter insists we speak gently.

"Respect" is literally the word fear (*phobos*), but when used of human relationships it usually refers to giving due honour. At times it may seem that our critics don't deserve any honour: their criticisms may seem unusually harsh or ill-founded. But it is precisely at times like these that we must remind ourselves that all men and women, no matter how belligerent, bear the image of God (James 3:9). They thus deserve our respect. This probably rules out calling non-Christians "crazy" as Captain Keane, mentioned earlier, is reported to have done!

I am reminded of a log in my own eye in this respect. I once got into a forthright conversation with a successful, self-made businessman. He was telling me all the things that were wrong with Christianity: science had disproved the Bible, the church was deeply corrupt and Christianity had gained its success around the world through violence and oppression. I was fairly calm and logical with the first two claims, but for some reason, the last one really got me going. I've read quite a bit about the early expansion of Christianity and yet nothing I said made him budge. "I don't believe you," he said. "Lots of books have shown how the church converted nations with the sword."

At that point I stupidly turned the corner from being calmly logical to outright arrogant. I raised my voice, reminded him I had a couple of degrees in this stuff and tried to embarrass him about his lack of knowledge on the subject. Graciousness, gentleness and respect were nowhere to be found. Even as my words left my mouth, I remember thinking: I'm doing exactly what I urge other believers never to do! I was trying to win the argument (for my sake) rather than the person (for Christ's sake). I suspect I achieved neither.

A response that lacks "cleverness" but is kind and courteous will often prove more valuable to the questioner than one that is just clever. Often the manner of our replies says as much about the kind of God we believe in as the content. After all, it is the content of our faith (in the God of grace) that is meant to fashion the manner of our speaking.

Evangelism training programs that focus on the doctrines of sin, atonement and grace without also stressing the need to be gentle, respectful and gracious are incomplete. Of course, this is simply an aspect of beautifying the gospel, discussed in chapter 7. I can hardly promote the Lord of love by speaking without love.

Church preachers have a special role here. They set the model for the congregation in a way that occasional courses cannot. Sometimes I hear preachers (in the safe environment of church) thundering against this or that moral departure in society or some outrageous argument from Richard Dawkins & Co., and I worry that the average Christian in the pew might try to take this mode of speech into their world. That is potentially disastrous. Just as bad, other believers know full well that such an approach will never work in their work, family or university environment and so they just keep quiet, unsure of the best way to speak up for Christ. But if congregations consistently hear in the weekly exposition a thoughtful, gracious engagement with the moral and intellectual viewpoints of society, they will be receiving the best kind of training possible for their daily conversations about Christianity. Preachers: please arm your people not just with *what* to say but *how* to say it.

Lives Worth Questioning

The final thing I want to say about answering for the faith is that we are to live lives worth questioning. Perhaps this goes without saying, especially since we explored this at length in chapters 6 and 7. Nevertheless, it is still worth noting that both apostles' exhortations to speak about Christ appear in the context of instructions about living godly lives. In Colossians 4:5 – 6 Paul prefaces his call for gracious answers with an exhortation to be wise in our conduct among those who don't believe:

> Be wise in the way you act toward outsiders; make the most of every opportunity. Let your conversation be always full of

grace, seasoned with salt, so that you may know how to answer everyone. (Colossians 4:5 – 6)

Throughout the Bible, "wisdom" is not a mental quality – like intelligence or cleverness – but an ethical outlook. Wisdom is knowledge of God's path of righteousness (see Colossians 1:9 – 10, 28; 2:23; James 3:17). When Paul urges the Colossians to conduct their lives before outsiders *wisely* (literally, "in wisdom"), he does not mean they should be shrewd in their dealings with unbelievers; he means that they should act (literally, "walk") in a godly fashion. Paul then adds the excellent words, "make the most of every opportunity". The expression is literally "buy up the occasion". It is an expression from the marketplace, which basically means *seize everything*. In context, Paul means we are to seize every opportunity to walk in wisdom, that is, to do good toward outsiders. And it is out of this call to enthusiastic godliness that the exhortation to speak up for Christ comes. Godly behaviour is the context of our speaking for Christ.

The same point is particularly clear in 1 Peter 3:

> Who is going to harm you if you are eager to do good? But even if you should suffer for what is right, you are blessed. "Do not fear their threats; do not be frightened." But in your hearts revere Christ as Lord. Always be prepared to give an answer to everyone who asks you to give the reason for the hope that you have. But do this with gentleness and respect, keeping a clear conscience, so that those who speak maliciously against your good behaviour in Christ may be ashamed of their slander. (1 Peter 3:13 – 16)

Notice that the call to defend the faith in verse 15 comes hot on the heels of a discussion about doing good (which actually begins back in verse 8). Moreover, verse 16 makes it clear that it is precisely the believer's "good behaviour" that provokes the "slander" that requires the gentle defence. The logic is pretty clear. Devotion to doing good is the context out of which we are to speak.

What exactly is the "good behaviour" believers are to practice and out of which they are to speak? Peter describes it beautifully at the beginning of this section of the letter:

> Finally, all of you, be like-minded, be sympathetic, love one another, be compassionate and humble. Do not repay evil with evil or insult with insult. On the contrary, repay evil with blessing. (1 Peter 3:8 – 9)

The life out of which we are to speak is not simply a moralistic life. It is a life of humility, compassion, nonretaliation and so on: in other words, a life of *love*. Christians will not stand out in this world simply by being "nice" and "ethical", but they will if they live the life described here, the life epitomised by the Saviour himself.

The point is simple: we are to live lives worth questioning and then offer answers worth hearing.

The Power of an Apt Reply

Steve is a plumber in Queensland, Australia, and for most of his life was a typical Australian sceptic when it came to things religious. He was not an atheist, but he never attended church, and his contact with Christians over the years had left him with the impression that many of them were hypocrites.

Steve did have time for one Christian he knew, a cycling friend. Each Saturday morning both of these men – in their forties – would hit the road for an hour or so, keeping the heart rate up and striking up the occasional conversation. One day riding along Steve began to pontificate about the hypocrites who go to church. "Some of those churchies," he said, "are real ratbags." His friend just listened. "They go to church on Sunday," Steve continued, "and then live pretty ordinary lives the rest of the week."

At that point Steve's mate responded. In a manner considered gentle and respectful only amongst Australian males, he said: "C'mon, mate. Don't go worrying about those people. God will look after them. You worry about yourself and God. That's the important thing." The two men rode on in silence.

These words powerfully affected Steve. For the rest of the day he pondered what a hypocrite he had been to criticise Christians when he was doing nothing himself to honour the Almighty. "You worry about yourself and God" – the words went around and around in his head. By evening Steve was convinced that he was the one with the spiritual problem. He got alone and uttered a prayer, an apology to the God he had been ignoring all his life. The next day, Steve took himself to church – along with all the other hypocrites – and to the surprise of everyone, especially himself, he devoted his life to Christ.

The next time Steve went riding, he told his cycling buddy that he had become a Christian. He also told him how much those few words had affected him. To Steve's amazement (and amusement) his friend replied, "What did I say? I can't remember." It was delightfully ironic – and when I met them, they joked about it – that something Steve's friend could not even remember saying was the means under God of drawing Steve to the Lord. Even the simplest comment about the faith can, because of God's Spirit, open a person's eyes to the truth of Christ.

To repeat what I said earlier in connection with Colossians 4:3 – 6, what bold proclamation is to evangelists, gracious answers are to believers in general. Both are activities with a profound capacity to promote the gospel.

CHAPTER 12

A Year in the Life of the Gospel

Bringing It All Together

There is rejoicing in the presence of the angels
over one sinner who repents.

Luke 15:10

I WANT TO FINISH by telling you a story. Unlike the numerous anecdotes scattered throughout the book so far, what follows is fictional in the details. It is an amalgam of a hundred different stories of faith I have heard over the years, crafted to illustrate the major themes of *The Best Kept Secret of Christian Mission*. As you read, I ask you to look out for examples of all of the gospel-promoting activities discussed throughout the book: flexible social relationships, financial support of the gospel, prayer, good works, the praise of God in church, answering for the faith and, of course, the work of evangelists.

Although the characters and details are fictional, the reality they represent is not. All of the factors described in my closing anecdote daily combine to promote the gospel of the one true Lord.

James is a twentysomething, soon to be thirtysomething, manager at his local pub. He has worked there since his twenty-first birthday and has slowly worked his way up through the ranks. He is confident, witty and well liked by the fifty or so staff around him.

Not so positive is James's relationship with the pub owner, Jack Sail. The Sail & Anchor is one of three pubs Jack owns. To him, they are simply money machines enabling him to renovate his beachfront house and keep his wife and kids in the manner to which they have become accustomed. Actually, Mrs Sail is part of the problem. She doesn't have any official role in the place but whenever she turns up – which is often enough – she bosses people around like it's her own home: "Move this table"; "Clean this toilet"; and so on.

In addition to being pushy, Mrs Sail is a "religious snob", as James once described her. At the recent staff Christmas party, she got talking to James and a few of the others about how immoral the world had become. "What people today need," she said with all the pomp of a headmistress, "is a dose of good Christian morals!" That is not exactly what she said, but it is how it came across to James. And the impression stuck: this bossy woman wants her bossy religion to run the show. "No thanks," James thought to himself.

James's impression of religion as essentially moralistic was moderated somewhat by two of his staff. Kim is the head chef of the Sail & Anchor's beautiful courtyard restaurant. She is a vivacious Chinese woman in her late thirties and she can cook anything. At least a couple of nights a week Kim cooks a meal for James after closing. She doesn't have to – she does it for several of the late night staff and she enjoys it. Although Kim is an employee, James sees her more as a fun big sister.

James first learned of Kim's "religion" when he saw her one night bowing her head before eating a meal. At first he thought she was upset about something, so he tried to catch her eye. When she looked up, she guessed what James was thinking and, without the slightest embarrassment, said, "I'm fine, James. I was just saying thank you!" James was impressed. Coming from Kim, saying "grace" didn't seem at all corny.

Kim's husband is the other Christian in the pub. Stuart doesn't work for the pub directly. He is an accountant in a small local firm, and he helps James with the books once a week on Wednesday afternoons. He also works part-time for his church — as an accountant, James assumed (wrongly). Stuart is a bit quieter than Kim, but he is incredibly reliable both financially and personally. Although the Sail & Anchor only pays him for five hours a week, there have been plenty of times when he has stayed back late, free of charge, to help James with various business-related problems — pay, employee entitlements and so on. He is a godsend for James, who hates the technical side of management.

The only other Christian James knows is his godmother, Auntie Judy. She has lived in the UK since he was five and, apart from the regular birthday cards, she has hardly featured in his life. James realised how seriously his Auntie Judy took religion two years ago at his wedding. She made a special trip out to Australia, which impressed James no end, and during the reception (at the Sail & Anchor, of course) she told him something he couldn't easily forget. "James, I know you and your family don't share my Christian beliefs," she said in a surprisingly non-judgmental tone, "but I just want you to know that I pray for you every single day."

James responded with a simple, "Thanks." He meant it; he just couldn't figure out why she would do that or how she could think of new things to say to the Almighty after twenty-seven years. He wanted to ask her what she prayed for, but he felt a little silly.

If you had asked James earlier in the year what influence these "religious people" had had on his life, he would probably have said "none". His picture of Christianity was fragmentary and a little contradictory. Like most Australians he assumed there was "probably a god out there somewhere". Beyond that, he rarely exercised his spiritual muscles.

His wife is a little different. Unlike James, Caitlin went to a private school with regular chapel services, so she has a half-decent idea about God and Jesus. If pushed she would probably admit to believing most of it, but she doesn't want to think about it too deeply. She has "issues" with God, she once confided in a friend.

James and Caitlin have lived together for eight years and have been trying to have a baby for almost three. Part of Caitlin's keenness to get married was a superstitious view that tying the knot properly might help her fall pregnant. It hasn't seemed to work. In February this year she had a miscarriage, her second, and she has been finding it a little tough. She has even resorted to saying the occasional Lord's Prayer, in the old form she remembers from school—"Our Father which art in heaven . . ." and so on. Sometimes she chokes on the words. Her attitude to "God" is part superstition and part disappointment, not that she ever talks to James about such things.

James's interest in things Christian took a positive turn one evening at the pub. All night he kept noticing a table of late twentysomething blokes out in the restaurant. They were laughing, eating and telling long-winded stories. They were loud without being rowdy. James assumed they were on a bachelor party or something.

At about 10:00 p.m. a scuffle broke out at the table right next to this group of guys. By the time the bouncers arrived on the scene one man, who had drunk so much he could hardly stand up anyway, was slightly concussed. He had knocked his head on the table and now had blood rushing down the side of his face. Just as James was working out who to throw out of the establishment, two of the guys from the other table asked if they could help.

"No thanks, guys," James said.

But before he had finished speaking, one of them was already helping the injured man to his feet and checking on his wound. "Hey, we should probably take this guy up to the medical centre," one of them said to his friend. Before James knew it, the two of them were escorting the half-conscious man out of the Sail & Anchor and up to the medical centre, 500 meters up the road.

The night was pretty tame after that and James couldn't help wondering what on earth those guys were doing taking a perfect stranger—an idiot at that!—up to the medical centre. It was an hour before they both came back and joined their other mates. When they did, James went over to their table, sat down and offered them a drink on the house for helping out.

"Thanks, mate," one of them said, "but we're about to head off."

"Church in the morning," said one of the others with a cheeky smile.

"A wedding?" James asked.

The lads burst out laughing. "Not really," one replied, "but it's in the same building." James looked perplexed, so one of them began to explain that they all went to the same church and tomorrow they were having a special service for friends and family.

"Old Mark here," one of them said putting his hand on the shoulder of one of the two who had helped the drunk bloke, "he's giving a little bit of a talk in the morning."

"You're giving, what, a sermon?" James said with obvious confusion. Whatever this Mark did for a living, he certainly couldn't have been a preacher, thought James.

"No," he said. "I've just been asked to give my testimo-"—Mark caught himself about to use some newly adopted jargon—"umm, I'm explaining how I came to put my faith in Christ."

As he was speaking, Kim walked out of the kitchen area and straight over to the table. "Hi guys," she said. "I see you've met my boss."

"You know these guys?" asked James.

"Sure," said Kim. "They're all at my church. In fact, tomorrow Mark, here, is going to . . ."

"Yeah, I know," interrupted James, "He's going to tell everyone how he became religious."

"Well, sort of," said Kim. "He's talking about his faith in Christ, which is not quite the same as being religious." James looked blankly. "Well, I mean religion is more to do with obey-ing rules," Kim continued. "It's bossy and moralistic."

"You mean like the lovely Mrs Sail," James said, remembering the Christmas party. By the look on Kim's face it was obvious she agreed. She just didn't want to criticise the boss's wife, James thought, or probably anyone, knowing Kim.

"So, do you want to come?" Kim said without any hesitation.

"Where?" he replied, honestly having no clue what she meant.

"To church in the morning, with all of us," she said. "A bit of music, a bit of talking, a bit of praying. Won't do you any harm. And you'll get to hear Mark explain how he didn't become religious!"

James didn't really know what to say. He liked Kim and her husband, Stuart. He thought this table of guys was pretty impres-sive, especially Mark and his mate. But, apart from his christen-ing and wedding, James had literally never been inside a church. "Well, I'm not really the religious type," he said, immediately realising what Kim would say next.

"I thought we just established it's not about being religious," Kim replied. "Look, that's fine, no pressure. We'll see you if we see you." Kim gave James the details of the church and left it at that.

As James was locking up later that night, he kept running through the events of the evening in his mind – the scuffle, Mark and the medical centre, Kim's invitation. He had no idea why he felt so taken with the things they'd spoken about.

The next morning James surprised Caitlin by announcing that he was not going for his usual Sunday morning run. "I was thinking of going to church," he said as casually as he could say such a thing.

"Where did that come from?" asked Caitlin. She wasn't trou-bled, just a little caught off guard. "My James going to church!"

"Well," started James, "there were these friends of Kim at work last night – a good bunch of guys." James told the whole story of how Mark and his friend had taken the injured man up to the medical centre and how Mark was due to give a speech at the church. "This Mark guy seemed like a really interesting person. I just want to hear what he has to say. And, besides, I think Kim and Stuart would really love me to turn up." Caitlin seemed satisfied with the answer, but made it clear she was going to stay in bed with the Sunday paper.

When James pulled up outside the church, a big old sandstone thing like the one he got married in, he suddenly felt a little hesitant. He wondered if everyone would know he was not a regular churchgoer. He even worried he might be underdressed. That fear was soon overcome when he spotted Stuart, who was dressed like he was going to the football game, not church. Stuart welcomed him and showed him into the building. They sat in the far back-right pew—James's choice of seating.

The first thing James noticed was the atmosphere. It was warm. He had expected it to feel cold and stale, especially on this winter's morning. There were a few people in the pews who looked pretty conservative, but even they were warm. One old dear in the pew in front of James gave him a big smile.

"Hello, nice to see you," she whispered with a smile that crumpled her whole face. James thought she must have recognised him from the Sail & Anchor. Little did he know Mrs Sheldon had never been near a bar in her life. She was just being her usual pleasant self. Mrs Sheldon always made a point of spotting and welcoming newcomers. She would probably add James to her prayer list too now. He was in danger.

The service started with songs. At first James felt out of place. He thought he was the only one who didn't know the words off by heart. Kim soon directed him to the words printed in the service sheet he had been given on the way in. At least then he could mouth the words. Actually, James found some of the tunes quite catchy. It wasn't his style of music at all—a bit too much piano for his liking—but he found standing in the middle of a hundred or so people singing at the top of their lungs pretty inspiring. One of the better songs had a line in it about "faith in

Jesus Christ", sung over and over. He remembered that was the phrase Mark and Kim had used to describe their "religion" the night before. He wondered what exactly it meant.

The man leading the service from the front gave small introductions to the various songs and prayers and readings. Most of what he said was surprisingly interesting, James thought. He began to introduce "a young man who has recently placed his faith in Christ". Mark walked up to the microphone – James was all ears.

It turns out that Mark had never been inside a church until twelve months ago. "My only churches," he said, "were the football club and the local pub." The congregation laughed, which surprised James a little. Even Mrs Sheldon giggled.

As Mark continued he told how he didn't have a bolt out of the blue or a blinding light. He simply had friends in his football team who would chat with him occasionally about spiritual things and who one day invited him to attend a course called Christianity Explained.

"The course is just so simple," Mark said with excitement in his voice. "You get to read one of the biographies of Jesus' life and ask whatever questions you want. This man, Jesus," he continued, "just impressed me so much I found myself wanting to know more. I wanted to trust him with my life." When Mark sat down, no one clapped, which James thought was very strange.

James didn't understand everything he heard in church that day. Some of the songs were a bit old-fashioned, the sermon was a bit dry and James kept missing the "amen" during prayers. Nevertheless, the whole experience, especially hearing Mark's story, was powerful, to say the least. His overriding impression was that these people really believed what they were saying and found great joy in it. Caitlin would have liked this, he thought at the end.

Over the next month or so James managed to get to church twice more – never with Caitlin, though, who seemed increasingly uncomfortable with the whole "God-thing". At work,

James found himself pondering spiritual things more and more. He even caught himself wondering what you were meant to say in "grace" before a meal. He was going to ask Kim one day, but he thought better of it. That was too personal, he thought. He wanted to know more about the faith but wasn't exactly sure how to go about it.

An opportunity to find out more was presented to him a few weeks later. Toward the end of his fourth church service (James was counting them), the man leading the service announced that another Christianity Explained course, just like the one Mark had done a year or so before, was commencing in three weeks. James was interested but dubious, until he heard where it was going to be held: in Stuart and Kim's home. It turns out, Stuart ran quite a few of these courses, including the one Mark had done. A member of the congregation some years ago had given the church money to employ someone two days a week to coordinate evangelism in the church. Stuart had been in the role for a couple of years.

James stayed for about ten minutes after the service, just enough time to drink his coffee, chat briefly with Mark and speak to Stuart about the course. "Would you be open to a sceptic like me coming to your seminar thing?" James was trying to sound more sceptical than he really was. "Absolutely," Kim interrupted, "and you'll get to eat some more of my cooking!"

Three weeks came around quickly for James, and soon he was sitting in Stuart's lounge room with eight or nine others exploring for the first time the life of Christ, as found in the Gospel of Mark. Some in the group were quiet; others, like James, had questions about everything, such as:

"What about evolution?"

"How do you know the Bible stories are not just made up?"

"Why would God let suffering exist?"

"What do you have to give up to be a Christian?"

Kim was great with the personal, practical questions. Stuart tended to handle the more technical ones. James was amazed how calmly and simply Stuart answered everything the group threw at him. For James, in particular, the air of trustworthiness in Stuart's professional and personal life carried over into his statements about Christ. James knew he was not listening to a "religious nut".

By the fourth week of the course people's questions were less confrontational and more about what it means to follow Christ. After looking at the meaning of Jesus' death, James asked, "But why would he do that?"

"Because he loves us," said Kim.

"Because he couldn't stand the thought of you and me not finding God's forgiveness," Stuart added. The response from the group was palpable. If this is true, thought James, it's important.

That night when James got home, Caitlin was already asleep. James went into the lounge room, grabbed a drink and decided to finish reading the Gospel of Mark. When he got to the end, he wanted to keep reading. He turned the page and started on the Gospel of Luke. About midnight he got to Luke 5:27–32, the calling of Levi the tax collector. The simple words "Follow me" and Levi's instant response struck James with great force. He sat, pondering everything he'd experienced over the last couple of months, and then whispered, almost unconsciously, "I want to follow you, Jesus! I want to follow you." Suddenly he knew the difference between religion and faith in Christ.

Caitlin had been aware of James's newfound interest in Christianity, but she did not expect to hear what she heard the next morning. "Darling," James said as he gave Caitlin her usual cup of tea in bed, "I don't know the right way to describe this, but all that stuff I've been learning about God and Christ: I believe it now."

"I've always believed it," Caitlin said, remembering her chapel days. "What do you mean?"

"Yes, but this is all new for me," continued James, "and I want to take it seriously. I want it to affect my life." Now Caitlin was nervous.

"In what way?" she asked. James had no idea. He just figured something this important was bound to do something to you.

Later that day at work James took Kim aside and told her what he'd read the night before and how he had decided to do what Levi did. As he was talking, he noticed that the ever-bubbly Kim had tears rolling down her face.

"James," she said with a quiver in the voice, "I am so happy for you. Stuart and I have been praying for you these last few weeks, really hoping that Christ would become real to you."

"Praying for you!" Those words suddenly reminded James of something he had heard two and a half years before from his Auntie Judy at his wedding reception—"I say a prayer for you every single day." James knew he had to tell her about his new-found faith.

Leaving staff to close up, James headed home about 11:00 p.m., looked up his godmother's UK details and rang the number. "Auntie Judy," he said, knowing how bizarre this must have seemed, "it's James—your godson."

"Oh, dear James," said the voice on the other end of the phone in exactly the joyful tone James remembered about her. "How wonderful to hear from you. Is everything OK? Caitlin, is she well?" Suddenly, she sounded concerned.

"Everything is fine," James assured her. "I just need to tell you about something that's been happening to me recently." James went on to tell Judy everything: his friendship with Kim, the night in the pub, his first church service, Mark's "testimony", Stuart's course, what he discovered in the Gospels—everything. He must have talked nonstop for five or six minutes. "Are you still there, Auntie Judy?"

"I'm here, James," she said with a quiver that reminded him of Kim's response earlier that evening.

"I have to ask," James said. "You once said you prayed for me every day. What have you been praying for exactly?"

His godmother explained that for almost thirty years she had been asking the Lord somehow to give James some Christian friends who could lead him to a real faith in Jesus. James listened dumbfounded.

"Well, I think your prayers got through," he said. "You might have to find something else to pray for now!" They laughed, chatted for a few more minutes and then said goodbye.

As he went to bed that night, James looked at Caitlin sleeping so peacefully and wondered how he could help her find what he had found.

In that moment, nothing seemed more important.

APPENDIX 1

Gospel Bites

IN WHAT FOLLOWS I want to illustrate how understanding the gospel as presented in chapter 8 might affect the way we talk about the faith with those who don't believe. If the gospel basically corresponds to the account of Jesus' life found in the Gospels, it follows that talking about the narrative of Christ will be a natural way of communicating our beliefs to friends and family.

I want to suggest that the sayings and deeds of Jesus, recorded in the Gospels, offer a rich source of answers for many of the most common questions put to us by people who don't share our faith. Briefly recounting something relevant Jesus said or did can provide our questioners not only with a satisfying answer, but also with an important glimpse into the substance of our faith, Jesus himself. The fact that Jesus is still highly regarded in wider society means that such "gospel bites", as you might call them, are particularly helpful in our current context.

Sadly, the "stories" of Jesus are sometimes viewed as childhood Sunday school material only. As a result, we can often miss their great usefulness for talking with others about the faith. The reality is, many questions and comments raised by those who don't believe relate quite naturally to events in his life. The following examples will hopefully illustrate what I mean. These "bites" do not explain the whole gospel (that's something I want to attempt in Appendix 2, "A Modern Retelling of the Gospel"), but they do point toward the gospel in a way that might, Lord willing, encourage further conversation and an opportunity to share the "whole" gospel.

A Question about Sin and Forgiveness

Imagine a friend declares (either with sincerity or a touch of pride): "I've done too many wrong things ever to be a Christian." How might you respond? The themes of sin, grace and forgiveness are beautifully embodied in many episodes of Jesus' life. Luke 7:36–50, for example, could provide the basis for the following possible reply:

> Well, then, you are exactly the sort of person Christ was interested in. He was at the home of a religious leader (Pharisee) one day when a prostitute came in looking for him. She was so overwhelmed she burst out crying. Everyone there wanted to condemn the woman and thought Jesus should do the same. Instead, Jesus condemned his self-righteous host and turned to the woman and said, "Your sins are forgiven." He forgave her and she was a changed woman because of it. Christ didn't come for the "good" people. He came to restore and forgive those willing to admit they are anything but good. Have you ever looked into Jesus' life?

The above reply would take less than a minute to offer. It addresses the questioner's comment and paints a picture of Christ that is biblical and, hopefully, memorable. The reply doesn't contain the whole gospel—from Jesus' birth to his exaltation. It doesn't even share all the details of Luke 7:36–50—remember, this is not meant to be a sermon, just a retelling of something Jesus said and did. In a way, it is similar to what you might do when roughly recounting a scene from one of your favourite movies. Importantly—and I believe this is one of the keys to successful conversation (about anything)—the response tails off with another question: "Have you ever looked into Jesus' life?" This provides people with the opportunity to continue the discussion if they wish. It also keeps the conversation focused on the substance of our faith, Jesus.

Other episodes from Jesus' life that lend themselves to speaking about the issue of sin and forgiveness include Matthew 9:1–8; Mark 7:24–30; Luke 19:1–10; 23:35–43; John 8:1–11. Why not look up these passages and ponder how you might recount them in a similar conversation?

A Criticism of Self-Righteousness

To demonstrate the flexibility of the gospel bite, let me use the same narrative (Luke 7:36–50) to illustrate a possible response to a different criticism: "I haven't got much time for religion; it often seems so judgmental and self-righteous."

> You've probably got more in common with Christ than you think, then. He always criticised that sort of religious attitude. On one occasion he was eating a meal at the home of a religious leader when a prostitute walked in and wept at his feet. She was obviously looking to him for acceptance. The religious leader was outraged, but Jesus actually defended the woman. He even offered her forgiveness and insisted that the religious leader was further away from God than this humble woman. "Religion" might be self-righteous, but Christ came to overturn all that stuff. True Christian faith is forgiving, not judgmental. Have you ever read much about Christ?

Again, there is no effort in the above response to tell the whole gospel. That would depend on how much more the questioner wants to know. Lord willing, this minute-long response might open up a larger conversation about an essential aspect of Jesus' mission: to welcome sinners into God's kingdom. Other episodes from Jesus' life that lend themselves to speaking about the issue of judgment and self-righteousness include Matthew 7:1–6; Mark 2:13–17; Luke 15:1–32; 18:9–14.

A Comment about Being the "Religious Type"

I wish I had a dollar for every time someone has said to me, "Look, John, I'm just not the religious type!" The Gospels are full of examples of the "unreligious" seeing in Jesus the answer to their deepest needs. One such episode is recounted in Matthew 8:5 – 13. Jesus' gracious dealings with a Roman centurion – a religious pagan and a political enemy – provide clear evidence that being the "religious type" is irrelevant with Christianity. A possible response follows:

> But being the "religious type" is irrelevant to true Christian faith. Jesus was always attracting and befriending people who were not the religious type. On one occasion a Roman centurion came to Jesus for help. Centurions were about as far from the religious type as you could get in Jesus' day. They were called the "godless" and were political enemies and occupiers. But this man came to Jesus, recognising something unique about this teacher. Jesus welcomed him and promised him a place in the kingdom to come – all without being religious. Have you explored much of Christ's teachings?

Other gospel bites on this topic include Matthew 15:21 – 28 and Luke 5:27 – 32. I'm sure you will be able to find others.

The Claim of "Being Good"

Many people today regard themselves as mostly "good" and, therefore, without need of God's forgiveness or commandments. It is often stated like this: "I might not be perfect, but I am a fairly good person." Jesus insisted that our fundamental obligation to the Creator is to love our neighbour and love our God (Matthew 22:34 – 40; Mark 12:28 – 34). And so I often say something along the following lines:

> I appreciate what you're saying, but doesn't it depend on what definition of "good" you're using? Jesus was once asked by a

religious scholar what was the single most important thing to do in life. He responded by saying there were actually two things—to love your neighbour as yourself and to love God with all your heart. Being kind and honest with people is only half of it. He insisted we also have to love our Creator. Would you say you're "good" on Jesus' definition?

Because Jesus is so highly respected in contemporary culture (at least as a teacher), you may find that people are unwilling simply to write off his words on this topic. This may also provide an opportunity for you to explain that even followers of Christ do not fulfil this command perfectly and so they too need his forgiveness.

The logic of loving God and neighbour as the fundamental obligation of humanity could be teased out in conversation a little more:

> According to Jesus, our fundamental obligation in life is to love both God and our neighbour. Most of us would rightly criticise people who claim to love God but ignore their fellow human beings. On Jesus' teaching, the reverse would be just as open to criticism. Treating people well while ignoring the Creator falls way short of what Jesus taught was our obligation. Jesus left no room either for the religious hypocrite who loves God but not neighbour or for the moral agnostic who cares for people but does not revere God himself. So, I guess it depends on whose definition of "good" we're going to accept. Have you ever looked into Jesus' life and teaching?

The Issue of Pluralism

I think most of us would agree that pluralism—the belief that all religions point to God—is one of the major challenges put to modern Christians. It appears in so many forms: "You Christians are so arrogant as to think you alone have the truth!" or "My own view is more open: I like to think of all religions as containing their own truth," or "What makes your religion so special when there are so many Muslims, Hindus and Buddhists in the world?"

There is no way a simple "gospel bite" is going to settle an issue this explosive. Nevertheless, one important aspect of our response might involve "blaming" Jesus for the views we hold as Christians. It was, after all, Jesus who made such grandiose claims. Christians can't help it if they find themselves convinced by what Jesus said. Any passage in which Jesus claims universal authority is pertinent to this topic (Matthew 28:16 – 20; Mark 14:60 – 65; Luke 24:45 – 47; John 14:5 – 6). In the following example I quote the famous passage from John's Gospel:

> I understand what you're saying, but it's important to realise that Christians don't think they possess the truth; not at all. They simply look at Jesus' life and find themselves convinced by his teaching and deeds. I mean, Jesus was the one who said he had universal authority over the world. He was once asked by a friend about the way to God. He replied "I am the way and the truth and the life. No one comes to the Father except through me." Christians didn't make that up. You can't really blame a Christian for taking seriously the words of Christ, can you? What do you make of Jesus?

A more philosophical approach might refer to John 14:8 – 10, where Jesus claims to be one with God the Father:

> You ask: "What makes Christianity so special?" Well, I think it boils down to a unique claim that Jesus made. One of his followers once asked him to show them what God was like. You know what Jesus said in reply? He said, "If you have seen me, you have seen God the Father." Jesus alone of all the great religious founders said that he himself was the revelation of God. People don't have to rely on religion or guesswork; they can just look at his life and see what God is like. Jesus is the "photo" of God, if you like. For me, that's what separates Jesus from the other religious claims. Have you ever thought much about Christ?

Such replies will not satisfy all of the questions relating to pluralism. For instance, people may respond to the above "gospel bite" with: "Yes, but how do you know all that stuff about Jesus is true in the first place?" This will give you an opportunity to talk about the historical reliability of Jesus and the Gospels, something I have written about elsewhere.[85] Christianity, uniquely among the world religions, is a historical faith. When people ask questions about history, they are on our turf. In any case, an answer similar to those above may provide a starting point for a helpful discussion about the truly unique claims of Jesus.

The Problem of Pain and Suffering

The question of suffering looms large in the modern mind, particularly in light of disasters such as the 2004 tsunami in Asia. Many of the issues need to be dealt with philosophically (does suffering disprove God's existence?) or theologically (is God powerless to do anything?). In no way am I suggesting that all, or even most, of the questions people might ask us relate immediately to some action or teaching of Jesus.

Nevertheless, there is an aspect of this particular problem that leads naturally to a discussion about Christ's life and, in particular, his death. Regardless of what we don't know about God's plans in this world, we do know his intentions. Jesus' sufferings provide a powerful counterpoint to the assumption that God might be distant, cruel and uninvolved. Hence, one aspect of my answer to the problem of pain and suffering comes back to the picture of God we have in Jesus' passion recorded in Mark 15:21 – 37:

> I don't have all the answers about suffering. But one thing I hold to, especially when I'm going through hard times, is that the God of Christianity is not distant and disinterested. In Jesus, God himself experienced human betrayal, horrible injustice and a gruesome death. The scene of his crucifixion, as described in the Gospels, is very moving. He bears incredible insult and injury and continues to act compassionately. This, according to the Bible, is the God who rules all things. He willingly experiences what we experience. This God is able to sympathise with those who suffer not simply because he is

all-knowing but because he has experienced pain first-hand. This helps me trust God when I don't understand what he's doing in the world. Have you ever looked at Jesus' life and death?

As I just said, in no way do I think this response answers the question of suffering. It simply provides a snapshot of one important aspect of the biblical notion of God as humble, loving and "familiar with suffering" (Isaiah 53:3).

I am not recommending you attempt a "gospel bite" each time you get into a spiritual conversation. The point of this appendix is simply to demonstrate that Jesus' life, teaching, miracles, death and resurrection are a rich source of answers to some common contemporary questions. Recounting a relevant part of that narrative may provide your friends with some satisfying answers. It may also open up an opportunity to outline the gospel more fully. In the next appendix I offer an example of what this might look like in a modern context.

APPENDIX 2

A Modern Retelling
of the Gospel

WHAT FOLLOWS IS AN ATTEMPT to outline the gospel more fully.
I have written this appendix as if speaking to an unbeliever. I
don't expect anyone to use these words in their own gospel conversations or even to follow the logical steps I take below. I am
simply illustrating what it might look like in a modern context
to explain what the New Testament calls "the gospel": the news
about how God has opened his kingdom to sinners through the
life, teaching, death and resurrection of Jesus Christ.

God of Common Sense

Belief in God is common sense. This is not intended as bait for
atheists. It is simply a historical observation: belief in God or
gods is a universal reality throughout time. Like the fascination
with art and music, or our quest for intimacy and social organization, reverence for a Creator is one of the few shared traits of
the whole human family. Even today, four out of five Australians
acknowledge the existence of God; only about one in twenty
describe themselves as atheists.[86]

Of course, the proposition that God exists is not provable in a
mathematical sense, nor can it be tested by science. Like love, art
and human consciousness itself, this truth sits outside the reach

of empirical testing. It is a macro-truth that makes sense of the world we live in and that has therefore made a lot of sense to a lot of people throughout time. It is common sense.

It may be true, as the minority argue, that the sophisticated orderliness of the universe and the mystery of the human mind are the result of blind, natural forces. But this explanation continues to strike most men and women – whether rich or poor, ancient or modern, educated or otherwise – as profoundly unlikely and deeply unsatisfying. More plausible, it seems, is the observation of the ancient biblical poet:

> The heavens declare the glory of God;
>   the skies proclaim the work of his hands. (Psalm 19:1)

If this is true, the question of God is the most interesting and urgent of all.

Whose God?

But the simple fact of worldwide reverence for a Maker raises an obvious question: whose god should we listen to? Perhaps there is a spiritual kingdom beyond the material one, but which version should we seek?

The unique and enduring claim of Christianity in all its forms is that the God of universal conviction – of our common sense – has broken into history for all to see. The "kingdom of God" has touched the world of humanity in a tangible way.

While churches have disagreed about many things through the centuries, the acknowledged core of Christianity is Jesus Christ, his teaching, healings, death and rising to life. And all of these – including the healings and resurrection – remain the subject of serious examination by scholars today.

Because Christianity's claims are uniquely tangible, having to do with historical events and not simply timeless spiritual truths, they are probed and evaluated in a manner without parallel in the study of the world religions. Archaeologists dig up Galilee and

Jerusalem to see if Jesus' stomping ground has been accurately described by the Gospels (the New Testament accounts of his life). Historians pore over the non-Christian evidence to see if Jesus' teaching, healings, death and resurrection rate a mention outside the Bible. And they analyse the New Testament writings themselves to assess their worth as independent historical sources. On all these counts Christianity fares much better than most of us realise. The Christian faith gladly places its neck on the chopping block of public scrutiny and invites anyone who wishes to take a swing.[87]

Healer

But when we open the pages of the Gospels, we are confronted with the claim that Jesus restored the sight of the blind, healed the sick and exercised mastery over nature itself. While the non-Christian references to Jesus corroborate his fame as a wonder-worker, can such claims be believed today?

How you and I answer this question depends not only on historical evidence, which in the case of Jesus' miracles is plentiful, but on our underlying beliefs about God. On the one hand, if we assume that the observable laws of nature are the only things governing the universe – that there is no Lawgiver behind these laws, no God – then claims of miracles, no matter how widespread the historical evidence, will be dismissed as nonsense. If, on the other hand, we hold that the laws of nature are not the only things governing the universe – that there *is* a Lawgiver, or God, behind the laws of nature – then, given the strength of the historical evidence in this case, openness to Jesus' miracles is perfectly rational.[88]

More important than this philosophical observation is an understanding of the meaning of Christ's reported deeds. According to Jesus, his healings were a tangible sign that "the kingdom of God has come" (Matthew 12:28).

What is "the kingdom of God"? It is the promise, first made in the Old Testament or Jewish Scriptures, that the Creator would one day prove himself to be king over his creation, that he would overthrow injustice and heal our frailty. If you have ever asked, "Why doesn't God do something about the evil and pain of the world?" you have, in a sense, hoped for what Jesus called "the kingdom".

Strikingly, Jesus insisted that his healings, exorcisms and mastery over nature were not only an indication of his kingly status in God's kingdom; they were a preview of the kingdom itself. His deeds were a pledge within history that what we all yearn for – the triumph of justice and the renewal of human life – God will one day accomplish.

Teacher

Jesus the Healer was also famous as a Teacher – the point hardly needs stating. Many of his sayings have become proverbial in Western culture: "Turn . . . the other cheek" (Matthew 5:39); "Do to others what you would have them do to you" (Matthew 7:12); "You are the salt of the earth" (Matthew 5:13); "It is more blessed to give than to receive" (Acts 20:35), and countless other expressions of what, after two millennia, seem like self-evident wisdom.

But what is the central obligation of men and women, according to Jesus? When asked this very question he replied: " 'Love the Lord your God with all your heart and with all your soul and with all your mind.' This is the first and greatest commandment. And the second is like it: 'Love your neighbour as yourself' " (Matthew 22:37–40).

According to Jesus Christ, the golden rule of God's kingdom is a simple, twofold directive: love your Maker and love your neighbour. The logic is seamless. If God exists, what could be more basic to authentic human life than wholehearted devotion to our Creator and selfless care for our fellow creatures!

Jesus leaves no room here either for the religious hypocrite who is zealous for God but uncaring toward others, or for the

ethical agnostic who aims to be a "good person" but who ignores
the Creator himself. Both fail the teaching of Christ.

Our culture rightly condemns those who "love God" but
lack a basic human compassion. In doing so, however, we should
recognise that the reverse is equally contemptible. Loving one's
neighbour while shunning the Creator is a grave distortion of the
shape of human life. It is to break what Jesus called "the first and
greatest commandment". Such a person may be "good" on their
own definition, but not on Christ's.

Judge

The Jesus who famously taught about love also spoke of judgment. There is no avoiding the topic.

Perhaps the modern aversion to the idea of divine punishment
comes partly from a justified revulsion at old-fashioned "fire and
brimstone" preaching. But there is probably another, more basic,
factor: we simply do not like it. The preferred God for many
today is the vague, distant Creator who kick-started the universe
but who now, if he thinks of us at all, warmly approves of most
of what we do.

But, according to Jesus, when God establishes his kingdom
and puts everything to right, he will condemn all that is opposed
to his just purposes. This will include ethical agnosticism no less
than religious hypocrisy. Love of God and neighbour, then, is
not simply the shape of an authentic human life; it is the criterion
of divine judgment. Jesus spoke of this regularly and without
embarrassment, and he even cast himself as the central character
in the theatre of judgment:

> Not everyone who says to me, "Lord, Lord," will enter the
> kingdom of heaven, but only those who do the will of my
> Father who is in heaven. Many will say to me on that day,
> "Lord, Lord, did we not prophesy in your name and in your
> name drive out demons and in your name perform many mir-
> acles?" Then I will tell them plainly, "I never knew you. Away
> from me, you evildoers!" (Matthew 7:21–23)

The idea of Jesus as Judge both comforts and disturbs. It is reassuring to know that someone as compassionate and just as Christ is entrusted with the judgment of our flawed humanity. Yet, as anyone who has read the Gospels will know, Jesus was uncompromising in his critique of our refusal to love (both God and neighbour).[89] Compassion and justice go hand-in-hand in the figure of Jesus. And, in the final events of his life, these themes became strangely intertwined.

Saviour

Christ's extraordinary life as Healer and Teacher (and future Judge) ended abruptly and in apparent failure. Crucifixion was the Roman empire's *summum supplicium*, "ultimate punishment", usually reserved for political dissidents. No one could talk of a coming "kingdom" and of his central place in it without provoking the wrath of Rome.[90]

But political explanations tell only part of the story. Far from being a failure, Christ's death was the ultimate expression of God's justice and compassion. On the eve of his execution, as he shared the Last Supper with his followers, he spoke of his imminent death as a sacrifice that would guarantee God's forgiveness and open up to us God's kingdom:

> Jesus took bread, and when he had given thanks, he broke it and gave it to his disciples, saying, "Take and eat; this is my body."
>
> Then he took the cup, and when he had given thanks, he gave it to them, saying, "Drink from it, all of you. This is my blood of the covenant, which is poured out for many for the forgiveness of sins. I tell you, I will not drink of this fruit of the vine from now on until that day when I drink it new with you in my Father's kingdom." (Matthew 26:26–29)

Within hours, Jesus' blood would indeed be poured out, not as a simple act of martyrdom but as a willing substitute for those facing judgment. By Christ's sacrificial death, we who have failed the divine imperative—to love the Creator and care for our fellow creatures—may be freely forgiven; more than that, we may share with Christ in his "Father's kingdom".

The Healer, Teacher and Judge is also the Saviour.

Lord

If the New Testament had left Jesus in a martyr's tomb, this would have been a perfectly respectable way to end the story of a great Jewish Teacher and Healer. But contrary to all expectations, the followers of Christ insisted that their Saviour had been raised from the dead. Their claim, for which many of them gave their lives, launched a movement that would utterly transform the world.

Most scholars agree about two things: (1) Jesus' tomb was empty shortly after his crucifixion, and (2) significant numbers of women and men claimed to have seen him risen from the dead. As with miracles generally, how you and I interpret these data depends not on historical evidence—which in this case is surprisingly good—but on our underlying convictions about God.

The first Christians had unflappable convictions about God and had no hesitation declaring that the Almighty had raised Jesus from the dead. He did this, they insisted, to establish Jesus publicly as the Lord in God's kingdom.

So strong is this connection between Jesus' resurrection and his status as Lord (or Messiah) that these two realities became the very touchstone of Christian faith. The apostle Paul, himself an eyewitness and eventual martyr for Christ's resurrection, put it bluntly: "If you declare with your mouth, 'Jesus is Lord,' and believe in your heart that God raised him from the dead, you will be saved" (Romans 10:9).

More than the Healer who previewed God's kingdom, the Teacher who called on us to love and the Saviour who died for our forgiveness, the resurrected Jesus is the divinely appointed Lord (and therefore our future Judge). And heartfelt acceptance of this reality is the beginning of the Christian life and the guarantee of future salvation in God's unending kingdom.

Epilogue: Portrait of a Christian

The God of common conviction—of our common sense—has opened up his kingdom to us in a tangible way in Jesus Christ. Christians seek to live in the light of this.

Christians believe that Christ's healings provide a glimpse of the restoration of all things in God's coming kingdom. They see in Jesus' teaching, especially in his call to love God and neighbour, the shape of an authentic human life. They revere Christ as the one entrusted with God's final judgments, and they rely on him as the one who died so that we might be freely forgiven. Above all, Christians believe that Jesus' resurrection establishes him as the divinely appointed Lord.

If all of this is true, nothing could more important, more urgent, than to express to your Maker your desire to trust in these realities yourself. When asked by his followers how to express oneself to God, Jesus taught them the so-called Lord's Prayer. It is a beautiful expression of trust in God, a plea for forgiveness from God, a request that the kingdom of God would shape our life here and now. If appropriate for you, please use the words to express your own desire to entrust yourself to God:

> Our Father in heaven,
> Hallowed [i.e., honoured] be your name.
> Your kingdom come.
> Your will be done
>   on earth as it is in heaven.
> Give us today our daily bread.
> Forgive us our debts [i.e., sins]
>   as we forgive our debtors [i.e., those who sin against us].
> And lead us not into temptation
>   but deliver us from the evil one.
> For yours is the kingdom,
>   and the power and the glory forever. Amen.[91]

Notes

1. Evangelists are referred to in three biblical passages: Acts 21:8; Ephesians 4:11; and 2 Timothy 4:5. We will look at the role of the evangelist in chapter 9.
2. See the first edition of *Hanging in There* (Sydney: Matthias Media, 1991).
3. The translation of the Shema quoted here comes from the Jewish prayer book (*The Complete Artscroll Siddu* [New York: Mesorah, 2003], 91).
4. For those with access to the primary documents the relevant passages are Josephus, *The Jewish War* 7.45; Philo, *On the Life of Moses* 2.41–44; *Special Laws* 2.62; see also Tobit 13:3–6.
5. *If I Were God I'd Make Myself Clearer* (Syndey, Australia: Matthias Media, 2002); *A Spectator's Guide to World Religions* (Oxford, England: Lion Hudson, 2007).
6. On the death of Jesus the Koran states, "They said, 'We killed Christ Jesus the son of Mary, the Apostle of God'; but they killed him not, nor crucified him" (Sura 4.157). On Jesus' status as the divine Son the Koran affirms, "They do blaspheme who say: God is Christ the son of Mary . . . They do blaspheme who say: God is one of three in a Trinity" (Sura 5.75–76).
7. Marcus Borg is professor of religion and culture at Oregon State University. The book is titled *The Heart of Christianity: Rediscovering a Life of Faith* (New York: HarperCollins, 2003). Pages 207–26 contain the argument with which I take issue here.
8. In 1 Corinthians 8:7–12 "the weak" are believers who feel they would be defiled if they ate meat that had been offered to idols. The strong in faith, on the other hand, know that mere food cannot affect one's status before God. Paul discusses the "weak" in Romans 14 also.
9. For more information on these banquet halls and Paul's teaching in 1 Corinthians 8–10 see my *Mission-Commitment in Ancient Judaism and in the Pauline Communities* (Tübingen: Mohn Siebeck, 2003), 228–61.

10. A good example is found in Romans 9:32 – 33. Speaking of those who reject Jesus, Paul says, "They stumbled over the 'stumbling stone'. As it is written: 'See, I lay in Zion a stone that causes people to stumble and a rock that makes them fall, and the one who believes in him will never be put to shame.' "

11. Max Lucado, *No Wonder They Call Him the Savior: Experiencing the Truth of the Cross* (Nashville: Nelson, 1986).

12. *CMS Checkpoint* magazine (Summer 2004 – 2005), 6.

13. For more on this see my *Mission-Commitment in Ancient Judaism and in the Pauline Communities*, 60 – 66.

14. R. C. Lucas, *Fullness and Freedom: The Message of Colossians and Philemon* (Downers Grove, Ill: InterVarsity Press, 1980), 173.

15. Some see the letter as written from a prison in Ephesus (in modern-day Turkey) or Caesarea (a coastal port in Israel), but I follow the majority of scholars in accepting Rome as the place from which Paul wrote Philippians.

16. Most commentators stress the financial meaning of "partnership in the gospel" (Philippians 1:5). With a number of scholars, however, I think the phrase might also include other gospel-promoting activities. I suspect Paul would have included prayer, godly living and speaking of Jesus under the heading of "gospel partnership".

17. C. E. B. Cranfield, *Romans*, The International Critical Commentary (Edinburgh: T&T Clark, 1979), 2:769 (footnote 4).

18. Source: Australian Bureau of Statistics, *Household Expenditure Survey*, 2005. The survey is conducted only every five years.

19. One could mount a similar argument about contributing to the poor. This too is a major theme in the New Testament: Matthew 25:31 – 46; Luke 10:25 – 37; Acts 24:17; Galatians 2:10; James 1:27; 2:14 – 15; 1 John 3:17. But that is for another book!

20. Of course, it is also (and particularly) true that Jesus himself is the "light of the world" (John 8:12).

21. The Greek plural *kala erga* ("good deeds") appears in numerous New Testament texts, where it always refers to acts of goodness/kindness: Matthew 5:16; 1 Timothy 5:25; 6:18; Titus 2:7, 14; 3:8, 14; Hebrews 10:24; 1 Peter 2:12. The synonymous phrase *agatha erga* ("good deeds") also refers to acts of goodness/kindness: Acts 9:36; Romans 2:7; Ephesians 2:10; 1 Timothy 2:10.

22. Scot McKnight, *A Light among the Gentiles: Jewish Missionary Activity in the Second Temple Period* (Minneapolis: Fortress, 1991), 67 – 68.

Numerous other Jewish texts point in the same direction: *Testament of Levi* 14.1–4; *Testament of Benjamin* 5.1–5 and 8.2–3; *Letter of Aristeas* 227; Josephus, *Antiquities* 20.75–76. The passages are discussed in my *Mission-Commitment in Ancient Judaism and in the Pauline Communities*, 51–60.

23. The famine itself is reported in biblical and nonbiblical texts (Acts 11:27–28; Josephus, *Antiquities* 20.101). Paul's poverty-relief program, known simply as "the collection" by New Testament scholars, is mentioned several times in his letters (1 Corinthians 16:1–4; 2 Corinthians 8–9; and Romans 15:25–27, in chronological order).

24. This is recorded by Eusebius (AD 260–340), bishop of Caesarea, in his famous *Ecclesiastical History* 6.43.11.

25. Emperor Julian, "Fragment of a Letter to a Priest," in *The Works of the Emperor Julian* (Loeb Classical Library 29), 2:337–38.

26. Emperor Julian, "Letter 22, To Arcacius, High-Priest of Galatia," *The Works of the Emperor Julian* (Loeb Classical Library 157), 3:67–73.

27. *The Rise of Christianity* (New York: HarperCollins, 1997), 209–15.

28. We see this already in Acts 8:4–5 and 11:19–21. For the second and third centuries see Eusebius, *Ecclesiastical History* 3.37.1–3 and 5.10.1–3.

29. In John 13:35 Jesus says that our love for one another will show the world that we are his disciples. John 17:20–21, furthermore, implies that Christian unity, a key consequence of our love for one another, can somehow move the world to believe in the Son and the Father.

30. That Peter intends us to read 1 Peter 3:1–2 ("won over . . . when they see the purity") as a concrete example of what he said in 1 Peter 2:12 (that "they may see your good deeds and glorify God") is suggested by his use of the same very rare term *epopteuô* ("see/ observe"), which occurs in the New Testament only in these two passages.

31. This point is not certain. The apostle's description of these husbands as "disobeying the word" may just be a stock way of describing those who do not yet obey the Word of God—whether or not they have actually had the word explained to them. I don't have a strong view on the matter.

32. See Philippians 4:5; Colossians 4:5; 1 Thessalonians 4:11–12. A discussion of the missionary significance of these and other passages can be found in my *Mission-Commitment in Ancient Judaism and in the Pauline Communities*, 262–92.

33. Christopher Hitchens, *God Is Not Great: How Religion Poisons Everything* (Boston: Twelve Publishing, 2007), 7.

34. Apollos was one of the great early evangelists: see Acts 18:24–28; 1 Corinthians 3:5. Tychicus was one of Paul's regular missionary workers: Acts 20:4; Ephesians 6:21; Colossians 4:7; 2 Timothy 4:12. We do not know anything more about Zenas or Artemas.

35. For the details of all of this see my article "Gospel as News: *Euangel-* from Aristophanes to the Apostle Paul," *New Testament Studies* 51 (2005): 212–30.

36. This Greek inscription is found in *Orientis Graeci Inscriptiones* 2:458. A full translation and discussion of the inscription and its accompanying documents can be found in F. W. Danker, *Benefactor: Epigraphic Study of a Graeco-Roman and New Testament Semantic Field* (St. Louis: Clayton, 1982), 215–22.

37. There was considerable speculation in the Jewish writings after the Old Testament about who this promised Isaianic gospel herald might turn out to be. In the Dead Sea Scrolls, for instance, he is identified with a quasi-divine herald named Melchizedek (Melchizedek Document, 11Q13) and even with a future Messiah (Messianic Apocalypse, 4Q521).

38. The word *gospel* appears without explanation in all of the following references: Romans 1:9, 15, 16; 11:28; 15:16, 19–20; 16:25; 1 Corinthians 1:17; 4:15; 9:12, 14, 16, 18, 23; 2 Corinthians 2:12; 4:3; 8:18; 9:13; 10:14, 16; 11:4, 7; Galatians 1:6, 7, 8, 9, 11; 2:2, 5, 7, 14; 4:13; Ephesians 1:13; 3:6, 7; 6:15, 19; Philippians 1:5, 7, 12, 16, 27; 2:22; 4:3, 15; Colossians 1:23; 1 Thessalonians 1:5; 2:2, 4, 8, 9; 3:2; 2 Thessalonians 1:8; 2:14; 1 Timothy 1:11; 2 Timothy 1:8, 10, 11; Philemon 13; Hebrews 4:2, 6; 1 Peter 1:12; 4:6, 17.

39. AD 33/34 is the date of Paul's first visit to Jerusalem after his conversion (Acts 9:26–31) in AD 31/32 (Jesus' death being dated in April AD 30). According to Galatians 1:18 Paul stayed with the apostle Peter during this fifteen-day visit and also met with James the brother of Jesus. Paul must have received much firsthand information about Jesus during this time (filling out what had been revealed to him personally by Jesus; see Galatians 1:16). Wouldn't

you love to have been a fly on the wall as Paul, Peter and James sat up late at night discussing the marvels of their Messiah? In any case, the creed Paul says he "received" (1 Corinthians 15:3) is most likely to have been passed onto him during this visit. In my opinion, the most reliable book on these chronological questions is by Rainer Riesner, *Paul's Early Period: Chronology, Mission Strategy, Theology* (Grand Rapids: Eerdmans, 1998).

40. Martin Hengel, *Acts and the History of Earliest Christianity* (London: SCM, 1979), 43–47.

41. If you have a cross-reference Bible handy, check out the Old Testament references in Matthew 27:38, 39, 46, 49; Mark 15:24, 29, 34, 36; Luke 23:30, 34, 36; John 19:24, 28–30.

42. In a statement reminiscent of Paul's creed, Luke records: "Then he [the resurrected Jesus] opened their minds so they could understand the Scriptures. He told them, 'This is what is written: The Messiah will suffer and rise from the dead on the third day, and repentance for the forgiveness of sins will be preached in his name to all nations, beginning at Jerusalem' " (Luke 24:45–47). Early gospel preaching unpacked both the event of Jesus' resurrection and its Old Testament background.

    Again, Paul's evangelistic speech in Acts 13:13–39 gives us an idea of how the apostle went about this: "God raised him [Jesus] from the dead so that he will never be subject to decay. As God said: 'I will give you the holy and sure blessings promised to David' [Isaiah 55:3]. So it is also stated elsewhere: 'You will not let your Holy One see decay' [Psalm 16:10]. Now when David had served God's purpose in his own generation, he fell asleep; he was buried with his ancestors and his body decayed. But the one whom God raised from the dead did not see decay" (Acts 13:34–37). The resurrection establishes Jesus as the one who inherits the eternal throne of David (as promised in 2 Samuel 7:12–14).

43. Actually, Luke here mentions only the "eleven" since Judas has gone his own way, so to speak! When Paul mentions "the Twelve", he is probably including Matthias, whom Luke later tells us was also present at these appearances (Acts 1:21–26).

44. Paul does exactly this in his Acts 13 sermon: "But God raised him from the dead, and for many days he was seen by those who had travelled with him from Galilee to Jerusalem. They are now his witnesses to our people" (Acts 13:30–31).

45. Dozens of scholarly articles have been written on Romans 1:3–4. Scholars find in this one sentence some intriguing details about the content and origin of early Christian belief. The structure and style of the sentence suggests that this little gospel creed was originally composed in Aramaic, the language of Palestine, before being translated into the (quite literal) Greek that appears here in Paul's letter. I won't bore you with the technical details. Suffice it to say that Paul establishes in this statement that his gospel is the normative ancient one, the one that originated in Palestine before he was converted and was believed by the Romans before he wrote his letter.

46. Note that I have changed the formatting from what is present in the TNIV text.

47. Luke, for instance, begins his account with the words: "Many have undertaken to draw up an account of the things that have been fulfilled among us, just as they were handed down to us by those who from the first were eyewitnesses" (Luke 1:1–2). Mark strikes the same note of "fulfillment" in his opening lines: "The beginning of the good news about Jesus the Messiah, as it is written in Isaiah the prophet: 'I will send my messenger ahead of you . . .'" (Mark 1:1–2). The opening chapters of Matthew and John are replete with references to Jesus as the fulfilment of the hopes of the prophets: see Matthew 1:1–2:23; John 1:1–45.

48. The importance of resurrection and Spirit in God's future kingdom can be seen in the following biblical passages: Ezekiel 36:24–30; 37:1–14; 39:25–29; Daniel 12:1–4; Romans 8:23; 2 Corinthians 5:15; Galatians 6:8; Ephesians 1:13–14; Philippians 3:20–21.

49. In Matthew's Gospel see 1:1, 6, 17, 20; 2:1–6; 9:27; 12:23; 15:22; 20:30; 21:9. In Luke's Gospel see 1:27, 32, 69; 2:4, 11; 3:31; 18:38–39. See also Mark 10:47–48; 11:10; John 7:41–42.

50. Peter Stuhlmacher is professor of New Testament at the University of Tübingen, Germany. This quotation comes from his superb commentary on the epistle: *Paul's Letter to the Romans* (Louisville: Westminster John Knox, 1994), 19.

51. Once again, the formatting has been changed from the TNIV.

52. John 12:1–7 names the woman "Mary", the sister of Lazarus, whom Jesus raised from the dead.

53. A point for the technically minded: in Greek the two halves of verse 9 are rhythmically and grammatically parallel, suggesting the

close connection between the gospel preached *unto the world* and the woman's deed declared *unto her memory*.

54. In addition to Mark 14 the episode is recounted in Matthew 26:6–13 and John 12:1–8. Scholars are divided as to whether the similar story in Luke 7:36–50 is another version of the same event or an account of a different event altogether.

55. Both themes, of course, are found throughout the Gospels (particularly that of Luke): Matthew 6:12; 9:2–6; 26:28; Mark 1:4; 11:25; Luke 1:77; 3:3; 7:47–48; 15:1–32; 18:9–14; 24:47; John 20:23.

56. This quotation comes from Hengel's influential book *Acts and the History of Earliest Christianity* (London: SCM, 1979), 43–47.

57. The ever-present Martin Hengel has written an entire book on this issue: *The Four Gospels and the One Gospel of Jesus Christ* (Philadelphia: Trinity Press International, 2000).

58. In this early period, even public readings (in church) from Matthew, Mark, Luke and John were themselves called "Gospels" because they declared (in part) the gospel.

59. Papias's note can be found in Eusebius, *Ecclesiastical History* 3.39.15.

60. Irenaeus, *Against Heresies* 3.1.1.

61. Eusebius, *Ecclesiastical History* 3.37.2.

62. Ibid.

63. For more technical information on "evangelists", please see chapter 4 and appendix 2 of my *Mission-Commitment in Ancient Judaism and in the Pauline Communities*.

64. The evidence for all of this, including a discussion of the oft-quoted Romans 1:15, is laid out in my article "Gospel as News: *Euangel-* from Aristophanes to the Apostle Paul," noted above.

65. For example, Peter O'Brien, *The Epistle to the Philippians* (Grand Rapids: Eerdmans, 1991), 481; G. Hawthorne, *Philippians* (Waco, TX: Word, 1983), 180.

66. See H. G. Liddell and Robert Scott, *A Greek-English Lexicon* (Oxford: Oxford Univ. Press, 1993 [1889]), 20.

67. The term "the brother" refers to Paul's missionary colleagues in the following passages: Romans 16:14, 23; 1 Corinthians 1:1; 16:11, 12, 20; 2 Corinthians 1:1; 2:13; 8:18, 22, 23; 9:3, 5; 11:9; 12:18; Galatians 1:2; Ephesians 6:21; Philippians 2:25; 4:21; 1 Thessalonians 3:2; Philemon 1, 7, 20. Four other instances could refer either to colleagues or to believers generally: Philippians 1:14 (the passage under discussion); Ephesians 6:23; 1 Timothy 4:6; 2 Timothy 4:21.

For the technically minded, there is yet another usage of the term "brother(s)" in Paul's letters. The expression appears numerous times in the customary "nominative of address", wherein a writer (in this case Paul) addresses his readers directly, usually to mark a change of topic. Being anarthrous (i.e., lacking the definite article) these instances of *adelphos* are not linguistically relevant for assessing the articular expression "the brother(s)".

68. First, Paul describes these preachers in 1:14 as "the brothers *in the Lord*". Throughout Paul's letters this exact phrase ("in the Lord/Christ") is frequently used as a specific title of honour for co-workers, meaning something like "in the Lord's service": four times in Romans 16:3 – 13, where, curiously, the expression again refers to *Roman* missionary colleagues; 1 Thessalonians 5:12; Colossians 4:7, 17; and Ephesians 6:21. Second, those who insist that "the brothers" in Philippians 1:14 are believers in general face the added difficulty of proposing a historically plausible account of verses 15 – 16. Are we really to think that believers *in general* were preaching in a manner designed to cause trouble for Paul's imprisonment? Is it not easier to imagine official preachers in Rome conducting their ministries with public antipathy toward Paul? Paul in fact implies as much in Philippians 2:20 – 22.

69. Timothy's previous evangelistic ministry is mentioned in Romans 16:21; 1 Corinthians 16:10; 2 Corinthians 1:19; Philippians 2:22; 1 Thessalonians 3:2.

70. "Desire" for a ministry may seem a lame indication of one's spiritual calling. However, Paul himself, in speaking about potential "overseers", says that desire indeed has a place: "Here is a trustworthy saying: Whoever aspires to be an overseer desires a noble task" (1 Timothy 3:1). By analogy, I am suggesting that people who set their hearts on evangelism may well be evangelists.

71. *Sunday Life*, in the *Sun-Herald* (17 October 2004), 26 – 27.

72. Rodney Stark has been researching and writing about the sociology of conversion since the 1960s. On the point mentioned above see the interview with Professor Stark in *Christianity Today* (July 14, 2003).

73. In some circles, the word "worship" is almost synonymous with "church service" or even with the "singing time" during a service (as in "praise and worship"). Others have reacted against this by avoiding "worship" terminology altogether when talking about church gatherings. They point out that "worship" basically means

service to God. The term therefore refers to the whole of life, not
just what we do for an hour on Sunday. In using the phrase "public
worship" I am deliberately describing our church gatherings as
a corporate, public and very significant expression of our larger
worship of God.

74. Josephus, *Jewish War* 7.45. Several other texts reveal the missionary
significance of Jewish public worship in the ancient world: Philo, *On
the Life of Moses* 2.41 – 44; *Special Laws* 2.62; Tobit 13:3 – 6. For more
on this, see my *Mission-Commitment in Ancient Judaism and in the Pauline
Communities*, 74 – 84.

75. Cassius Dio 57.18.5a. The other sources are: Josephus, *Jewish
Antiquities* 18.81 – 84; Tacitus, *Annals* 2.85; Suetonius, *Tiberius*
36. For further details on this Jewish expulsion from Rome and
an earlier one in 139 BC (for the same reason), see my *Mission-
Commitment in Ancient Judaism and in the Pauline Communities*, 24 – 33.

76. In an article titled "1 Peter – A Mission Document?" *The Reformed
Theological Review* 63:2 (August 2004): 72 – 86, Mark Boyley
proposed that *exangellô* in Psalm 9:14 refers to a declaration of
God's greatness *outside* of a liturgical context and that, therefore,
the word can quite naturally mean any kind of proclamation. The
verse in question reads: "that I may declare [*exangellô*] your praises
in the gates of Daughter Zion". Because the "gates" mentioned here
were thought to refer to public spaces in Jerusalem (rather than the
temple), Mark Boyley concludes that the "declaration" here was a
form of personal preaching on the part of the psalmist. This was
then used to support the notion that 1 Peter 2:9 calls for personal
preaching on the part of Christians. However, the liturgical context
of Psalm 9:14 is clear from the words of verse 11: "Sing praises to the
LORD, enthroned in Zion." Unless we are to imagine this pious Jew
walking around Jerusalem singing to his friends, this whole stanza
can only be interpreted as part of Israel's public worship. Moreover,
the "gates" of Zion (Jerusalem) were not just civic space; they were
an important location for public worship as Psalm 100:4 makes
clear: "Enter his gates with thanksgiving and his courts with praise;
give thanks to him and praise his name." Psalm 9:14 refers to Israel's
public praise, not to personal preaching. The only real exception in
the use of *exangellô* in the Bible is in Proverbs 12:16, where it refers
to a fool "showing" his anger to all. This is obviously not a liturgical
declaration (nor a personal proclamation).

77. Timothy J. Keller, "Reformed Worship in the Global City," in *Worship by the Book*, ed. D. A. Carson (Grand Rapids: Zondervan, 2002), 218.

78. It is perhaps difficult for some to imagine that praise could be so high on God's list of priorities for his people. This is partly why some read 1 Peter 2:9 as a reference to gospel preaching, which seems (to them) like a more plausible purpose to live for. However, let us remember that Isaiah 43:21 and 1 Peter 2:9 are by no means the only passages that describe "praise" as a raison d'être of God's people (old and new). The apostle Paul also considered "praise" to be a fundamental aspect of our Christian calling (see Romans 15:7 – 11). Indeed, in Ephesians 1:3 – 14 Paul describes the whole plan of salvation as designed for the praise of God.

79. For example: Earle Ellis, *Prophecy and Hermeneutic in Early Christianity: New Testament Essays* (Tübingen: Mohr Siebeck, 1978); David E. Aune, *Prophecy in Early Christianity and the Ancient Mediterranean World* (Grand Rapids: Eerdmans, 1983); Christopher Forbes, *Prophecy and Inspired Speech in Early Christianity and Its Hellenistic Environment* (Peabody, MA: Hendrickson, 1997).

80. This story was reported in the Melbourne *Age* newspaper, February 9, 2004, under the title "As God Is My Co-Pilot".

81. For a detailed discussion of Ephesians 6:15 – 17, see my *Mission-Commitment in Ancient Judaism and in the Pauline Communities*, 114 – 22.

82. To get more technical, when Paul uses the term *logos* ("word") as a grammatical absolute (as in verse 3's "the word"), he always means the message of the gospel. When he uses *logos* in a non-absolute way, either by modifying it (as in verse 6's "your word") or by leaving out the definite article ("a word"), he means "speech" of any kind, as in Colossians 3:17: "And whatever you do, whether in word [*logos*] or deed, do it all in the name of the Lord Jesus." "Conversation" is a perfectly good translation of *logos* in Colossians 4:6.

83. The grammatical parallel in Colossians 4:4 and 6 is clear. In verse 4 Paul uses the word "ought" (*dei* in Greek) followed by a speaking verb in the infinitive mood (*lalçsai*): the apostle "ought to proclaim". In verse 6 he again uses the word "ought" (*dei*) followed by a speaking verb in the infinitive mood (*apokrinesthai*): believers "ought to answer". To the first Greek listeners of Paul's letter this parallel would have been obvious.

84. R. C. Lucas, *Fullness and Freedom: The Message of Colossians and Philemon* (Downers Grove, IL: InterVarsity Press, 1980), 173.

85. John Dickson, *The Christ Files: How Historians Know What They Know about Jesus* (Sydney: Blue Bottle Books, 2005).

86. Those who acknowledge God: 80.1 percent; those who are atheists: 5.3 percent respectively. Source: *World Values Survey*, Inter-university Consortium for Political and Social Research (Ronald Inglehart et al. 2000).

87. A starting point for investigating the historical basis of Christianity can be found in my *The Christ Files: How Historians Know What They Know about Jesus*.

88. An accessible introduction to the historical data concerning Jesus' reported miracles, along with an explanation of their meaning according to the Christian Gospels, can be found in my *A Spectator's Guide to Jesus: An Introduction to the Man from Nazareth* (Sydney: Blue Bottle Books, 2005), 35 – 48. Representative of the mainstream scholarly conclusion that Jesus performed deeds that friend and foe alike took to be miraculous is the 500-page discussion by prolific US scholar John P. Meier, *A Marginal Jew: Rethinking the Historical Jesus* (New York: Doubleday, 1994), 2:507 – 1038.

89. Some of Jesus' teaching on God's judgment can be found in Matthew 25:31 – 46; Luke 13:22 – 30; John 5:22 – 27.

90. The account of the Roman trial of Jesus can be found in John 18:33 – 37.

91. The Lord's Prayer, as it is called, can be found in Matthew 6:9 – 13. The last two lines have been inserted from the TNIV footnote.

Scripture Index

Genesis
1:1 .... 26, 34

Exodus
29:18 83

Leviticus
4:31 83

Deuteronomy
6:4 27

2 Samuel
7:12 – 14 ...... 124, 223

1 Kings
8:22 – 53 67
8:41 – 43 ...28, 30, 67, 158

Psalms
9:11 – 14 160
9:14 227
16:10 223
19:1 212
47:1 161
56:4 – 13 160
57 .... 29, 161
57:9 – 11 157
66 .... 29, 161
66:1 – 8 157
71:14 – 18 160
73:28 160

79:13 160
96 .... 27 – 30, 30 – 33, 157 – 158, 161, 170, 183
96:1 – 9 157
96:1 – 5 28
96:3 – 5 37
96:4 – 5 31
96:4 25
96:5 38
96:7 – 9 29
96:8 .... 36, 38
96:10 – 13 32
100:1 – 5 161
100:4 227
102:18 161
105:1 161
105:2 161
107:21 – 22 160
108 .... 29, 161
108:1 – 5 157
117 .... 29, 30, 161
117:1 158
119:12 – 14 160

Proverbs
12:16 227

Isaiah
2:1 – 4 161
8:12 – 13 181
40:9 114
42:8 160
42:12 160

43:20 – 23 162
43:21 .... 160, 228
49:6 .....87, 88, 89, 91
52:7 .... 29, 114
53:3 210
55:3 223
56:6 – 8 161
61:1 114
63:7 160

Jeremiah
31:31 – 34 120

Ezekiel
34:23 63
34:31 63

Micah
5:2 – 4 63

Matthew
1:1 – 2:23 224
2:6 63
4:23 114
5 – 7 89
5:5 89
5:7 89
5:9 89
5:13 214
5:14 – 16... 87 – 89, 91, 95, 160
5:15 88
5:16 ....85, 89, 96, 99, 103, 220

5:27 – 32 89
5:37 89
5:39 .... 89, 214
5:44 89
6:1 – 2 .... 89, 96
6:2 89
6:9 – 13 229
7:1 – 6 205
7:1 89
7:12 214
7:21 – 23 215
7:22 – 23 ......127, 132
8:4 147
8:5 – 13 206
9:1 – 8 205
9:35 – 10:5 ..... 62 – 66
9:36 63
9:37 – 10:1 64
9:37 – 38 ....61, 71
9:38 65
10:5 – 10 80
10:10 .... 65, 80
11:19 49
12:28 213
15:21 – 28 206
16:16 118
16:27 ....127, 132
19:28 ....127, 132
21:15 – 16 164
22:34 – 40 206
22:37 – 40 214
24:14 114
25:31 – 46 .... 220, 229
25:31 – 33 .....127, 132
26:6 – 13 225
26:12 – 13 128
26:13 129
26:26 – 29 216
26:26 – 28 120
26:27 – 29 127
28:16 – 20 ...... 33 – 37,
                 208

28:18 – 20 26
28:18 – 19 183

Mark
1:1 – 2 224
1:1 .... 128, 129
1:14 – 15 114
1:17 127
2:13 – 17 205
2:14 127
2:15 – 16 .... 49, 55
7:24 – 30 205
7:36 147
8:29 118
11:17 158
12:28 – 34 206
13:10 22
14 128
14:8 – 9 128
14:9 129
14:32 – 36 127
14:60 – 65 208
15:21 – 37 209
15:40 – 16:3 121
16:7 122

Luke
1:1 – 2 224
3:16 134
5:27 – 32 ..... 199, 206
7:36 – 50 .... 127, 204,
               205, 225
7:37 – 39 50
8:56 147
9:20 118
9:51 – 56 147
9:60 147
10:1 – 24 147
10:1 – 7 80
10:7 80
10:25 – 37 220
13:22 – 30 229

13:23 – 27 .....127, 132
15:1 – 32 ...... 127, 205
15:1 – 2 50
15:10 190
18:9 – 14 ..... 127, 205
18:22 127
19:1 – 10 ..... 127, 205
19:1 – 7 50
19:9 – 10 51
19:10 54
19:28 – 40 ... 164 – 167
19:37 – 40 164
23:35 – 43 205
23:39 – 46 127
24:33 – 43 122
24:34 122
24:45 – 47 .... 208, 223

John
1:1 – 45 224
1:43 127
5:22 – 30 ......127, 132
5:22 – 27 229
8:1 – 11 205
11:27 118
12:1 – 8 225
12:1 – 7 224
13:35 221
14:5 – 6 208
14:8 – 10 208
17:20 – 21 221
18:33 – 37 229
21 122

Acts
1:21 – 26 223
2 .... 168, 169
2:11 168
2:16 – 18 168
2:22 – 39 21
2:22 – 36 130
2:44 – 45 146

3:12 – 21 131
4:8 – 12 21
5:42 135
6:1 – 7 92
7:55 183
8 147
8:4 – 5 221
8:5 135
8:12 135
9:19 – 20 135
9:22 135
9:36 220
10:34 – 43 ...... 21, 132
11:19 – 21 221
11:27 – 28 221
13:13 – 39 .... 119, 121, 223
13:16 – 41 21
13:23 – 39 .... 133, 135
13:30 – 31 223
13:34 – 37 223
13:38 – 39 134
16:11 – 40 78
17:2 – 3 136
17:18 – 21 ... 134 – 135
17:22 – 31 .... 134, 135
18:5 136
18:24 – 28 222
18:28 136
19:13 136
20:4 222
20:21 136
20:24 – 25 136
20:24 136
20:35 214
21:8 ..... 143, 147, 219
24:17 220
28:30 – 31 136

Romans

1:1 – 4 124
1:1 79

1:2 – 4 21
1:2 124
1:3 – 4 123 – 125, 126, 128, 129, 134, 224
1:3 137
2:7 220
2:16 ..... 120, 127, 132
9:32 – 33 220
10:1 68
10:9 .... 122, 217
10:17 99
12:1 163
12:3 – 8 152
14 219
15:7 – 11 228
15:8 137
15:24 81
15:25 – 27 221
16:21 65

1 Corinthians

3:5 222
3:9 65
8 – 10 57
8:1 55
8:4 – 6 27
8:7 – 12 219
8:10 56
9:13 – 14 80
9:14 76
9:16 33
9:19 – 23 54
10:31 – 11:1 .... 48, 54, 56
10:31 60
10:33 – 11:1 57
10:33 46
11:1 53
11:23ff. 137
11:23 – 25 119
12:1 – 11 152
12:27 – 31 152

13:8 74
14 168
14:3 – 4 169
14:23 – 26 ... 167 – 170
14:24 170
14:26 169
15:1 – 8 .... 21, 117
15:1 – 6 116
15:1 .... 111, 112
15:3 – 6 112
15:3 – 5 ...... 116 – 123, 124, 125, 128, 129
15:3 ..... 119, 137, 223
15:4 .... 120, 121
15:5 122
16:1 – 4 221
16:6 81

2 Corinthians

5:10 – 11 .... 32 – 33
8 – 9 221
8:18 .... 144, 145

Galatians

1:16 222
1:18 222
2:10 220
2:11 – 21 53
2:14 53
4:4 137

Ephesians

1:3 – 14 228
2:10 220
4:2 44
4:8 – 12 .... 148, 152
4:11 .... 141, 143, 144, 152, 219
5:19 163
6:15 175
6:19 – 20 71

6:19 71
6:21 222

Philippians
1:3 – 5 78
1:5.......... 79, 82, 220
1:14 – 17...... 145, 146
1:14 147
2:6 – 11 137
2:25 .... 65, 78
4:2 – 3 145
4:3 65
4:5 222
4:14 – 18.............. 79
4:15 79
4:18 .... 78, 79, 82
4:21 – 22 146

Colossians
1:7......................145
1:9 – 10..............187
1:28 187
2:23 187
3:16 ....149, 163
4:2 – 6 174
4:2 – 4 72
4:3 – 6 189
4:3 – 4 176
4:3 73
4:4 228
4:5 – 6 ....20, 176,
                    186 – 87
4:5 .... 174, 222
4:6 ..... 176, 178, 183,
                    184, 228
4:7......................222
4:12 – 13.............145

1 Thessalonians
3:2 65
4:11 – 12.............222

2 Thessalonians
3:1..................... 72

1 Timothy
2:1 – 4................. 69
2:10 220
3:1 – 10 151
3:1.....................226
5:25 220
6:18 220

2 Timothy
2:8 – 9 126
2:8 ....21, 126, 128,
                    129, 134
2:15 65
4:5 ....20, 143, 147,
                    175, 219
4:12 222

Titus
1:9 – 14 106
2:1 – 10 ...... 103 – 109
2:5 ......104, 105, 106
2:7......................220
2:8 ......104, 105, 106
2:9 – 10 .... 106, 110
2:10 .....97, 106 – 107,
                    109
2:14 220
3:8 220
3:12 – 13.............106
3:13 81
3:14 220

Hebrews
10:24 220
13:15 163

James
1:27 220
2:14 – 17.............149
2:14 – 15.............220
3:9 185
3:17 187
4:15 182

1 Peter
1:3......................179
1:12 160
1:21 179
1:25 160
2:5 .... 162, 163
2:9 .... 155, 159 – 163,
                    170, 227, 228
2.12 ..... 99, 160, 220,
                    221
3:1 – 2 ...99 – 103, 221
3:1............. 101, 160
3:8 – 9 188
3:13 – 16...... 174, 187
3:13 – 14.............178
3:14 – 15...... 180, 181
3:15 ....20, 35, 37,
      102, 160, 172, 174,
      176, 178, 179, 183
3:16 178
4:4 179
4:6 160

1 John
3:17 220

Subject Index

Abbott, Stephen, 182
afterlife, 40–41
allegiance to Christ, 35, 180–83
answering for the faith, 23, 175–77, 186
Antioch, 158–59
apokrinomai, 178
Apollos, 222
apologia, 178, 179–80
apostolic gospel, 129, 135–36, 138
Arak, Eleazar ben, 174
assistance, financial, 22
atheism, 93, 94
atonement, 120, 123, 125, 127
authority, universal, 208

banquets, 55–58
bearableness, 44
behaviour
    Christian, 97–110
    godly, 22, 23, 99–103
    good, 188, 206–7
Bible
    basic doctrine, 26–27
    prayer and mission in, 67
    shortest summary of the Gospel, 126
Borg, Marcus, 42–43
Buddhism, 40, 41
burial, Jesus', 120–21, 123

Cassius Dio, 159
charitable giving, 76–84, 220. *See also* financial assistance

Christ, 118–19. *See also* Jesus
    allegiance to, 180–83
    death of, 209, 216
    mission of, 55–58
    speaking up for, 101–3
Christian behaviour, 97–110
Christian living, 56–58
Christianity, 43
    core of, 212
    criticisms of, 104–5
    world's view of, 182
Christians
    and good deeds, 90–91, 93–94
    ordinary, 46–60
    responsibility, 129, 175–77
    social life, 57–58
Christological monotheism, 115, 183
Christology, 181
Chrysostom, John, 82
church
    early, 137–38
    and gospel promotion, 85–96
    local, 141–54
Church Missionary Society, 66
church services, 155–71
Clowney, Edmund, 161
common sense, 211–12
compassion, 62–66, 215
conversations, 22–23
    promoting the gospel through, 172–89
conversion, 159, 167–70
    without a word, 99–102
Cranfield, Charles, 80

creed, 116–17
crucifixion, 120, 216

Dawkins, Richard, 73, 104
death, Jesus', 118–19, 120, 123,
    209, 216, 219
Denton, Andrew, 97
didaskalia, 106
dining, 49, 55–58
disciples, 34–35, 65
    Jesus 'appearance to, 122
doxazô, 88–89, 96
doxological evangelism, 161, 163, 168
duty, universal, 27–30

early church, 137–38
eating, 49, 55–58
employee-employer relationship,
    102
Epaphras, 145
Ephesus, 147–48
Eusebius, 138, 150–51
evangelism, 17–19, 23, 24
    and compassion, 64
    doxological, 161, 163, 168
    in early church, 138
    and godliness, 106
    immediate goal of, 139
    and local church, 141–54
    in Old Testament, 28–29
    and prayer, 65–66
    and self-consciousness, 18–19
    training, 21
evangelists
    determining who they are,
        149–54
    meaning of, 143–44
    in New Testament, 144–49
Everyday Evangelism (Abbott), 182

faith, 100, 127
    answering for, 23, 175–77, 186
    Christian, 140

financial assistance, 22, 220
financial partnerships, 76–84
food, 55–58
forgiveness, 107, 127, 131, 134,
    204–5, 207, 216
    God's, 206
friend of sinners, 46–60

Gemmell, Nikki, 155–56
generosity, 107
Gentiles, 28, 30–33, 69, 91, 158
gentleness, 184
glory, 56, 60, 88–89
God
    forgiveness of, 206, 216
    glory of, 56, 60
    grace of, 59, 94, 184
    judgment of, 32, 229
    kingdom of (*See* Kingdom of
        God)
    lordship of, 28, 33
    love for, 207, 214, 215
    mercy of, 94
    mission to the world, 36
    pleading with, 68–71
    praising, 30–33
    role of prayer in mission, 67
    worship of, 95
God Is Not Great (Hitchens), 104
God-talk, 182–83
godliness, 106, 107
godly behaviour, 22, 23, 99–103
godly life, 90–91
gods, pagan, 31, 40
good behaviour, 188, 206–7
good deeds, 89, 90–91, 106, 220
    and gospel proclamation, 109
    power of, 107
    and Roman Empire, 92–96
goodness, 89
gospel, 222
    bites, 203–10
    bookend summary, 123–25

clarity, 153
connection with gospel, 126–28
content of, 115–16
core content of, 139–40
in early church, 137–38
first messages, 129–37
as founding message, 144
and gospel, 126–28
and kingdom of God, 112–15,
    124–25
making it beautiful, 103–9
message we promote, 111–40
modern outline of, 117
modern retelling of, 211–18
as necessary cause of faith,
    100–101
prayer for work of, 72–73
proclaiming, 23, 109
as proclamation of Messiah's life
    and death, 131–32
reducing, 21–22
what it is, 111–40
year in the life of, 190–201
gospel promotion, 23–24, 30–33,
    60, 72, 120
goals of, 110, 119
with money, 76–84
with prayer, 61–75
through Christian behaviour,
    97–110
through daily conversation,
    172–89
through good deeds, 95–96, 106
through public praise, 155–71
through works of the church,
    85–96
grace, 21, 59, 94, 127, 136, 184,
    204
Great Commission, 26, 33–34,
    35, 37

Harris, Sam, 73, 104
harvest, 64–65

Hengel, Martin, 118, 136
Hinduism, 40–41
Hitchens, Christopher, 73, 104–5
Holy Spirit, 168
honesty, 106, 107
honour, 81–83, 185
hope, 179
humility, 106

idols, 31, 38, 57, 157–58, 178–79
Ignatius, 70
intolerance, 44–45
Irenaeus, 138
Isaiah, 113
Islam, 40
Israel, 227

Jerusalem, 87, 164
Jesus. See also Christ
    appearance to disciples, 122
    burial of, 120–21
    claims universal authority, 208
    at core of Christianity, 212
    death of, 118–19, 120, 209, 216,
        219
    as divine Son, 219
    enters Jerusalem on Palm
        Sunday, 164
    as friend of sinners, 46–60
    as fulfillment of promise to
        David, 124
    as healer, 213–14
    as judge, 215–16
    lordship of, 183, 217
    loyalty to, 183
    as Messiah, 115, 119, 123, 125,
        128, 134
    ministry of, 49
    and mission, 64
    mission of, 62
    resurrection of, 118–19,
        121–22, 217

as Saviour, 216–17
social life, 48–51
suffering of, 209
as teacher, 214–15
Jews/Judaism, 28, 40, 68–71, 91,
    159
John the Baptist, 132
Josephus, 158–59
judgment, 32, 127, 132, 205,
    215–16, 229
Julian, Emperor, 93–94
justification, 134

Keller, Tim, 161–62
kindness, 89
kingdom of God, 112–15, 212, 216
    connection with gospel, 124–25
    theme of, 118
    what it is, 213–14
Koran, 40, 41, 219
kosmeô, 106
kyrios, 180, 183

Last Supper, 119, 120, 216
light of the world, 85–96
lives worth questioning, 186–88
local church, 141–54
logos, 228
Lord, 37, 38–39
    promoting, 28, 37
Lord's Prayer, 74, 218, 229
Lordship, 27, 28, 33, 34, 35, 115,
    183
love
    for God, 207, 214, 215
    of neighbour, 207, 214, 215
loyalty to Jesus, 183
Lucado, Max, 58
Lucas, Dick, 72, 177

Macedonia, 144–45
marriage relationship, 102

McKnight, Scot, 91
meals, 49, 55–58
mercy, 94, 107
Messiah, 40
    deeds of, 115–16
    life and death of, 131–32
    role in final judgment, 132
ministry, Jesus', 49
mission
    activities, 22–24
    gifts to, 82–83
    God's, 36, 67
    hidden, 61–75
    of Jesus, 55–58, 62
    mind-set, 47–48
    and monotheism, 31, 45
    and Paul, 53, 54
    and prayer, 67, 73
    and public worship, 158
    why to get involved in, 25–37
mission equation, 30–33, 33–37
missionaries, 66, 80
missionary mind, 46–60
money, 76–84
monotheism, 27, 63, 115
    Christological, 115, 183
    and mission, 31, 45

neighbours, loving, 207, 214, 215
New Atheism, 73, 104–5
New Testament, 144–49
No Wonder They Call Him the Savior
    (Lucado), 58

Old Testament, 27, 28–29

pagan gods, 31
pagans, 29, 30, 57
pain, 209–10
Palm Sunday, 164
Pantaenus, 150–51
Papias, 138

parent-child relationship, 102
partnerships, 77–83
passion-resurrection narrative, 121
Pastoral Epistles, 148
Paul, 53–55, 78–79, 92, 106,
    144–45, 176–77, 178, 217,
    225–26
Pentecost, 129, 168, 169
Peter, 159–60, 178
Pharisees, 164
Philip, 147
Philippi, 77–79, 145
Philo of Alexandria, 68–69, 90–91
Pluralism, 38–45, 207–9
poor, caring for, 107
popular pluralism, 39–41
praise, public, 22, 28, 30–33,
    155–71, 228
prayer, 22, 23, 61–75
    for an unbelieving world, 70
    on behalf of Jews, 68–71
    and compassion, 62–66
    and evangelism, 65–66
    and mission, 67, 73
    role in God's mission, 67
    for those who proclaim the
        gospel, 71–72
    for the work of the gospel,
        72–73
propempô, 120
prophesying, 167–70
public worship, 155–71, 227
purity, 55

Reality, ultimate, 42–43
reincarnation, 40–41
relationships, 102
religions, 38–45
religious type, 206
repentance, 127
respect, 185
restaurants, 56

resurrection, 41
    Jesus', 118–19, 121–22, 123,
        124–25, 217
Retief, Frank, 108–9
Roman Empire, 92–96
Romans, conversion of, 159
Rome, 145–47

sacramentalism, 42–43
sacrifice, 82–83, 162, 163
salvation, 57–58, 67
salvation cringe, 47–48, 49
salvific mind-set, 59–60, 68
self-consciousness, 18–19
self-righteousness, 205
Sermon on the Mount, 89
services
    church, 155–71
    synagogue, 158–59
Shema, 27
shepherd, 63
sin-atoning death, 123, 125
sinners, 46–60, 127
    God's grace toward, 59
sins, 21, 120, 127, 204–5
    forgiveness of, 131, 134
social life, 48–51, 56–58
sophisticated pluralism, 41–45
speaking, 22–23
Stark, Rodney, 94–95, 156
Stuhlmacher, Peter, 125
suffering, 209–10
synagogue services, 158–59

teacher-student relationship, 102
temple, 162
Thomas, Len, 98, 100
Tiberius, Emperor, 159
Timothy, 147–48
Tobit, 88
tripitaka, 41
triumphal entry, 164–67

trustworthiness, 106, 107
Turkey, 145

universal authority, 208
universal duty, 27–30
Upanishads, 41

Winton, Tim, 97–98, 100
wisdom, 187
Word of God, 106
workers, 64–65

world-saving light, 87–89, 91
worship, 22, 29, 155–71, 226–27.
    See also praise, public
    and good deeds, 95
    of idols, 57, 157–58, 178–79
Worship by the Book (Keller), 161–62

Yahweh, 39

Zacchaeus, 50–51

Share Your Thoughts

With the Author: Your comments will be forwarded to the author when you send them to *zauthor@zondervan.com*.

With Zondervan: Submit your review of this book by writing to *zreview@zondervan.com*.

Free Online Resources at
www.zondervan.com

Zondervan AuthorTracker: Be notified whenever your favorite authors publish new books, go on tour, or post an update about what's happening in their lives at www.zondervan.com/authortracker.

Daily Bible Verses and Devotions: Enrich your life with daily Bible verses or devotions that help you start every morning focused on God. Visit www.zondervan.com/newsletters.

Free Email Publications: Sign up for newsletters on Christian living, academic resources, church ministry, fiction, children's resources, and more. Visit www.zondervan.com/newsletters.

Zondervan Bible Search: Find and compare Bible passages in a variety of translations at www.zondervanbiblesearch.com.

Other Benefits: Register yourself to receive online benefits like coupons and special offers, or to participate in research.

ZONDERVAN

ZONDERVAN.com/
AUTHORTRACKER
follow your favorite authors